AESTHETICS OF THE COMMONS

T0366495

AESTHETICS OF THE COMMONS

EDITED BY
CORNELIA SOLLFRANK, FELIX STALDER,
AND SHUSHA NIEDERBERGER

DIAPHANES

PUBLISHED AS VOLUME 24 OF THE INSTITUTE FOR CONTEMPORARY ART RESEARCH
SERIES, ZURICH UNIVERSITY OF THE ARTS

ISBN 978-3-0358-0345-7

LAYOUT AND PREPRESS: 2EDIT, ZURICH
PRINTED IN GERMANY

WWW.DIAPHANES.COM

Contents

Preface

The present book is the result of an experimental research project. In the beginning there was art—16 projects by artists. Since they neither correspond to traditional art forms nor are they congruent with political activism, we were interested in *what* they actually do, *how* they do it and also how they *locate* themselves. Already by relating these projects to each other we have opened up a new space. We have marked this newly emerging space with a thesis and a question. Our thesis was to define these projects as both *commons* and *art*. The question was to investigate what happens when these two fields of reference are brought into exchange with each other, to explore what these artistic projects could contribute to the commons discourse in a new and specific way, and, vice versa, what new perspectives on aesthetics would result from viewing them through the lens of the commons, a concept that has its origins in economics and political science.

Before inviting the ten authors of this volume to work with these questions in the light of their respective expertise, the editors conducted a three-year research project entitled *Creating Commons*, which—in several phases, both theoretically and practically—not only reflected and worked on these projects, but also collaborated with the artists who run the projects. The results of three workshops, a total of 17 interviews, and the documentation of an exhibition are the research materials we have made available to the authors with the request to build on them and to elaborate one aspect of the newly formulated *Aesthetics of the Commons*.

Since the authors themselves come from very different disciplines, the results are correspondingly diverse. The result is therefore not a self-contained theory developed within one discipline, but rather an offer to readers to make cross-connections and concatenations according to their preferences, and thus to carry the considerations made in this book into their own fields of work and continue them—in theory and practice.

Acknowledgments

We want to thank all the authors for engaging intensely with the materials produced by our research, and the artists, activists and theorists for the inspiration and the pleasure of collaborating:

Panayotis Antoniadis (mazizone.eu/nethood.org, Zurich/Athens), Dušan Barok (Monoskop.org), Zeljko Blace (MaMa/ccSPORT), Anna Calabrese (University of the Arts, Berlin), Ruth Catlow (Furtherfield, London), Annet Dekker (Universiteit van Amsterdam), Paul Keller (Kennisland, NL), Sean Dockray (aaaaarg.fail), Daphne Dragona (Berlin), Marc Garrett (Furtherfield, London), Jan Gerber (0xdb.org), Olga Goriunova (University of London), Alessandro Ludovico (neural magazine, IT), Sebastian Luetgert (0xdb. org), Marcell Mars (Memory of the World), Annette Mächtel (University of the Arts and ngbk, Berlin), Tomislav Medak (Memory of the World), Michael Murtaugh (Constant, Brussels), Mauricio O'Brian (goteo.org, Barcelona), Rahel Puffert (Braunschweig University of Art (HBK)), Mario Purkathofer (Dock18, Zurich), Laurence Rassel (ERG, Brussels), Patricia Reis (Mz* Baltazar's Laboratory, Vienna), Urban Sand (openki.net, Zurich), Femke Snelting (Constant, Brussels), Spideralex (Donestech, Catalonia), Penny Travlou (University of Edinburgh), Marek Tuszinsky (Tactical Tech Berlin), Lioudmila Voropai (HfG Karlsruhe), Eva Weinmayr (AND publishing, London), Peter Westenberg (Constant, Brussels), Stefanie Wuschitz (Mz* Baltazar's Laboratory, Vienna).

The public lectures, research workshops, and the exhibition would not have been possible without the support and engagement of Sabine Himmelsbach (HeK Basel) and Robert Sakrowski (panke.gallery Berlin).

The production of the research project, the exhibition, and this publication would not have been possible without the skills and the help of Thomas Isler, Reto Stamm, Piet Esch, Jo Zahn, Manfred Miersch for video recording and post-production, Camilla Coutinho for graphic design for the exhibition and catalogue, Valentine Pakis and Michel Chevalier for translation, Tobias Ruetschi for transcription of interviews and Nigel Johnson for advice on grant writing.

We are very grateful for the support we received from the Institute for Contemporary Art Research (ifcar) at the Zurich University of the Arts, particularly Christoph Schenker and Barbara Preisig, who provided the congenial institutional home for our research. We also thank Cynthia Matumona, Julia Prütz, Dora Bohrer and Manuela Balsamo-Christen who steered us through the administrative jungle.

We also want to thank our publisher, Diaphanes, who managed to combine the best of two worlds, a print and an electronic open access publication, in particular Michael Heitz for his support, valuable advice, and openness to experimental cover design, as well as Catherine Lupton for careful proofreading and copyediting.

The cover is both a product and a process. It has been designed by Alex Leray and Antoine Gelgon from Open Source Publishing (OSP), Brussels. OSP is a collective created in 2006 by artists and graphic designers to question the role of digital tools in visual creation, and to invent alternative practices privileging sharing and mutual aid rather than secrecy and competition.

This cover is typeset in Meta Old-French, a Libre parametric font by the design collective Luuse, inspired by early 20th century US interpretations of classical french typography. Instead of proposing a ready-to-use specific cut, it is a boilerplate program describing the skeleton of the font. This basic infrastructure is an invitation for multiple interpretations, variations, uses and misuses. This font is a follow-up of Metahershey, a 2013 collective type-design experiment based on the Public Domain Hershey font collection, interpreted by Metafont and drawn using pen plotters. All through pre-90's technology.

The research project *Creating Commons* was financed by the Swiss National Science Foundation (grant: # 100016_169419), with additional funds from the Institute for Contemporary Art Research.

Introduction

What do a feminist server, an art space located in a public park in North London, a "pirate" library of high cultural value yet dubious legal status, and an art school that emphasizes collectivity have in common? They all demonstrate that art can play an important role in imagining and producing a real quite different from what is currently hegemonic; that art has the possibility to not only envision or proclaim ideas in theory, but also to realize them materially.

The sphere of culture is dominated by the logic of commodification, extending the imperatives of private property and competition, of buying, selling, owning, and trading into areas that have long been shaped by very different norms, from public funding to community organizing (in traditional cultures or in "subcultures") to reciprocity in everyday practices. Within communication, nearly all modes of relating—from the most public and to the most intimate ones alike—have been subsumed under powerful technical systems optimized for "engagement," irrespective of the quality or content of that interaction. They follow strictly commercial imperatives of data extraction and advertisement-driven nudging, with little regard to psychological or societal consequences.[1] What the revelations by Edward Snowden did for government surveillance, the scandal over Cambridge Analytica did for social media. They made the general public aware that our lives unfold within technological infrastructures over which we have no control and of which we have limited knowledge—just sufficient to realize that the very tools we are working with often work against us. Yet, we still use them, often grudgingly, because they provide real value and have become essential to navigate the complexity of today's world. Global capitalism—with all its contradictions—traverses us. It has colonized not only almost all aspects of our lives and relationships that make up our human and more-than-human environment, but also our imagination, the way we think of ourselves, of our possibilities of being in the world.

There will be no way out of this trap without new social and technological "imaginaries." As Felwine Sarr, in his call for reimagining Africa, explains: "for the very reasons that societies first and fore-

---

1   Franco Berardi, *Heroes: Mass Murder and Suicide* (London and New York: Verso, 2015).

most establish themselves through their imaginaries, these imaginaries become the forges from which the forms that a society grants itself can emanate."[2] Social imaginaries are not just ideas or personal fantasies. Rather, they are a set of collectively-held, basic assumptions and beliefs that cannot be proven but are taken as self-evident. They shape intuition and common sense, and inform both individual action and collective institutions.[3] The imaginary of liberal modernity centered around the notion of "ownership" and the "individuality" that ownership, first of one's own body and then of things produced or acquired, confers. It was rational to acquire more, and it was moral to be rational.[4] We are both at height of this imaginary—everything can be owned—and at its end—its destructive implications have become highly visible.

But what could replace it? How to rethink the world and ourselves as collectively shared, rather than individually owned? Culture, it would seem, is a relatively obvious case, because culture—to the degree that it's not only about ownership—is about meaning and thus can never be fully individual. In the digital context, abundance overflows the confines of private property. Yet, also here, the grip of the conventional is still strong.

In this process of re-imagining and re-doing, the role of art is indispensable. It helps in articulating powerful affective dimensions beyond the immediately useful and draws lines towards the speculative and unknown. Ascribing such a role to art, however, also requires rethinking its role in society. Imaginaries do not emerge from a distance, from the splendid position of "absolute individual autonomy" and "freedom of purpose," but rather from immersion in compromised situations, from collective interventions into messy realities. And the goal, for the time being, is not to build utopia, but to create a culture that is, as Laurence Rassel, director of the École de Recherche Graphique in Brussels, put it, "less toxic."[5]

---

2   Felwine Sarr, *Afrotopia*, trans. Drew Burk and Sarah Jones-Boardman (Minneapolis: University of Minnesota Press, 2020), p. XII

3   Cornelius Castoriadis, "Imaginary and Imagination at the Crossroads," in *Figures of the Thinkable (Including Passion and Knowledge)* (Stanford: Stanford University Press, 2007), pp. 123–152.

4   C. B. Macpherson, *The Political Theory of Possessive Individualism: Hobbes to Locke* (Don Mills, Ontario: Oxford University Press, 2011 [1962]).

5   Laurence Rassel, "Rethinking the Art School," Talk (March 1, 2018), Hek, House of Electronic Arts, Basel, http://creatingcommons.zhdk.ch/rethinking-the-art-school/ (All URLs in this text have been last accessed October 20, 2020).

This publication examines a series of artistic and cultural projects—drawn from what one could loosely call the (post)digital—that take up this challenge in different ways and contexts. What unites them, however, is that they have what we call a "double character." They are art in the sense of placing themselves in relation to (Western) cultural and art systems, developing discursive and aesthetic positions, and at the same time they are "operational," i.e. creating recursive environments and freely available resources whose uses exceed these systems. The first aspect raises questions about the kind of aesthetics that are being embodied, the second aspect creates a relation to the larger concept of the "commons." The commons here are not understood as a fixed set of principles that need to be adhered to in order to fit a definition, but as a "thinking tool."[6] In other words, we are less interested in the question of whether these cases constitute a commons according to some definition, or in creating a new definition based on these cases, but in what we can make visible by applying the framework of the commons as a heuristic device.

COMMONS

The commons we refer to in this publication are—implicitly or explicitly—the *digital* commons, but not because we want to suggest some separate digital reality, far from it. Rather, because our lives are, and will remain, shaped by the affordances of (digital) tools and infrastructures, and because the various practices of commons-oriented digital cultures have been a potent source for new imaginaries, in both online and offline practice.

After its early history as a form of common land use, the commons re-emerged, in the English-speaking world, as a major theoretical, political and cultural horizon during the 1990s, and have been articulated within a number of larger perspectives that often refer to one another.

---

6   Femke Snelting first suggested this concept for the Feminist Server, using it to describe a material practice that raises fundamental questions that would otherwise remain unarticulated. See Cornelia Sollfrank, "Forms of Ongoingness, Cornelia Sollfrank in conversation with Femke Snelting and Spideralex," *Creating Commons*, 2018, http://creatingcommons. zhdk.ch/forms-of-ongoingness/

The economic

Economists, building on the foundational work of Elinor Ostrom, have viewed the commons as a set of institutions for governing "common-pool resources"—meadows, irrigation systems, fisheries, forests, and so on—rather than private assets.[7] Extensive empirical studies were successful in repudiating Hardin's infamous "tragedy of the commons,"[8] in which he argued that utility-maximizing, competing individuals would necessarily destroy the physical commons and that only private (or state) property regimes could prevent that. Contrary to this schematic and, actually, racist view,[9] Ostrom and her collaborators found a plethora of institutional arrangements through which communities were able to coordinate collective action around shared resources over long periods of time.[10] Indeed, these institutions turned out to be so manifold and diverse, often responding to very local conditions, that the researchers abstained from synthesizing a single model. Rather, they identified a set of challenges that these institutions need to solve, ranging from including and excluding people from the use and management of the commons, to setting and enforcing rules of (self-)governance and managing the relations with the wider social environment.[11] For economists, the resources are at the center of the commons, and the social institutions and cultural forms developed through them have the purpose of (re-)producing these resources. While they break with the view of individual self-maximization, however, they retain an understanding of actors as primarily rational, with rationality leading to cooperation in that case.

7   Elinor Ostrom, *Governing the Commons* (Cambridge: Cambridge University Press, 1990).
8   Garrett Hardin, "The Tragedy of the Commons," *Science* 162, no. 3859 (1968): pp. 1243–1248.
9   Matto Mildenberger, "The Tragedy of the Tragedy of the Commons," *Scientific American Blog Network* (April 23, 2019), https://blogs.scientificamerican.com/voices/the-tragedy-of-the-tragedy-of-the-commons/
10 Ostrom's argument was so convincing that Hardin revised his original claim, by narrowing it to "unmanaged commons," which is a contradiction in terms, as the commons are all about collective management of shared resources. Garrett Hardin, "The Tragedy of the Unmanaged Commons," *Trends in Ecology & Evolution* 9, no. 5 (1994): p. 199, https://doi.org/10.1016/0169-5347(94)90097-3
11 Michael D. McGinnis and Elinor Ostrom, "Design Principles for Local and Global Commons," conference paper for "Linking Local and Global Commons," Harvard Center for International Affairs, Cambridge, MA, April 23–25, 1992, http://hdl.handle.net/10535/5460

The digital

Given the rural and agricultural orientation of much of the early commons research, it was unexpected that the notion of the commons was taken up in the context of the production of knowledge-intensive digital goods, first in the field of software, then across the full range of digital culture. Perhaps the most significant difference between physical and digital commons is that digital data is "non-rivalrous" in use. While meadows can be overgrazed, digital information cannot be overused. Use does not subtract from the resource; on the contrary, it adds to it. The challenge for digital commons thus lies more in finding the necessary number of people willing and capable of producing and contributing to the resource than in the prevention of overuse. Indeed, the capacities of networked digital infrastructures allow many forms of (re-)production to be organized outside of a market logic, through voluntary cooperation. As the hurdle for using the resource tends to be extremely low, this also allows relatively small groups of people, ranging from a single producer to more formally organized communities, to produce resources that could become relevant to a large number of people. Cooperation is facilitated by the digital in two ways. First, by making it easier for like-minded people to find each other and coalesce around shared interests, and second, by creating differentiated infrastructures—from mailing lists, to wikis, shared database and others—that enable large communities to collaborate with relatively little organizational overhead. Yet, there are not only differences between physical and digital commons, but also between types of digital goods, in particular between software and works of art and culture. If, in software, there is no free version of a program, it can always be reimplemented by writing the same functionality in different code (unless the functionality itself is patented). Hence there is something like "Libre-Office," which is functionally very similar to "Microsoft Office" but with open source code and a free license. In the cultural context, this is not possible—with a few exceptions like Wikipedia having started as a free version of commercial encyclopedias. Notwithstanding Pierre Menard, Jorge Luis Borges' fictional twentieth-century writer who tried to recreate (rather than merely translate) *Don Quixote*,[12] works of art

---

12 Jorge Luis Borges, "Pierre Menard, Author of the Quixote," (1939), in *Collected Fictions*, trans. Andrew Hurley (New York: Penguin Books, 1998).

cannot be redone without creating a new and different work.[13] In most cases, access to the actual work is needed, irrespective of the licensing terms. Hence, many cultural commons that build on existing works operate in a legal gray zone, where traditional copyright claims might well exist, but often are not enforced, either by tacit agreement of the rights holder, or because the works are "orphaned."[14] Technically such practices may be seen as piracy, while in fact they embody elements of a commons, in that they create and maintain "shared resources" available for reuse.

The legal

To the degree that commons are a type of property regime they have always been regulated by the law.[15] Throughout modernity, there has been a tension between shared and private resources, which was usually resolved in favor of private ownership through processes of enclosure.[16] Digital property is regulated by copyright and the field of software was the first to encounter the use of copyright as a means for enclosure. In the early days of computing, software was an add-on to large and expensive hardware, rather like a user manual, and the sharing of software improvements among programmers/users was normal. Only since the mid 1970s, with companies such as Microsoft appearing, did software become regarded as a product in its own right and copyright law was used to enforce claims of exclusive ownership.[17] Within ten years, virtually all software was shipped with a license that prohibited changing and redistributing it. The social roles of the programmer who writes a particular piece of code and the user who simply applies the software, were separated by a hard, legal boundary expressed in the licensing agreement that users had to accept before using the software. In the mid 1980s, Richard Stallman started

---

13 Indeed, there are entire artistic genres, from appropriation art to re-enactments, that play with this difference.

14 A work is regarded as orphaned if technically it still falls under copyright protection, yet no rightholder comes forward to enforce his or her rights.

15 Hartmut Zücker, "The Commons. A Historical Concept of Property Rights," in *The Wealth of the Commons: A World beyond Market and State*, ed. David Bollier and Silke Helfrich (Amherst MA: Levellers Press, 2012), pp. 125–131.

16 Peter Linebaugh, *Stop, Thief! The Commons, Enclosures, and Resistance* (Oakland: PM Press, 2013).

17 Bill Gates, "An Open Letter to Hobbyists," *Homebrew Computer Club Newsletter* 2, no. 1 (1976): p. 2.

a counter-movement for what he called Free Software. Having been socialized in the then vanishing early hacker culture based on sharing and collaboration within an elite group of programmers in major research laboratories, he felt it was time for strategies against this enclosure. "Free" refers to four crucial "freedoms" users should have in respect to software: the right to run, the right to study and change, the right to redistribute identical copies and the right to distribute transformed copies. The first two rights focus on the protection of individual freedom, the second two focus on the needs of a community to share and collaborate freely. These rights were made enforceable through a particular license, the GNU General Public License (GPL), whose first version was published in 1989 and the most recent version (3.0) in 2007. This license was itself a product of hacker culture, insofar as it used an existing system for an entirely unintended purpose. Copyright law has always been used to create private property out of an intangible work by granting the supposedly original author near absolute control over its use.

The GPL uses this power of the author in order to subvert individual control, by granting these four basic rights to everyone with only one condition: any transformed work must be distributed with the same rights. This "viral" clause guarantees that any work put under this free license would remain freely useable and any improvements were given back to the communities on whose works the improvement relies. Partly owing to the collaborative nature of software development, partly to the political leanings of the founder(s) of the Free Software Movement,[18] the focus on the development of communities has been as strong as on the rights of individual creators. By the early 1990s, the Internet had become widely available in universities, particularly among computer science students. The GPL quickly became the standard license, because it was already established and ideally suited for collaboration based on shared interest, rather than institutional affiliation. The vast expansion of social space through the Internet made it much easier to find people with whom to collaborate. In the early 1990s, Linus Thorvalds, then a student in Finland, contributed not only the missing piece of software to create an entire free operating

---

18 Eben Moglen, "Anarchism Triumphant: Free Software and the Death of Copyright," *First Monday* 4, no. 8 (1999), https://doi.org/10.5210/fm.v4i8.684

system (GNU/Linux), but also pioneered a new development process with frequent updates. This was highly motivating for contributors, who saw their improvements quickly accepted, and released and reoriented software development from finished product to open process. By the end of the decade, this approach had gained mainstream attention, and in order to appeal to business sensitivities, it was re-branded as "Open Source,"[19] and conceptualized as a new "mode of production" for knowledge-intensive goods.[20] In the software context, the different terms—free software or open source—denote different political attitudes that could be described with radical versus pragmatic. In the cultural context, the term "open source" is used most often, not as an affirmation of one of these attitudes, but for its greater metaphorical scope that lends it more easily to be applied to contexts other than software. By the late 1990s the Internet had become a mass medium in the US and file-sharing exploded onto the scene.[21] It looked like the experience made with software would be repeated. Against a largely non-commercial practice of sharing culture—texts, images, sound and video— existing copyright was being enforced ever more aggressively through new enclosures, threatening not only online culture, but civil liberties more generally.[22] One way to address this issue was to port the idea of a free license from software to culture. A first attempt, called Free Art License, was initiated by the French artist Antoine Moreau in early 2000.[23] However, it was the Creative Commons project, launched a year later, that brought such licenses to the cultural mainstream. While the free software movement was revolutionary in intent, the CC project, headed by leading law professors in the US, has always been

19 Eric S. Raymond, "Goodbye, 'Free Software'; Hello, 'Open Source'," Catb.Org (February 8, 1998), http://www.catb.org/~esr/open-source.html.
20 Steven Weber, *The Success of Open Source* (Cambridge MA: Harvard University Press, 2004); Yochai Benkler, *The Wealth of Networks: How Social Production Transforms Markets and Freedom* (New Haven: Yale University Press, 2006).
21 Napster was launched on June 1, 1999 and had to close after being sued on July 1, 2001. At its peak, it had more than 24 million users, which was seen as a very large number. Many other filesharing services followed, most notoriously the bittorrent-based Piratebay, which was launched in 2003 and still exists today.
22 James Boyle, "A Politics of Intellectual Property: Environmentalism for the Net?," *Duke Law Journal* 47, no. 1 (1997): pp. 87–116.
23 Aymeric Mansoux, "Sandbox Culture: A Study of the Application of Free and Open Source Software Licensing Ideas to Art and Cultural Production," Centre for Cultural Studies, Goldsmiths, University of London, 2017, https://monoskop.org/log/?p=18777

reformist.[24] So, rather than putting the needs of an active community at the center of their approach, CC focused on the individual creator who could freely choose from a set of licenses, ranging from granting limited right of access and non-commercial use to granting full rights of re-use, including the condition of propagating the same rights to everyone else. Community was an afterthought and the commons were imagined primarily as an aggregation of individual works, donated by enlightened authors. Today, the Creative Commons licenses are the de facto standard within the cultural field, used by millions of individual creators and major projects such as Wikipedia, Open Street Map and Open Access publications in science (such as this one).

The political

The fourth perspective on the commons, which sometimes takes both physical and digital resources into view, draws on political science that conceptualizes commons as a holistic social system. As Massimo de Angelis put it:

> Commons are not simply resources we share—conceptualizing the commons involves three things at the same time. First, all commons involve some sort of common pool of resources, understood as non-commodified means of fulfilling people's needs. Second, the commons are necessarily created and sustained by communities—this, of course, is a very problematic term and topic, but nonetheless we have to think about it. Communities are sets of commoners who share these resources and who define for themselves the rules according to which they are accessed and used. Communities, however, do not necessarily have to be bound to a locality, they could also operate through translocal spaces. They also need not be understood as "homogeneous" in their cultural and material features. In addition to these two elements—the pool of resources and the set of communities—the third and most important element in terms of conceptualizing the commons is the verb "to common"—the social process that creates and reproduces the commons.[25]

24 Lawrence Lessig, *Free Culture: How Big Media Uses Technology and the Law to Lock Down Culture and Control Creativity* (New York: Penguin Press, 2004).
25 Massimo De Angelis and Stavros Stavrides, "On the Commons: A Public Interview," *e-flux Journal*, no. 17 (June 2010), http://www.e-flux.com/journal/on-the-commons-a-public-interview-with-massimo-de-angelis-and-stavros-stavrides/

Such a view takes material, social and institutional dimensions into consideration as highly interdependent, and positions them as a potential alternative to the dominant neoliberal regime of commodification and privatization. While De Angelis has always been careful to point out the danger of co-optation and the need of capitalism to have a reproductive "outside,"[26] a more popular and activist discourse had few such reservations. Here, commons are viewed as operating simply "beyond market and state," with a tendency to idealize commons as self-sufficient islands of shared values and consensual decision-making.[27] While the flattening of the concept might be justified as part of an activist approach to very real and urgent issues, it remains conceptually problematic because it is unable to elaborate its own assumptions and thus produces its own theoretical and practical blind spots.

Michael Hardt and Antonio Negri expand the notion of the commons beyond physical or digital resources in the conventional sense. They consider as part of the commons "also and more significantly those results of social production that are necessary for social interaction and further production, such as knowledge, languages, codes, information, affects, and so forth."[28] In such a view, the commons is primary, and capitalist production is secondary. To the degree that capitalism colonizes and encloses the commons, it cuts itself off from a vital source. Since social life, by its very definition, depends on shared language, codes and affect, the commons cannot fully disappear, but constitute part of "altermodernity." More than that, cognitive capitalism, with its emphasis on languages, codes, and affects, unwittingly expands the commons, even as it tries to enclose and commodify them.

The feminist

Feminist perspectives also see the commons as an expansive sphere of the social but with a different emphasis. Silvia Federici, for example, starts from a focus on reproductive work that "begins with the real-

---

26 Massimo De Angelis, "Crises, Capital and Co-Optation: Does Capital Need a Commons Fix?," in Bollier and Helfrich, *The Wealth of the Commons*, pp. 184–191, http://wealthofthe-commons.org/essay/crises-capital-and-co-optation-does-capital-need-commons-fix

27 Bollier and Helfrich, *The Wealth of the Commons*; David Bollier, *Viral Spiral: How the Commoners Built a Digital Republic of Their Own* (New York and London: New Press, 2009); see also popular websites such as https://shareable.org

28 Michael Hardt and Antonio Negri, *Commonwealth* (Cambridge MA: Belknap Press of Harvard University Press, 2009), p.viii.

ization that, as the primary subjects of reproductive work, historically and in our time, women have depended on access to communal natural resources more than men and have been most penalized by their privatization and most committed to their defense. (...) Women have also led the effort to collectivize reproductive labor both as a means to economize the cost of reproduction and to protect each other from poverty, state violence, and the violence of individual men."[29] She takes a very broad view of reproduction, which includes not only physical reproduction, but also culture and social memory as important dimensions of community. And Maria Mies maintains that there cannot be a commons without community, hence she takes a very critical view of notions such as "global commons" or "shared heritage of mankind," which are in practice often used to take existing commons managed by a specific community (for example seeds and plants) and turn them into an "open access" regime (genetic information) ready for exploitation by transnational corporations.[30] Thus commons, in these (eco-) feminist perspectives, are institutions of self-governing and often self-sufficient local economies in which "production" and "reproduction" are not split into separate domains, but form an organic unity.[31]

While the emphasis on the inseparability of production and reproduction, and the notions of care and mutuality play an important role also for the commons in this book, for Federici the idea of "digital commons" is a contradiction in terms. In her opinion, technology, in particular digital technology, has no potential for the commons, because "with computerization, the abstraction and regimentation of labor is reaching its completion and so is our alienation and desocialization. The level of stress digital labor is producing can be measured by the epidemic of mental illnesses—depression, panic, anxiety, attention deficit, dyslexia—now typical of the most technologically advanced countries like the U.S.—epidemics that can also be read as forms of passive

---

29 Silvia Federici, "Feminism and the Politics of the Commons," in Bollier and Helfrich, *The Wealth of the Commons, pp. 48-49,* First published in *The Commoner,* no. 14 (2010). http://wealthofthecommons.org/essay/feminism-and-politics-commons

30 Maria Mies and Veronika Bennholdt-Thomsen, "Defending, Reclaiming and Reinventing the Commons," *Canadian Journal of Development Studies / Revue Canadienne d'études Du Développement* 22, no. 4 (2001): pp. 997–1023, https://doi.org/10.1080/02255189.2001.9669952

31 The underlying trinity of women, reproduction and nature is not without its critics, but to elaborate this would exceed the focus of this book.

resistance, as refusals to comply, to become machine-like and make capital's plans our own."[32] There is no denying that digital technology supported the commodification of the world and more intensive relations of exploitation.[33] It seems problematic, however, to locate the root of this within technology rather than within capitalist relations, and thus preclude the question in which ways technology could support other types of relations that can sustain commons and thus reflect a contemporary trans-local experience, rather than a rural and local one.

The transversal

This review of some of the main perspectives on the commons is by no means an attempt to provide an exhaustive overview. The theory of the commons has grown in scope and cultural diversity significantly over the last few years, and many additional theoretical perspectives are provided in the texts included in this publication. The aim here is to provide a context for the transversal dimension in our conceptualization of the commons as a "thinking tool." Thus we start from the assumption that commons are not just built around resources, but also affects. They are not just aggregations of individuals or homogenous communities, but demand and produce a range of subjectivities beyond these two types. Commons are structured by relations of care rather than ownership. They emerge from entanglement with, rather than separation from, an often hostile environment. To create such different relationships, commons need adapted (technological) infrastructures, and they bring forth their specific institutional forms. This, it is important to stress, does not create ideal situations or replicable models, but practical tools, experiences and stories through which to think, because, "it matters what stories tell stories."[34] And to tell different stories, we need different aesthetics.

---

32 Silvia Federici, "Re-Enchanting the World: Technology, the Body, and the Construction of the Commons," in *Re-Enchanting the World: Feminism and the Politics of the Commons*, (Oakland: PM Press, 2018), pp. 188–197, here p. 192.

33 Nick Couldry and Ulises Ali Mejias, *The Costs of Connection: How Data Is Colonizing Human Life and Appropriating It for Capitalism, Culture and Economic Life* (Stanford: Stanford University Press, 2019).

34 Donna Haraway, "It Matters What Stories Tell Stories; It Matters Whose Stories Tell Stories," *a/b: Auto/Biography Studies* 34, no. 3 (2019): pp. 565–575, https://doi.org/10.1080/08989575.2019.1664163

AESTHETICS

The artistic projects at the heart of this publication open up the field of art to areas in which current social contradictions are being negotiated and processed. On the one hand, these efforts to "open up" art have the effect that specific forms of artistic perception, organization, and activity can leave behind the traditional reference system of art and operate "effectively" outside of it. At the same time, conversely, a movement is taking place to ensure that certain problems and sets of questions emerge within the field of art. This two-way exchange raises questions of autonomy and contributes to an emancipatory transformation of the art field and its borders, while also enriching the set of tactics and strategies outside the field.

The artistic projects discussed are of a highly heterogeneous sort, but they all have certain aspects in common. Each of them is concerned, for example, with creating social formations, whether in the form of physical locations where people can gather and do something together, or in the form of technical infrastructures such as platforms, servers, or websites, which facilitate communication outside the logic of surveillance capitalism, enable access to certain resources, or allow networking to take place on the basis of common interests and shared values. In each case, the primary concern of the respective projects is to establish connections and relations and thus create human and more-than-human socialities.

Inside out
The notion of the field goes back to the French cultural sociologist Pierre Bourdieu, who describes various social spheres according to their prevailing inherent dynamics and thus differentiates them from one another. Every field possesses its own unique logic, which constitutes it and determines its internal manner of functioning. He thus devotes attention to culture or the arts as a field whose autonomy is of particular significance, though at the same time he underscores its dependence on other social fields, especially that of economy. On the one hand, as Christiane Schnell has pointed out, he "emphasizes the defiant potential of the artistic field, in which the rules of play and the logic of value differ from those of market competition. On the other hand, however, Bourdieu also demonstrates how this field and the

values produced there are fed back into society and its hegemonic structures."[35]

In a historical examination of the nineteenth century, Bourdieu analyzed the origin of art's field-specific rules, which largely arose as an effort to distance art from the spread of capitalism and its ideals of utility and productivity.[36] What emerged was the idea of the artistic field as an "island of market-free aesthetics" and the notion that art serves only its own ends (l'art pour l'art). Accordingly, artists are disconnected from having any responsibility toward society; their only obligation is to "anti-utilitarianism" (freedom of purpose) and to their own individual drive to express themselves. In Bourdieu's view, however, it is precisely this "particular logic," which is "based on the very nature of symbolic goods," that makes room for an "inverse economy."[37] Here, the value of art is created by its own inherent mechanisms, which have more to do with "faith" than with transparency. Moreover, the logic of the field requires that the existence of these mechanisms of value creation and marketability has to be denied. This also means that the field of art has limits that even the most free-thinking artists cannot cross without sacrificing their credibility within the art world: "The boldest artistic ideas are only thinkable *within* the system that determines what is possible."[38] This immediately raises the question of how such transgressions might look and what consequences they might have.

Despite the hegemonic nature of cultural praxis, which typically entails that those with certain privileges—those, in other words, who possess social and cultural capital—determine the legitimacy of art, art nevertheless became enormously differentiated in the twentieth century and thereby, time and again, also experienced or transgressed its limits. In particular, artistic practices that deviate from the traditional paradigms of authorship/work/originality and, by utilizing participatory and interactive formats (for example), leave behind the artistic venues of galleries and museums run the risk that their cultural value

35 Christiane Schnell, "Der Kulturbetrieb bei Bourdieu," *Jahrbuch Kulturmanagement* 1 (2010): pp. 43–53, here p. 44.

36 Pierre Bourdieu, *The Rules of Art: Genesis and Structure of the Literary Field*, trans. Susan Emanuel (Stanford: Stanford University Press, 1996).

37 Ibid., p. 141.

38 Schnell, "Der Kulturbetrieb bei Bourdieu," p. 46.

as "works of art" can be denied or diminished. Such works transgress boundaries, and the extent to which this is accepted or even rewarded is a matter of negotiating the terms of legitimate art. Finally, the field as a whole will not survive if it opens itself up indiscriminately. Thus, boundaries are always shifting, and it is part of the dynamic of the artistic field that this will continue to be the case.

Regarding this process of negotiating the limits of the field of art, our focus here is on a select group of projects that we not only perceive as commons but also as art. Projects that attract recognition and achieve effects, not only within the field of art, but also outside of it, are treated here as fully belonging to the field of art, and this publication is an attempt to legitimize this position from various points of view. We have no intention of defining in general "how art operates" or promoting a universalist discourse; rather, we make a point of stressing that there are numerous forms of artistic praxis that have developed their own inherent logic and have therefore tested out the limits of the field anew and consciously gone beyond them. Part of the self-defining power of these projects is that they can decide whether they want to expand the limits of their field as a whole or, when faced with the challenge of traditional paradigms, leave the field altogether.

In what follows, we will introduce perspectives that seem relevant to us. Together, they provide a broad framework within which we situate the *Aesthetics of the Commons*.

The operational
In a social situation that is deeply influenced and pervaded by the operational logic of networked media, and in which digital technologies provide the infrastructure of social production in general and artistic production in particular, Walter Benjamin's question concerning the "aesthetics of production" is perhaps more relevant than ever. Because the question of whether one should use digital media was answered long ago, the only remaining question is that of how. Benjamin addresses this latter question in terms of the production of art, for which he argues that it is not only necessary to produce radical content but also to position this content in such a way that the conditions of its production are integrated into the production of critique. Otherwise, the bourgeois apparatus of production will simply be able to assimilate the radical content in question: "[T]he bourgeois apparatus

of production and publication can assimilate astonishing quantities of revolutionary themes—indeed, can propagate them without calling its own existence, and the existence of the class that it owns, seriously into question."[39] It is not only necessary, that is, to use the apparatus of production but also to transform it, an act that Benjamin (borrowing from Brecht) calls an *Umfunktionierung*—a "functional transformation," by which he means "the transformation of the forms and instruments of production."[40] This demand goes back to Benjamin's clear goal of placing aesthetic production in the service of class struggle, which, he hoped, would appropriate and functionally transform the means of production (including media-based means). He counters the myth of "indifferent" art by claiming that art always operates with a particular interest and thus always takes a position— either in agreement with or against the prevailing conditions. Regarding the argument that a political position automatically annuls the quality of art, Benjamin turns this on its head by drawing a connection between artistic quality and political quality. Such political quality arises from the position that a work of art takes within the artistic conditions of production. This position is determined by what he calls "technique." In this regard, a work's political "tendency"—that is, its political orientation—is interrelated with its artistic quality: "There is a functional interdependence between the correct political tendency and progressive artistic technique,"[41] which means that the quality of a work always arises from its position with respect to the conditions of production. Drawing upon the ideas of Sergei Tretyakov, who referred to the revolutionary author as an "operating writer," Benjamin argues that this situation gives rise to an operational aesthetics that is always in pursuit of "new conceptions of artistic forms or genres." These latter conceptions tend to take into account the technical circumstances of the present, for it is these that characterize an era's means of production.

---

[39] Walter Benjamin, "The Author as Producer," in *Selected Writings: Volume 2, Part 2, 1931– 1934*, trans. Rodney Livingstone et al. (Cambridge MA: Belknap Press of Harvard University Press, 1999), pp. 768–782, here p. 774.

[40] Ibid., p. 773.

[41] Ibid., p. 770.

The organizational

The notion of "organizational aesthetics" is a suggestion made by the cultural theorist Olga Goriunova.[42] With this concept, she tries to do justice to emerging phenomena of the Internet and to understand the "aesthetics" of technological platforms, without reducing aesthetics to its usual Western definition. Her main point of reference is the aesthetic theory of the Russian literary scholar Mikhail Bakhtin. Bakhtin's understanding of aesthetics is not limited to the field of art or to visual phenomena or other sensual experiences. Rather, he understands the aesthetic relation as a correlation between the subject and the dynamics in which he or she is embedded, aesthetics being central to the processes of subjectivation and to the production of the subject.[43] Because subjectivity is not thought of as "a whole, one, centered and stable subjectivity," it requires a productive force that constantly produces such subjectivity as a fiction. This productive force is the aesthetic relation. It is responsible for "making sense" of things in a constantly evolving process of experiences, encounters, ambitions, and actions that relate the subject to the world.

In the specific case studies that Goriunova uses to develop her theory, the correlation is between the subject and Internet platforms that are intrinsically related both to the materiality as well as to the ecology of networked media technology. Both the organizational structure and the techno-cultural objects it brings together would not exist without such technology. Furthermore, the platform and the type of practice that is being organized through it mutually depend on each other. In this sense, an art platform does not just organize an existing field; it plays an important role in the emergence of the respective practice while remaining variable itself. It is this concept that Goriunova refers to as "organizational aesthetics."

The relational

The notion of "relationality" plays a central role in almost all the projects examined in this publication. To understand the creation of

---

42 Olga Goriunova, *Art Platforms and Cultural Production on the Internet* (London: Routledge, 2012).

43 See Mikhail Bakhtin, *The Dialogic Imagination: Four Essays*, trans. Caryl Emerson and Michael Holquist (Austin: University of Texas Press, 1982); and Mikhail Bakhtin, *Toward a Philosophy of the Ac*t, trans. Vadim Liapunov (Austin: University of Texas Press, 1993).

environments in which new relationships can be established as an artistic practice entails a radical reconceptualization of the idea of what an artist is, of what he or she "creates," and how. Here, relationships do not have to be limited to those between humans; rather, they can also be understood in an expanded way as referring to non-human actors and to the "world" as a whole. Inhabiting newly created environments with its own ways of interacting and coexisting recursively creates new forms of subjectivation and being in the world—also for the creators themselves.

When Nicolas Bourriaud introduced the concept of "relational aesthetics"[44] as a framework for a number of exhibitions he curated, it was met with huge interest—both from the side of those who were interested in expanding art into the social realm and from the side of those who were strictly against such "functionalization." In his own definition, relational aesthetics is an "aesthetic theory consisting in judging artworks on the basis of the inter-human relations which they represent, produce or prompt."[45] He derived his theory from the artworks he was exhibiting, and he defined their common concern as that of inventing models of "sociability" and "conviviality." More specifically, this meant spending time together and meeting people— temporarily, at special events created by artists—whom one would not have met otherwise.

Although Bourriaud has been an effective advocate for the then contemporary tendency to emphasize process, performativity, openness, social contexts, transitivity, and the production of dialogue over the closure of traditional modernist objecthood, visuality, and hyper-individualism, he made sure that the experimental encounters he considered would remain within the confines of art institutions (museums and gallery spaces), where they could function as exhibitable "artworks." Moreover, what at first sight may have seemed like emancipatory—not to mention radical—aesthetic practices were in fact not meant to be more than entertainment. Contradicting himself, Bourriaud made sure that the works he selected would have no ambition whatsoever "to overcome the system of organized exploitation and

---

44 Nicolas Bourriaud, *Relational Aesthetics*, trans. Simon Pleasance et al. (Paris: Les presses du réel, 1998).
45 Ibid., p. 112.

domination"[46] that is responsible for the social misery and alienation typical of our societies, although he had claimed that the works in question were "responses" to such circumstances. In fact, relational art was about "learning to inhabit the world in a better way, instead of trying to construct it based on a pre-conceived idea."[47] As the Radical Culture Research Collective has pointed out, "[r]elational artists tend to accept what Bourriaud calls 'the existing real' and are happy to play with 'the social bond' within the constraining frame of the given."[48] Despite Bourriaud's use of it as a conservative aesthetic concept, the relational still contains the potential to be actualized as a more radical and politicized form of aesthetics.

The educational

Within artistic practices of commoning, the educational is a fundamental category.

Being a praxis of exchange and sharing, the commons open up new spaces for "other" ways of relating and learning. Following the thinking of Gayatri Chakravorty Spivak, learning is not a simple, linear process, and it is not just about accumulating skills and knowledge. Rather, education is a complex process of subjectivization which plays an important role for (cultural) hegemonies to create and maintain the social order. According to Spivak, it is important to recognize the interdependence between learning and education and power and authority, and thus the violence inherent to processes of learning.

Spivak's analysis of the role of education as an instrument for establishing social power relations leads her to the notion of *unlearning*. Unlearning, first of all, requires an understanding of the historicity of all subject positions—which implies that they have been "made" and thus could also be "unmade." The unlearning of privileges is what her approach suggests as a starting point: "Unlearning one's privilege as one's loss,"[49] sums up what is core to her thinking and also resonates with earlier feminist standpoint theories: privilege implies a lack

---

46   The Radical Culture Research Collective (RCRC), "A Very Short Critique of Relational Aesthetics," (2012), https://greekleftreview.wordpress.com/2012/01/01/a-very-short-critique-of-relational-aesthetics/
47   Bourriaud, *Relational Aesthetics*, p. 13.
48   RCRC, "A Very Short Critique of Relational Aesthetics."
49   Donna Landry and Gerald MacLean, eds., *The Spivak Reader: Selected Works of Gayatri Chakravorty Spivak* (London: Routledge, 1996), p. 4.

of access to "other" standpoints, i.e. the ones related to experiences of discrimination. María do Mar Castro Varela therefore suggests not being ashamed of the privileges we have by birth or through class mobility, but rather understanding that *any* position within a social system comes with a specific and therefore also limited power to act.[50] Nevertheless, unlearning one's privileges is not just a gesture, and it is only possible through critical thinking *and* acting that involves the risk of challenging one's own position. In this sense, unlearning is a deconstructive practice that means to "constantly and persistently look into how truths are produced."[51]

Learning from post-colonial theory, the aesthetics of the commons involve the realization of an "epistemic violence" that underlies all processes of social formation. In that sense, the role of commoning projects can be to conceive education as a powerful engine for social transformation, as a "counter-hegemonic weapon"[52] that enables the creation of imaginaries and practices beyond the established forms of discrimination.

The institution critical

Despite their art historical canonization, including the creation of an art genre with the name "institutional critique," critical aesthetic practices that include a reflection of their own field, its mechanisms of inclusion and exclusion, its entanglement with social, political and financial power are still evolving today. They may or may not actively relate to this tradition, and they may or may not call themselves "institution critical," but in the context of the aesthetics of the commons, it is of interest to trace this development and analyze its influence.

It has been suggested to speak of different phases of institutional critique,[53] starting with the first one in the 1960s and 1970s with artists who brought the spirit of the protest movements of the time (anti-war, anti-racism, feminism etc.) to the art world; but turning it

50 María do Mar Castro Varela, "(Un-)Wissen. Verlernen als komplexer Lernprozess," Migrazine 1, 2017, http://www.migrazine.at/artikel/un-wissen-verlernen-als-komplexerlernprozess
51 Landry and Maclean, *The Spivak Reader*, p. 27.
52 Do Mar Castro Varela, "(Un-)Wissen."
53 Gerald Raunig, "Instituent Practices. Fleeing, Instituting, Transforming," *trans-versal* (January 2006), http://transform.eipcp.net/transversal/0106/raunig/en.html

into conceptual and formal works within the institution.[54] It was during the second phase, from the 1980s onwards, that the term "institutional critique" was coined by the artist Andrea Frazer. The newly created genre was characterized by works that criticized art and its institutions in a self-reflexive and immanent way—"limiting all possible forms of institutional critique to a critique of the 'institution of art' (Peter Bürger) and its institutions."[55] However, if "institutional critique is not to be fixed and paralyzed as something established in the art field and confined within its governing rules, then it has to continue to develop along with changes in society and especially to tie into other forms of critique both within and outside the art field, such as those arising in opposition to the respective conditions or even before their formations," as Raunig writes in 2006. What has been called "phase change,"[56] describes a new phase in which *transversality* is an important aspect. It helps to theorize "the assemblages that link actors and resources from the art circuit to projects and experiments that don't exhaust themselves inside it, but rather, extend elsewhere."[57] Adopting Holmes' ideas, the projects that can be related to this new area involve an "extradisciplinary" way of working and are less concerned with art as an institution that needs to be criticized than with the urgency of the counter-institutional positions they relate their practice to. This "transversal exchange of forms of critique" establishes a new form of institutional critique which expresses a critical attitude and, at the same time, is an instituent practice.[58] It does not exhaust itself in the classical gestures of negation and rejection of the institution or the reintegration of critique into institutional apparatuses, but rather is aware of its involvement in the criticized while actualizing the social potencies that unfold the knowledges of alternative ways of institutionality.[59]

54 Kastner speaks here of an "Artistic Internationalism" that aimed at transgressing the borders of the art field. Jens Kastner, "Artistic Internationalism and Institutional Critique," *transversal* (November 2006), http://transform.eipcp.net/transversal/0106/kastner/en.html
55 Raunig, "Instituent Practices."
56 Brain Holmes, "Extradisciplinary Investigations: Towards a New Critique of Institutions," *transversal* (January 2007), http://transform.eipcp.net/transversal/0106/holmes/en.html
57 Ibid.
58 Raunig, "Instituent Practices."
59 Stefan Nowotny and Gerlad Raunig, *Instituierende Praxen: Bruchlinien der Institutionskritik,* 2nd Edition (Vienna: transversal texts, 2016).

The beautiful

With reference to Rancière (though intentionally reinterpreting his work), one could argue that the projects discussed in this book may indeed be political in nature, but not in the sense that they plainly and directly address social problems or denounce injustices (they do not, that is, "disseminate political content" and thus merge with the political). Rather, they correspond throughout to Rancière's idea of thinking about art as a "sensorium of exception": "Art is primarily political in creating a space-time sensorium, in certain modes of being together or apart, of defining being inside or outside, opposite to or in the middle of,"[60] as he suggests. Though largely outside of traditional artistic venues, the projects that are of interest here enable an experience that can very well be called aesthetic, for this experience is not exhausted by knowledge or desire but rather creates, in its own unique way, connections and tensions between the collective and the singular, the special and the mundane.[61] They can therefore be thought of not only as "oppositional" but also as "beautiful"—understanding beauty as that which cannot be fully grasped conceptually nor be simply consumed.[62]

Aesthetics of the Commons

The *Aesthetics of the Commons* emerge from relating two broad frameworks with one another. The quality of both, in our understanding, is that they not only produce openings, and offer space for negotiation and material practice, but they both even require it, structurally. Art as well as commons live from a permanent process of vision and implementation, of experimentation and evaluation, of responding to the contemporary condition by creating new forms, formats and formations and questioning them again. Connecting these two frameworks, certainly raised more questions than answers, but it has also produced a series of propositions of how to think about practices that try to respond to some of the crises that make up the present moment. These crises are extensive and run deep, right into the heart of the modern liberal project, and thus also the projects and theories presented here

---

60 Jacques Rancière, "Die Politik der Kunst und ihre Paradoxien," in *Die Aufteilung des Sinnlichen. Die Politik der Kunst und ihre Paradoxien*, ed. Maria Muhle (Berlin: b_books/ Polypen, 2006), pp. 75–100, here p. 77.
61 See Jens Kastner, "Rancière," *Graswurzelrevolution* 332 (2008): pp. 15–16.
62 See Jacques Rancière, *Ist Kunst widerständig?* (Berlin: Merve, 2008).

are extensive and raise fundamental questions, while making proposi-tions for new imaginaries. However, this publication will not provide a unified theory, but a set of conceptual tensions and openings from which to rethink ways of encountering present crises. It was never in our interest to answer the question what art is, or what the commons are, but we highly appreciate and value the negotiation of both, of what happens when they meet and how they can enrich each other. This is a collective and open-ended process and we hope to provide materials that are inspiring to you.

Organization of the Book

The ten texts that make up this book are organized in three sections that highlight the transversal character of the *Aesthetics of the Commons*: Agency & Subjectivity, Care & Infrastructure, Affect & Organi-zation. Drawing on a wide range of theories, they articulate mutual constitutions of commoning as social practice and as aesthetics; that is, specific forms through which these practices unfold. While the texts balance the two sides differently, depending on their particular theo-retical concerns, none of them separates them into different domains; rather it is their inseparability and transversal relations that gives the *Aesthetics of the Commons* its unique character.

Agency & Subjectivity

Olga Goriunova offers a perspective on the aesthetic dimension of com-moning projects, in particular shadow libraries, focusing on the subject positions they articulate. Subject positions, she argues, are abstracted subjects, not individual subjectivities, and they are generated through specific practices, including technological systems. Following Bakhtin, Goriunova identifies an aesthetic dimension, since these subject posi-tions open up specific ways of being in the world, making sense of it and acting in it. Against the backdrop of historic subject positions, she discusses how these relate to their socio-political conditions: how they open up ways of alternative being (the pirate), but also become objects of oppression (the witch). Goriunova discusses how the very pragmatic practice of commoning knowledge resources—including

33

small gestures of care, affection and tending, but also bigger gestures like setting up a system—is articulating specific subject positions that then produce environments and discourses, and also have the power to introduce new ways of seeing the world into other fields.

Jeremy Gilbert starts from the question: "What lies in the zone between temporary, relatively short-lived exercises in the construction of 'commons' and the possibility of large-scale institutional innovation and reform?" The relation between the creation of new artistic forms and social change has been rethought repeatedly since Plato first posited it, disapprovingly, with respect to music. One way of conceptualizing this potentiality, Gilbert notes, is in terms of the capacity of such practice to engender an affective experience of possible worlds. These act as a prefiguration of different worlds, offering a stark contrast to dominant patterns of affective relations, providing joy and hope on the smaller scale for a world that looks exceedingly bleak on a larger scale. This provides a resource available for action in other fields. There is a constant danger, though, that this resource is appropriated by capital, thus using artistic innovation merely as a training ground for the subjects of the most advanced forms of digital capitalism, to infuse it with a "new spirit". In respect to commoning practices, the crucial dimension for Gilbert is the relationship between abundance and scarcity. Commoning practices—even if their output might be meager—are always based on abundance, from natural resources that are replenishing themselves to digital information which is non-rival (use does not subtract, rather multiplies it). Capitalism always requires the scarcity of the commodity form, hence there is the continuing practice of enclosure. Within a comprehensively commodified world, commons projects have the potential to "dis-enclose" resources, liberating them from the commodity-form, developing affective structures of care based on abundance, providing subjectivities and agencies for a different future.

Judith Siegmund, in her contribution, enquires into the specific idea of aesthetics which are at play in artistic practices of archiving and publishing. She dissects the Kantian notion of aesthetics, then in order to retain the dimension of autonomy, she puts it on a different footing. Rather than grounding it in the distance of art from other social fields which supposedly allows for indifferent reflection and individualized pleasure, she develops the notion of autonomy rooted in a particular type of agency. An agency that stems from the subjects' acknowledgment of their deep entrenchment in social structures and yet, at the same time, from their striving for something of their own. The goal is neither to gain sovereign mastery nor to act in an individually self-determined way. Rather, autonomy stems from an agency that contains the idea of responsiveness, which can only be fully understood in scenarios that involve interdependence, yet allows for high degrees of freedom in this responsiveness.

Care & Infrastructure

Daphne Dragona investigates a changing understanding of commons as a response to the current global situation of interconnected crises. Taking up the idea of commons as "affective infrastructures," she is particularly interested in the potential of art projects to build affective relations by constituting "active points of relation" and "spaces for affective encounters." She explores four different artistic initiatives, in different parts of the world, and their specific ways of "opposing hegemonic worlds" and "decolonizing social space," thus offering the ground for transition and transformation. Being embedded in "ecologies of resources, people and relations" they all link to the sociopolitical conditions of their time and play an important role in building commons as affective infrastructures both in a "literal" but also "metaphorical" sense. The artists work with the commons in relation to the earth and its resources, knowledge, and information, but also cultural and social spaces, and have raised questions over appropriation and ownership. Their emphasis lies on accommodating heterogeneity and embracing uncommon knowledge, thus enabling unprecedented forms of assemblage. Dragona characterizes these as producing a new aesthetics, an "aesthetics of openness and ongoingness, of transversality and multiplicity which embraces change and social transformation. It is an aesthetics that challenges given understandings of the world, and invites people to co-shape, inhabit, and explore new possible visions of it."

Magdalena Tyżlik-Carver takes the exhibition *OPEN SCORES: How to Program the Commons*, which took place in late 2019 at panke.gallery in Berlin, as the reference point for a wide-ranging examination of the challenges of data curation. Its basic operations—harvesting, cleaning, filtering, analyzing, and displaying—have become generalized techniques of living and acting in contemporary worlds that are producing and are produced by data on all levels. They are conducted continuously in specialized and everyday practices. The challenge for art curation, she identifies, is to transform these ongoing practices in an exhibition which can function as a "temporary location for meaning making, a moment for disrupting knowledge in order to invent it." Here, the *score* takes on a double function. One the one hand it translates, as she writes, "collaborative processes into data and information, thus making them accessible beyond the conditions in which each project originated." Extending the tradition of Fluxus, they create an aesthetic which results in a tension between object and time, opening a perspective for action beyond the confines of the temporary location of the exhibition. On the other hand, they point to the ambivalent character of the contemporary condition, whose ubiquitous scores are sometimes executed by machines, sometimes by humans, and, most often, in complex assemblages. Through the respective focal points of the works, the exhibition represented an opportunity to inquire into contemporary forms of care and re/production through aesthetic means, that is, commoning *with* digital technologies.

Gary Hall, based on his own work as an academic who does not just write theory, but also builds environments and knowledge infrastructures for the production and sharing of theory, develops what he calls the "anti-bourgeois theory" (ABT). ABT demands to "intra-act with the world instead of just representing it," and one of the shared aims of the "pre-figurative projects" he is involved in "is to disarticulate the existing playing field and its manufactured common sense of what it means today to be a theorist, a philosopher, an academic, an artist or a political activist." In this sense, he calls for expanding traditional conceptions of authorship by including activities of care, thus proposing a new understanding of theory altogether: as *implementing* different ways of being instead of just *imagining* them. Hall positions his work in the postdigital era—"a technical condition that … is constituted by the naturalization of pervasive and connected computing processes … in everyday life," and a political landscape characterized by the crisis of representative democracy and growing populism. As a response, he suggests new models for political communication based on postdigital technologies for purposes grounded in principles of social responsibility, solidarity, and mutual care, coupled to the collective redistribution of knowledge and resources. Commons, for Hall, serve as a conceptual framework that enables such new ways of thinking and acting while remaining an open and diverse territory.

Affect & Organization

Ines Kleesattel investigates the praxis of "Feminist Servers" from the point of view of institutional critique, in particular feminist positions that highlight the role of maintenance and care (in contrast to production and possession), such as Mierle Laderman Ukeles' *Manifesto for Maintenance Art (1969)*. These practices, she argues, are best characterized as "Situated Aesthetics": "an aesthetic relationality ... of differentiation, of partial connections, and an ongoing precarious commoning." This opens a perspective to rethink, ground and extend the notion of a relational aesthetic, but also bring in the materiality and (more than human) sociality of the relations, the affective work—tensions, conflicts and agreements—that go into creating and maintaining the relations and the specific social spaces that are built through becoming related in that way. From this, a more complex notion of aesthetics and functionality emerges, one in which the two are intertwined, dynamic and continuously (re)produced.

Sophie Toupin focuses on the role of "techno-social imaginaries," noting that a broad vision of the future, often speculative, underlies different articulations of socio-technical systems. Currently, these are dominated by the capitalist imaginaries exemplified by Amazon and Facebook, creating technological systems aimed at extraction and profit-making. Commoning projects, on the other hand, are animated by different imaginaries, focusing on collaboration, sharing, and self-organization. Toupin is particularly interested in feminist and intersectional imaginaries, which connect the technological with the social, the informational with the material, in particular the body. Such speculative endeavors, she maintains, play an important role in articulating a different future, and generate new forms of organizations to fight for it.

37

Rahel Puffert starts from her understanding that all art emerges under specific socio-political conditions and thus necessarily relates to them, even if this is ignored in most discourses about art. She opens a perspective on what she calls the "sensus communis" (a sense of what is shared) through the lens of critical art education, as work on the relations between art, aesthetic practices, and the public. Going beyond the modernist notion of the autonomy of the artwork, and the Kantian notion of the detached aesthetic experience, she is striving to open art up into a socio-political question, which also includes its institutional dimensions. Against this backdrop, she investigates three projects (a feminist hackspace, a public art school, and an artist-run space) on how they realize this sense of the shared within their own institutional conditions. Of specific interest are ways of building and sustaining communities, the relationship to the outside and the "other," and the sensibilities for educational aspects in institution building. "Instituting"—to use one of the terms brought up by one of the projects—includes learning as a way of becoming a commons.

Christoph Brunner takes seriously the artists' claim that "a functioning piece of software can function as an argument: one that is impossible to make if you can only refer to an idea, or a plan, or a theory." Based on a detailed analysis of the video platforms 0xDB and pad.ma, which run on a custom-developed platform, he elaborates the notions of "concatenated commons" and "operational aesthetics" by drawing on theories by William James, Deleuze and Guattari, and Donna Haraway. His focus on the commons is on "temporalizing activations rather than groups, or places," foregrounding how unique instances of commoning (places or groups) are held together by specific types of movement. Commons, then, is first and foremost "a potential of relating, of resonating across different durations, a power to concatenate that can take many forms but does not predetermine the form it takes." Operational aesthetics, he writes, "engage bodily capacities of sensing but extend these capacities into an ecological situatedness that is material, processual and transtemporal." Thus, it encompasses both "part of the programmed and coded structure, as much as the confluence of material, embodied, perceptual and conceptual infrastructures of sense-making."

Felix Stalder and Cornelia Sollfrank, July 2020

Agency & Subjectivity

Olga Goriunova

Uploading Our Libraries:
The Subjects of Art and Knowledge Commons

In this article, I explore digital libraries and repositories of texts, films and other forms of art and knowledge as commons in relation to the subject positions they formulate and from which they are made. Libraries are technically not always commons, although they are increasingly discussed as ecological infrastructures for a good life.[1] Shadow libraries and repositories, as discussed below, are non-state, no profit archives, precarious libraries, public knowledge ecosystems[2] that form new types of culture and knowledge commons. These radically open knowledge infrastructures[3] are unstable, ephemeral, inventive commons, whose subjects see and make the world differently.

PART 1
Introduction to Subject-Positions

The idea of the commons directly relates to the questions of subjectivity and subject (or subject-position). The subject here is taken to mean an abstracted position, almost a logical placeholder, which is distinct from subjectivity or self as a complex and indeterminate lived experience. The subject may abstract from self and maintain a connection to it, or may be a figuration, acting as quasi-subject or "model subject" and being unrelated to any particular individual. We know abstracted subject positions from role models, conceptual descriptions, and novelistic

1 Shannon Mattern, "Library as Infrastructure," *Places* (June 2014), https://placesjournal. org/article/library-as-infrastructure (all links in this text were last accessed October 21, 2020).
2 Cornelia Sollfrank, "The Surplus of Copying. How Shadow Libraries and Pirate Archives Contribute to the Creation of Cultural Memory and the Commons," *originalcopy* (November 2018), http://www.ocopy.net/essays/cornelia-sollfrank/
3 Alexandra Elbakyan, Transcript and Translation of Sci-Hub Presentation (2016), https:// openaccess.unt.edu/symposium/2016/info/transcript-and-translation-sci-hub-presentation

or cinematic figurations. They also take part in the processes of subjectivation, albeit their zone of actualization is art, literature, or culture more broadly. Subject-positions also develop in digital media systems, formulated in relation to technological infrastructures and platforms.

Before setting out to describe the subjects of the projects generating and maintaining knowledge commons, the subjects of shadow libraries and repositories and the subject positions offered to and invented by their collective users, it is important to mark two important claims, from which the notion of the subject or subject position that I want to pursue here stems. The first is that subjectivity is a process rather than an essence. Subjectivity as a process relies on interactions with other humans and non-humans, with forces, laws, institutions, power—overall, on development and exchange in complex systems. Subjectivation, another term to emphasize the processual nature of becoming, is used to describe the flow of life that individuates into a particularity, and here the individual is never quite fully achieved in the sense of being final and whole: an individual is always in the process of being made, relying on the pre-individual, the collective, and the non-individual.

The second claim concerns aesthetics. An argument made by Mikhail Bakhtin is that aesthetics is core to the processes of subjectivation and to the production of the subject.[4] This aesthetics is not a characteristic of something that belongs to the world of art, neither it is something that is primarily visual or perceived by the senses. Aesthetics is a broader category. For Bakhtin, it is the aesthetic relation—that is, primarily a productive, creative force—that *makes sense* of a multitude of features, judgments, responses of a person. This becomes clearer if we take as our starting position the idea presented above that one unique subjectivity is a fiction. A human consists of multiple and multi-directed drives, actions, desires, thoughts—with this multitude dynamically evolving and permanently making sense in relation to the world in which one lives. A whole, one, centered and stable subjectivity is constant work, a fable. This fable, for Bakhtin, is told by aesthetics. It is the aesthetic relation that makes sense of the multiplicity of things

4   Mikhail Bakhtin, *Estetika slovesnogo tvorchestva* (Moskva: Iskusstvo, 1979). The essays included are published in English in Mikhail Bakhtin, *The Dialogic Imagination: Four Essays* (Austin: University of Texas Press, 1982) and Mikhail Bakhtin, *Toward a Philosophy of the Act* (Austin: University of Texas Press, 1993).

taking part and undergoing processes of subjectivation. The aesthetic relation is the one that makes sense, *creates the subject concretely*, in embodied reality, and *abstractly*, in abstracted meaning. Such aesthetic relation is of the person and of the world towards the person; here aesthetic relation is what creates both the person and the world.

When Bakhtin talks about the aesthetic protagonist (in Dostoevsky's novels), he suggests that a protagonist offers *a point of view*. The protagonist here is not a manifestation of socio-political forces (a classical Marxist view on literature), or a constellation of individual characteristics to produce a realist character (Tolstoy's achievement), but a specific point of view on oneself and the world, a conceptual and axiological position: a position from which meaning-making and judgment, evaluation of the world and oneself is made. Such a conceptual subject-position is fictional, i.e. it is literature, and yet a point of view from which a certain new version of the world can be created, and in that, it is aesthetic.

In a certain way, such a proposition is conceptually close to what Deleuze and Guattari describe as a "conceptual persona," of which they write: "The role of conceptual personae is to show thought's territories."[5] A conceptual persona maps and lays out a plane, a cut of the world, with its own coordinates and a horizon of possibility, and within which a mode of living or other form of difference can be invented and produced. Although Deleuze and Guattari say that conceptual personae are not "literary or novelistic heroes,"[6] they write: "the plane of composition of art and the plane of immanence of philosophy can slip into each other to the degree that parts of one may be occupied by the entities of the other."[7] "Great aesthetic figures of thought"[8] offer a point of view, a position, from which a territory can be mapped and creatively produced.

The subject positions described below are abstracted from the work and structures of shadow libraries, repositories, and platforms. They are formed as points of view, conceptual positions that create a version of the world with its own system of values, maps of orientation and horizon of possibility. A conceptual congregation of actions,

5   Gilles Deleuze and Félix Guattari, *What is Philosophy?* (London: Verso, 1994), p. 69.
6   Ibid., p. 65.
7   Ibid., p. 66.
8   Ibid., p. 65.

values, ideas, propositions creates a subject position that renders the project possible. Therefore, on the one hand, techno-cultural gestures, actions, structures create subject positions, and on the other, the projects themselves as cuts of the world are created from a point of view, from a subject position. This is neither techno-determinism, when technology defines subjects, nor an argument for an independence of the human, but for a mutual constitution of subjects and technology through techno-cultural formulations.

Similarly to how Sianne Ngai discussed the problem of the "tone of the text," as a general feeling that neither the reader nor any of the protagonists necessarily feel,[9] there are subject positions in and of a technical system that arise in complex ways. Such positions are figured by a range of possibilities and forms of engagement in a system, but are not necessarily prescribed in such a way that there is a subject position corresponding to a sequence of clicks through the interface. It is not possible to pin a subject position on a technical function alone; neither is the "user" set up through the design process. Sometimes such a subject position is not worth speaking about—it can be formulaic, offer a speck of a subject—but at other times it is a point of view, of meaning-making, of value, that makes a claim for another version of the world. Techno-cultural projects, including the ones I attend to below, form subject positions, both in terms of a position from which the project is created and maintained, and as a collective user/participant, developed through the project's technical realization, content, forms of interaction, and evolution over time.

I have previously developed the notion of organizational aesthetics to explain how the configuration and development of techno-cultural platforms and their practices contribute to the creation of an art movement and of artist and curator as subjects.[10] Subject-positions can be formed by software processes in relation to complex forms of organization of the repository. They can be constructed, among other factors, by specific computational configurations of networks, platforms, use functions, back-ends, software tools, interfaces, html-versions and connection speeds, as well as complex sets of ideas, decisions, chances,

9   Sianne Ngai, *Ugly Feelings* (Cambridge MA: Harvard University Press, 2005), p. 69.
10 Olga Goriunova, *Art Platforms and Cultural Production on the Internet* (London: Routledge, 2012).

and cultural forms. Such subject-positions are aesthetic because they are creative processes that act productively, make sense of and create different cuts of the world and new forms of inhabiting it. In this article, it is the access to the changing structures of art and knowledge, and their changing position in larger infrastructures of society that is negotiated by the subjects under consideration.

There is a tradition for thinking technology in relation to subjectivation (as developed in the work of Gilbert Simondon), but in this text I am more concerned with abstracted subject positions, and how they work in the project of society, rather than going into detail about what they do to subjectivities. My proposition of the subject as a subject-position grows out of Bakhtin's offering. However, I suggest being cautious of the Cartesian tradition, followed by Bakhtin, of regarding a subject as always produced in relation to one human, or human mind, which turns back on oneself and realizes that it can think both the world and itself, thus splitting reality into an object of thought and the thinking subject, conscious of itself. This subject has been announced dead by the poststructuralists. It was decimated by feminist and post-colonial work that showed that such a subject is produced by subjugating the world and otherness, that such a subject is always precoded as white, male, and able. What I would like to do in this text is to argue away from such a subject, and instead think a subject position that acts aesthetically in the world, and in relation to subjectivities. If a subject is a process of abstraction, of turning back on oneself, or a falling out of immanence, as Deleuze called it,[11] there are many ways of abstracting subjects and many different kinds of abstracted subjects operating in the world.

The subject by virtue of its abstracted nature is inscribed in various structures of power (Althusser said that they are generated in response to them[12]), acting back on the self. Very different traditions can be brought together when thinking such subjects. One tradition that concerns itself with people and their subjects is grounded in the social sciences. Here, the formation of the subject is often about rendering people as units, by counting them and recording them as data, fitting

11 Gilles Deleuze, *Pure Immanence: Essays on a Life* (New York: Zone Books, 2001), pp. 26–28.
12 Louis Althusser, "Ideology and Ideological State Apparatuses" (1970), https://www.marxists.org/reference/archive/althusser/1970/ideology.htm

them into categories, and calculating average persons. Well-known arguments, such as that of Ian Hacking, in the article "Making Up People," focus on the claim that statisticians make people up by creating categories and models, which are then filled in by people making themselves in the image of a category or rather society molding people in terms of the category.[13] This is a nominalist position: one names something and it comes to exist, not only as a label, but as embodied reality. The article is staged as an argument between a nominalist and a realist, seemingly with no side winning. Radical nominalism, after all, and perhaps especially after Duchamp, is indistinguishable from poetry or art.

Here is where the operations of counting, identifying, classifying cross to the art and humanities side, another tradition of thinking subjects: people also make themselves and others in the image of creatures of literature, art and film. A term suited to talking about this is that of a poetic figure, figuration, a persona or a subject-position. Here, a subject is an aesthetic position created by an art project, a Bakhtinian point of view offered by a novel's protagonist or a cinematic figuration.

Rancière called these two distinct domains the logic of fact and the logic of fiction. Fiction is not false: it has rigorous logic. I suggest that in computational, data-intensive cultures the logic of fact and the logic of fiction cross wires, creating abstract subject positions that are aesthetic, meaning productive and creative, and which partake in the processes of subjectivation as well as the creation and maintenance of society. There are many such subject positions. Some are very significant and all-encompassing, while others are "flecks of identity,"[14] elements of figurations created by techno-cultural gestures.

In Marxist readings of history, the problem I am trying to capture is normally addressed in terms of an opposition between the form of an individual forged by capitalist systems of relations, and a re-thinking of such an isolated self-managing subject in relation to the notions of collective subjectivation, collective knowledge and action, and alternative property regimes, amongst other things. Such an analysis

---

13 Ian Hacking, "Making Up People" (1986), https://serendipstudio.org/oneworld/system/files/Hacking_making-up-people.pdf
14 Matthew Fuller, *Media Ecologies: Materialist Energies in Art and Technoculture* (Cambridge MA: MIT Press, 2005).

emphasizes that the production of an individual as a self-consistent unit functioning within an order of time and space of work is primarily the result of a transformation of people into disciplined labor power, which is to be further expropriated and turned into capital. The logic of capital governs the copyright system directly (in terms of laws protecting profits, whether immediate or imaginary) and by instilling habits and beliefs, a process of training that is so long that Felix Stalder calls for "unlearning copyright."

But how are such things learned in the first place? The early modern transformation of people into working subjects is explored in the work of Silvia Federici. Federici argues that the person that is homogenized, fixed in time and space, identical to itself, is an invention of capitalism seeking to produce a capable and willing, regularized workforce out of people orientating themselves around chance, magic, and different notions of time and need. This concerns, Federici says in *Caliban and the Witch*, not only the productive labor force, but also the reproductive labor force, primarily women, who were individualized, cut off from the commons, and subjugated into dependence on a man in a nuclear family unit in the early period of capitalist development.[15] Federici's argument emphasizes that historical commons, such as forests in England, were sites of subsistence, collectivity and cooperation. The use of the commons, her argument goes, produced and sustained knowledges and practices involved in the production of difference. This was the difference of how to be female—in relation to plants and the knowledge of herbs, which entailed relation to one's own body, including controlling reproductive capacities, and in relation to other women, their knowledge and shared practices. The common forest was also the source of food and warmth that entailed support for different modes of living and survival. Alongside the dispossession of people by way of enclosures and terminating the communal use of the forest, women were condemned as witches and executed in large quantities, with their forest-reliant knowledges and practices lost as a result.

Here, I would say, a witch is a subject-position. Today, people may decide to explore the option of being a witch, to figure themselves in the image of a witch, to develop a practice to communicate with what

15 Silvia Federici, *Caliban and the Witch* (New York: Autonomedia, 2004).

Stengers calls the "unknowns" of modernity.[16] Such figuration would be conceptual, as well as collective, expressed in specific collective practices. At the same time, as Federici demonstrates, it is a category historically used in Europe to exterminate women to the order of hundreds of thousands during the sixteenth and seventeenth centuries. A figuration here crosses into a legal category, which, once applied to the person, provides grounds for her torture and execution. The tension between the aesthetic function of a subject-position, its political force and its utilization in juridical terms are core to the notion of the subject. The aesthetic figuration of a subject position can be militarized, turned into a weapon or put into shackles.

Overall, I argue that the shadow library projects considered below create subject positions that re-define horizons of possibility through intervening into and widening the processes of subjectivation. To do this is always a political as well as an aesthetic matter. The commons is a site of nourishment of various kinds, of knowledges and practices that sustain alternative political imaginaries of education, social relations, art, culture, economy, and the making of forms of solidarity. Commons are practices, forms of knowledge, action and cooperation, dynamic technical infrastructures that have corresponding subject-positions: they nurture and sustain specific subjects. Such subjects are techno-aesthetic figurations; as such, they may be formed as targets of state control or be targeted so that certain behaviors they represent can be eliminated. Similarly to how the witch hunt, when expressed in cultural, societal suspicion of women, attacked certain forms of feminine power, the copyright regime attacks certain powers: of a habit of knowing, of sharing, of experimental forms of art, of different orders of cultural importance, of building alternative infrastructures. Subject positions can and have repeatedly crossed into categories targeted by law: for instance, when launching a piece of software running a DDoS attack started to constitute criminal behavior rather than a form of political demonstration. Here, for example, acting in the image of a hacker, a member of *Anonymous* supporting Wikileaks against the blockade by Visa or PayPal (a thread of a subject-posi-

16   See work by Isabelle Stengers, including "Experimenting with refrains: Subjectivity and the challenge of escaping modern dualism," *Subjectivity* 22, no. 1 (2008): pp. 38-59, and Philippe Pignarre, Isabelle Stengers, *Capitalist Sorcery: Breaking the Spell*, trans. Andrew Goffey (London: Palgrave, 2011).

tion), in some cases quickly led to people ending up in prison. The damaging lawsuits against individuals who started shadow libraries is another example: an individual is singled out and framed as a criminal in specific nationally delimited legal systems that attempt to narrate the world and people in their own logic and language. The notion of the bourgeois subject is profoundly linked to the notion of individual property. Evasive murky subjects of commons, with their multiple and undefined roles, can offshore responsibility constituted in the terms of current copyright law and its enforcement. Multiple subjects of commons can allow not only for disidentification, but also for play and evasion of this regime.

In what follows, I review a number of the projects sustaining art and knowledge commons in the digital age in terms of the subject positions that arise from the way they have developed and work, as the positions of those who create, maintain, safeguard and use the commons and as the ways of understanding them. There are a few such figures: historically, a pirate, an outlaw, and, more recently, meta and underground librarian, public custodian, general librarian, critical public pedagogue, multiform bibliographer, fancy general archivist, and cultural analyst. All of these are ways of ordering reality and thus creating knowledge, art, and collaborative action. These subjects are not some whim, they are acting in and producing lived reality and the processes of subjectivation of those reliant, even if only occasionally, on them.

PART 2
Pirate, Thief and Otherwise an Outlaw

One of the important figures for the formulation of the commons in response to the rise of networks in the 1980s and 1990s, was that of the pirate. Bruce Sterling's 1988 *Pirates in the Net* described enclaves dedicated to "data piracy," but it was Hakim Bey's work on pirates, appearing in different formats, including *Pirate Utopias*, and culminating in his proposition of the concept of the Temporary Autonomous Zone (TAZ) that became influential for net critics, filesharers, media artists, and activists.

The historical pirates, in his account, held land in common in pirate enclaves; their wealth was held in common treasury.[17] Shared resources meant temporary liberation of land as well as imagination, and implied specific forms of self-governance and sovereignty. The TAZ, inspired by the figuration of an anarchist pirate, is a temporary free enclave that takes the form of a network, tactics, or organization. A TAZ is not necessarily a place in time per se, but is embedded in the Web, which is an "open structure of info exchange."[18] The Web is the necessary support system for a TAZ, which acts within the ethics of the counter-Net, leeching off the official, hierarchical, state-or-corporate-controlled Net. The "actual data piracy,""illegal and rebellious use" of the Net relies on having the structures, tactics, and ways of organizing via the Web. But it's not only that: the Web can also "*inform* the TAZ, from its inception, with vast amounts of compacted time and space which have been 'subtilized' as data."

In Bey's vocabulary, Net and counter-Net seem to act as infrastructures, whereas the Web is a form of their use, a mode of organization, a multiplicity of infrastructural features to support the TAZ, and provide it with time and space in the form of data. What would have been a network of locales, markets, knowledges of routes as well as songs and epics as shared infrastructure of pirate subsistence is "subtilized" into data and the Web.[19] The new formulation of a plastic techno-system, together with its practices of use, strategies, and poetics coalesce around the figure of the pirate. This pirate is a subject position that allows for the invention of new socio-political forms of life. In Bey's account, although he does not use the term, the Web as infrastructural commons enhances and supports forms of life, spaces and time rather than substitutes for them. The ideas come from elsewhere: the pirate imagines and actualizes new forms of society, relying on the common forms of organization, tactics, and resources of the Web.

The founder of *Sci-Hub*, Alexandra Elbakyan, uses related vocabulary today, setting up a fascinating context for her work in one of her

17 Peter Lamborn Wilson, *Pirate Utopias: Moorish Corsairs & European Renegadoes* (New York: Autonomedia, 1995), p. 195.
18 Hakim Bey, T.A.Z.: The Temporary Autonomous Zone, Ontological Anarchy, Poetic Terrorism, (1985/1991), https://theanarchistlibrary.org/library/hakim-bey-t-a-z-the-temporary-autonomous-zone-ontological-anarchy-poetic-terrorism
19 Ibid.

interviews.[20] "We are the thieving magpies," was Bey's premise to his version of the commons. Elbakyan says that science was historically regarded as a theft of secrets from nature. While the figures of the pirate and heroic outlaws, such as Robin Hood, are also an important source of inspiration for her, she also activates a large variety of resources, from Ancient Greek mythology and Thomas Moore to the Soviet scientific community, to advocate for the abolition of private ownership of the process and the results of scientific enquiry. The figures of the pirate, the outlaw, and of cunning Hermes, a God of crossing boundaries, set up an ideational horizon that make the work of *Sci-Hub* possible.

Meta librarian

The context that Tomislav Medak sets up for his work with Marcell Mars includes the policy of austerity following the 2008 financial crisis, the crisis of mass education, and the underemployment of skilled workforces, read against the background affordances of technical infrastructures. Following the rise of American monopolies, such as Google, Facebook or Twitter, the channeling of information networks into private platforms, and the aggressive campaigns of publishing giants such as Elsevier, new figures and subject positions come to prominence.

Marcell Mars and Tomislav Medak initiated Memory of the World as a proof of concept for the project Public Library in 2012. Memory of the World was built in response to the specific situation when Croatian libraries were disposing of books. Staged as a response to the financial cuts, this disposal was also used as an opportunity to get rid of undesired political histories and knowledge. The librarians were throwing out Marxist books, books by Serbians or those written in the Cyrillic alphabet.[21] In response, Medak and Mars asked people to bring books and journals that were being chucked out; they were then scanned and

20 Elbakyan. Transcript and Translation of Sci-Hub Presentation (2016), https://openaccess. unt.edu/symposium/2016/info/transcript-and-translation-sci-hub-presentation

21 Croatians use the Latin alphabet for transcribing a language that was described as a single Serbo-Croatian language during the Yugoslavian period. It is possible to transcribe it either in the Latin or the Cyrillic alphabet. For more context, see "Knowledge Commons and Activist Pedagogies: From Idealist Positions to Collective Actions." Conversation with Marcell Mars and Tomislav Medak (co-authored with Ana Kuzmanić), https://monos-kop.org/images/7/7f/Jandric_Petar_Kuzmanic_Ana_2017_Knowledge_Commons_and_Activist_Pedagogies_From_Idealist_Positions_to_Collective_Actions_Conversation_with_Marcell_Mars_and_Tomislav_Medak.pdf

made available to the readers (*Written-Off*, 2015). For example, the entire catalogue of the Yugoslav Communist research group journal *Praxis*, which was going to be destroyed, was put online: this opened up a worldwide discussion of the legacy of this group (*Digital Archive of Praxis and the Korc ula Summer School*, 2016).

The subject position of a *meta librarian* arises here in response to the crisis in the project of continuation of knowledge. A meta librarian is the next level up from the librarian; a librarian of librarians, it comes onto the stage when normal librarians fail. Mars and Medak emphasize the position of the institution of the library as a conflictual site. [22] Torn between the promise of universal knowledge and universal enlightenment, i.e. access to that knowledge, on the one side, and repression of otherness in the construction of universality, on the other, the institution of the public library has to serve multiple purposes. When it primarily acts as the regulatory institution of nation building, keen to serve a particular version of national identity to support the functioning of the nation-state, the preservation of multiplicity of knowledges requires disobedience, forking and complexification of the institution of the library and the subject of the librarian. The versioning of the position of the public librarian into a meta librarian institutes a new library.

The subject position of meta librarian is that of the one who intervenes and takes on the role of the public librarian, while being an amateur. A meta librarian safeguards and makes available knowledge and practices preserved in undesired or unavailable books. Here, two further notions converge under the general auspice of the meta librarian: a *public custodian and a general librarian*.[23]

Public custodian

Techno-cultural gestures and infra-structural actions inform and organize subject positions. The work of creating Memory of the World is physical labor: one person, working on it full time, was scanning 50

---

22   Tomislav Medak, "The Future After the Library. UbuWeb and Monoskop's Radical Gestures," in *Javna knjižnica / Public Library*, ed. Tomislav Medak, Marcell Mars, and WHW (Zagreb: WHW & Multimedia Institute, 2015).

23   "Before and After Calibre," Memory of the World: "When everyone is librarian, library is everywhere." It was accessible via this link during the time of writing: https://www.memoryoftheworld.org/blog/2012/11/27/before-and-after-calibre-2/

titles a day, delimiting the project's capacity of creation. This kind of work cannot be automated and does not scale well. Scanning and post-processing requires time, which poses a clear bodily limit. This means that the titles need to be selected; with old books and magazines, one has to take individual decisions on what to preserve, and to what degree of precision in terms of resolution or annotation. Here, the custodian comes on stage. *Custodians.online*, a collective of shadow librarians, published letters in support of Library Genesis and Science Hub in 2015: here, shadow librarians use the term "custodian" as a self-definition.

The custodian preserves culture and knowledge, but in contrast to the private custodian who safeguards a collection entrusted to them until times change for the better, the *public custodian* is compelled to activate the collection. This might include converting formats, making files readable by a variety of e-readers, and organizing material, including references, but more generally, the public custodian is committed to making the collection available for public use.

The subject position of Memory of the World is that of a public custodian. It is called into existence by a crisis in the politics of memory. As an amateur historian, a public custodian is keen to preserve and create access to alternative pasts and futures. Anyone who participates in creating the project, bringing or scanning material, takes on themselves parts of this subject position, while also contributing to it as the main conceptual principle of the resource. It is from the point of view of the position of the public custodian that the claim to a different version of political and social history, and a different relationship to the library and to the public, is made.

But the custodian is not only the position from which to salvage, to preserve and to take care of disappearing paper books. Shadow librarians use the idea of custodianship as an umbrella concept: they are united, as Mars and Medak state, by "gestures of disobedience, deceleration and demands for inclusiveness."[24] These gestures are actions that help constitute the position of the public custodian. The subject position of a public custodian here can be maintained by a com-

24 Marcell Mars, Tomislav Medak, "Against Innovation: Compromised Institutional Agency and Acts of Custodianship," *Ephemera* 19, no. 2 (2019), http://www.ephemerajournal. org/contribution/against-innovation-compromised-institutional-agency-and-acts-custodianship

mitment to hosting a mirror, by registering and re-registering domain names, and by a multitude of other gestures. One doesn't need to be a giant of custodianship to be a custodian. Small gestures contribute to the subject position from which a claim to advocacy, construction and maintenance of "online infrastructures" of art and knowledge can be made. Shadow librarians specify them in course syllabi and online materials: digitizing a book on a scanner, PDF authoring, adding metadata, managing sub-libraries, converting file formats, leaking files, removing DRM and syncing cataloguing software and e-readers are techno-cultural gestures performed from the subject position of custodian.[25] All these radical gestures reverse "property into commons" and "commodification into care."

General librarian

Public Library—a project and a conceptual proposal by Mars and Medak—is a catalogue of books shared through Calibre (open source software to organize PDF and EPUB files into virtual libraries), an index and a set of tools and tutorials. There is a minimal definition of a new kind of public library, developed by Medak and Mars: make your own collection of books available to the public through the catalogue (Calibre in their case). The catalogue software organizes the collection, adds and manages metadata and connects the collection and their readers. The readers contact librarians through the catalogue; librarians seed collections directly from their laptops.

This is a vision of a *general librarian*: similar to the notion of the general intellect, it is a librarian distributed through software—a librarian everywhere; everyone a librarian. The key technique of the subject position of a general librarian is the catalogue. The maintenance of the catalogue is the core gesture of the general librarian: because the catalogue is an abstraction, separated from the library, and a software tool, it semi-automates and partially liberates the librarian, while still requiring maintenance. The subject positions are sustained by actions and techno-cultural infrastructures, which they both create and are defined by. The general librarian is not a function of software, but a

---

25 Tomislav Medak, Marcell Mars, "Amateur Librarian – A Course in Critical Pedagogy," https://www.mondotheque.be/wiki/index.php?title = Amateur_Librarian_-_A_ Course_in_Critical_Pedagogy

subject position mutually constituted by the book collection, the cata-loguing tool, work put into managing catalogue software and some key concepts and values. "Let's share books" here becomes a point of view, a position from which a possibly universal but also polyvocal knowledge can be created by a very large network of small collections.

Underground librarian

In contrast, the subject-position of *underground librarian* relates to that of a heroic outlaw. Someone might contact a public custodian or a general librarian with an offer of 50,000 liberated books. They would not want to take care of the files, but seek to pass them on, for some other subjects and structures to process and absorb them into the pool of common resources. The aim of the underground librarian is to get the files and release them from constraints. Acting more like a leaker or interceptor of data, their key aesthetic is the move from something that is constrained or shackled to something unshackled, and whether it is used or not is of lesser concern. Custodians and librarians, by contrast, deal with rather small, selective collections. The gestures of stripping DRM or PDF watermarks and moving information flows that the underground librarians busy themselves with are perhaps on a continuum with those of the public custodian and a general librar-ian, but have a different aesthetic intensity and duration: intervention, detouring, leaking, making untrackable are their main gestures.

Critical public pedagogue

Aaaaarg, a text repository, was established by Sean Dockray to serve as a library for the Public School. An intervention into the field of education, it is rare among repositories as it has produced a strong community of users that catalogue, annotate, contextualize and dis-cuss books. The position of Aaaaarg as an open collaborative website generated many ways of filtering content: one can go by discussions, recommended translations, thematic collections, related material, and many others. Sebastian Luetgert calls it a missing university library on a global scale, with a social layer of context around it.

It's hard to find junk on Aaaaarg. By deliberately slowing things down, impeding automated uploads and "sharing what you love rather than sharing everything," the techno-cultural gestures and structures of Aaaaarg come close to the communal investment of public custodians.

But there is also a strong legacy of critical pedagogy, whereby education is political through and through.

The role of education is to teach how to learn. Pedagogy is (ideally) guided by the aim of endowing the learner with the tools of learning. Here, curricula or syllabi, among other educational instruments, organize and evaluate knowledge, raising critical awareness. In the last five years, the rise of online syllabi as a response to political struggles signaled a new turn for public education, both inside and outside the classroom. In "Learning from #Syllabus," Graziano, Mars and Medak analyze #Syllabus as an object that fuses the social justice movements' tradition of using educational tools, including teaching material, to "support political subjectivation"[26] with the materiality of new media. #Syllabus is a web-based ordered list of links, circulated with the support of a social media hash tag, which abandons boundless user taxonomy and Google's indexing in favor of the creation of a crowd-sourced list of available resources and makes a pedagogical intervention on a specific politically urgent topic.

Critical pedagogy, self-education and public intervention as manifest in #Syllabus create the context for one of the subject positions of Aaaaarg: that of a *critical public pedagogue.* Such a pedagogue activates knowledge in specific ways, so that their students can undergo a critical transformation. Here, pedagogue and students can swap places. Everyone is an eternal student, and, quite likely, also a pedagogue.

Multiform bibliographer

Monoskop acts not only as a library, but as a system of knowledge maps that includes references pointing far beyond Monoskop. Sean Dockray suggests that by disaggregating the repository function and the referencing function, its founder Dusan Barok makes the entire Internet his archive. Barok himself calls this work "indexing."[27] Barok's indexing activates records by linking to them; it directs users

---

26 Valeria Graziano, Marcell Mars, Tomislav Medak, "Learning from #Syllabus," in *State Machine: Reflections and Actions at the Edge of Digital Citizenship, Finance, and Art*, ed. Yannis Colakides, Marc Garrett, Inte Gloeirich (Amsterdam: Institute of Network Cultures, 2019), p. 119.

27 Dušan Barok, "More Than Numbers, Less Than Words," *Javna knjižnica / Public Library* conference, Nova Gallery, Zagreb, June 2015. https://monoskop.org/Talks/More_Than_Numbers_Less_Than_Words

by providing context, resources, and further bibliographies. In fact, the subject position of Monoskop is partially that of a researcher librarian, but overall it is that of a *multiform bibliographer*.

In the print era, a student starting work on a thesis was often advised to consult a bibliographic dictionary. Such a reference book on a specific topic looked like an encyclopedia, with entries on topics followed by an extended annotated bibliography of further reading. Monoskop is such a system for and of study, except that it also includes biographies, texts, a variety of media, different kind of references (for instance, to events), and generally such a huge variation of material, that the bibliographer in the making becomes richly multimedia and radically multiform.

Wiki is the technology of this subject position. Creating knowledge, but also re-organizing and activating the material of the web, wiki acts as a recording, pointing and mapping system. Research and annotation of knowledge in Monoskop is more than a curated index: the subject of Monoskop—a position from which it lives and grows and a user position from which to start the exploration of a topic—is that of an enhanced human browser. True to the original horizon of possibility of the World Wide Web, a universe of linked knowledge, here the hypertext mapping is updated to carefully constructed, but necessarily open narratives. The technically led subject-position of Monoskop, the logic of its construction, is that of a virtuoso forager, able to find results where there are none and follow their interests in constructing a wide range of knowledge frameworks. Encyclopedist, organizer of material, hypertext narrator, such a subject position is a curious combination of a classical formation of knowledge, the promise of hypertext, resistance to contemporary logics of walled gardens, where all links stay within one platform, and the contemporary informational condition of being overwhelmed by useless material but being unable to find anything beyond it.

Monoskop started as a mapping initiative; an impulse that still remains. Students are asked to make entries on Monoskop: a documentation of a learning process, mapping knowledge and history, creates a subject position from which to see oneself and the world in the mode of a wiki. Incomplete, fragmentary, light, it is multiple; mapping on the Monoskop wiki is a mode of research and of pedagogy, the Internet of the future, the discovery of Eastern Europe by

Eastern Europe,[28] and many other multimodal, multimedia and multiform things.

Fancy general archivist and postmodern curator of the avant-garde
UbuWeb is a curated repository of artworks, extended by a multitude of related material to what Cornelia Sollfrank called "the cultural
memory of the avant-garde."[29] The subject position of UbuWeb is that
of an archivist of a radically new kind. Such a new archivist does not
ask for permission. Browsing the dark corners of the Web for files,
they upload them to their archive, which over time acquires coveted
status. If the copyright holder complains, the archivist enters into communication with them, sometimes succeeding in convincing them to
allow access to their work in exchange for being part of a distinguished
collection of artists. Such an archivist is a new, although critical, gate-
keeper. Archiving becomes curation, and the archive starts functioning as an art institution.

Established 20 years ago, and still running on html 1.0, UbuWeb
grew out of collections of modern and contemporary art that people
at times personally gave to its founder. Widely used in teaching art
and small in size, it leads a precarious existence. Each file is provided
with a download link bearing the imperative: "if you find something
on the internet, save it." The technical-organizational aesthetics of the
archive formulate a subject position that offers and challenges everyone to be an archivist, although of a different status. The *fancy archivist*, the curator, licenses certain kinds of art histories. As the archive
can disappear any minute, everyone must become an archivist, a *general archivist*, fancy or not. Building on interpersonal networks, the
fancy archive is always temporary, un-indexed, invisible, but hugely
important. For its birthday, UbuWeb got a present from the custodians: mirrors.

Cultural analyst
0xDB, started in 2007, is an experiment in software development for a
database of movies. Initially developed as part of the *Oil of the 21cen-*

28 Nanna Thylstrup, "The Licit and Illicit Nature of Mass Digitization," in Nanna Thylstrup, *The Politics of Mass Digitization* (Cambridge MA: MIT Press, 2018).
29 Sollfrank, "The Surplus of Copying."

tury project, it actualized, through software, an imaginary world: "this is how it could look." 0xDB offers a multitude of ways to represent, watch, understand, cut through, and study a movie. One can sort films by budget, genre, color, number of cuts, cuts per minute, the words in subtitles, and multiple other means. The result of the sorting is information intensive: it is a data visualization. 0xDB treats time-based media as a database, and offers creative ways to query it. The subject position of the project is that of a *cultural analyst*, where data analytics is applied to art and culture.

An intervention into software as a cultural system and a system for culture, Sebastian Luetgert and Jan Gerber's methodology is to start with the imaginary result and walk back. Here, the transversality of roles is emphasized: a software developer can have a creative role, and a point of view: what one sees is political. Working with Pad.ma, an online archive of video material, the team also developed a platform for alternative activist video that documents events such as mass murder during riots in Western India and Gujarat. This video material is not finished, cannot be attributed to authors and most often, cannot be published. This raw material, which is a process rather than an item, Luetgert says, requires fluid and dynamic handling from the technical system, in contrast to treatment of finished and authored films as individual complete units. Software here must protect the identity of the author, act as a guard, and aid in enquiry. Proposing the position of a forensic film analyst, Pad.ma moves closer to the work of Forensic Architecture and to Wikileaks, where software is a weapon of investigation.

Conclusion

Subject positions offer points of view from which to make interventions, to create new relations, and to affirm alternative imaginaries. Such subject positions are maintained by gestures, actions, and ideas performed in techno-cultural structures. These two statements already present a program.

Firstly, a subject position is created not, or not solely, as a response to power, out of the self turning back on itself, but in relation to technology and information infrastructures, which shape relations to knowledge and art. The shadow libraries and repositories discussed above intervene in the organization of information and structuring of knowledge, art and culture. Their multiform cutting-through existing structurations creates conditions of possibility for the emergence of a diverse range of subjects. Above, I explored only a few subject positions, formulated specifically in relation to the question of intervention upon structuration of knowledge and art. But it is the optionality afforded by these projects as part of the commons that forms the basis on which subjects that can offer difference, whether in how to be a woman, how to act politically, or how to study, understand and act, can be developed. Difference starts with the possibility of choosing and creating subject-positions, rather than absorbing them by prescriptive encoding. This process relies on nutritious substrate, which can be made available or withdrawn, and where the means of availability or formulations of restriction are increasingly technical.

Secondly, it is a pragmatic program: doing things creates subjects, and ways of technical doing, including small gestures and long-term tending to the systems, figure subject-positions. Affection is key to creating and maintaining contemporary commons. Tending to the projects that constitute commons is a continuous individual and collective action. Care, affection, filiation are performed by small gestures of software installation or big gestures of registering domain names and hosting mirrors.

Bahktin also used filiation as the grounds of aesthetic construction and the holding together of the subject. What is core to such a principle is that it makes relation the basis and condition of living: acquiring a subject position is achieved through relations, which, in these projects, are mediated and realized also by technology. The relations are multidirectional, and so it is also true that by creating a certain subject position, a re-formulation of a cut of the world takes place. The subject position is not only produced but produces—practices, environments—which, in turn, trickle further away, introducing changes to spaces perhaps not very much concerned with the questions at hand. Once a subject-position, a point-of-view, a techno-cultural gesture is established, it travels: in networks, in space-time, in methods, in disciplines, in politics, in imaginaries. In that, the subject-positions explored in this text exhibit capacities to transform things beyond their immediate fields of operation. The transformations these subject positions bring about concern principles of the organization of knowledge and ways of knowing, politics of memory and geopolitical histories, modes of abstraction and distribution of authority and care alike, with and through technical systems, disciplinary reproduction or undoing of domination through pedagogy, techniques of vision and learning, agency, and many others. They concern processes and infrastructures of societal life that need to keep changing in order to sustain and generate inhabitable spaces.

Jeremy Gilbert

The Commons, the Public, and the Aesthetics of Solidarity

What lies in the zone between temporary, relatively short-lived exercises in the construction of "commons" and the possibility of large-scale institutional innovation and reform? Today there can be little question that the question of creating and defending "commons"—shared fields of relation and collective resource—is a crucial activity on many scales. The direct connection between the neoliberal destruction, enclosure and privatization of commons and the devastating effects of global heating is undeniable.[1] One of the reasons why "commons" remains such an attractive and potentially useful concept is its ability to designate spaces and sets of social relationships that are organized according to non-capitalist logics of collectivity, democracy and creativity at many possible scales: from the very local to the wholly global. At the largest operable scale, the environmental crisis has made very clear that the entire planetary ecosystem must at the same time be understood as a single field of interdependent processes, rather than divisible and commodifiable substances. At the smallest, there is clearly a strong tradition wherein various cultural practices are used to try to create a localized zone of engagement and mutual interaction—a sort of "micro-commons"[2] for participants: exhibitions, happenings, festivals, raves, etc. At the far end of this continuum we might consider Hakim Bey's influential idea of the "Temporary Autonomous Zone": a space outside of capitalist relations and state administration, that might be no more permanent or substantial than a dinner party.[3]

1   Naomi Klein, *This Changes Everything: Capitalism vs. The Climate* (London: Simon and Schuster, 2014).
2   Massimo de Angelis, *Omnia Sunt Communia: On the Commons and the Transformation to Postcapitalism* (London: Zed Books, 2017), p. 78.
3   Hakim Bey, *TAZ: The Temporary Autonomous Zone* (Seattle WA: Pacific Publishing Studio, 2011).

The question I want to address here is a crucial one if small-scale, local and even relatively large-scale attempts at commons-building—outside of significant political and economic structures—are to be regarded as having any wider political and transformative potential. This is the question of how it might be possible to develop insights and practices drawn from such interventions and apply them in different and/or larger-scale contexts, and in what ways such localized projects might be actively aligned and coordinated with larger-scale efforts to constitute permanent or semi-permanent commons.

Hope and Solidarity

The idea that localized social or aesthetic practices might serve as implicit or explicit prefigurations of future changes to wider social relationships has a long history. Plato remarked (disapprovingly) that changes in musical form are often associated with political and social change.[4] Artists have hoped that aesthetic experiment might have social repercussions at least since the revolutionary phase of the "romantic" movement.[5] Utopian communities have deliberately tried to exemplify potential new societies and new types of social relations at least since the early days of the modern socialist movement.[6] Discussions of the potential value of participatory and "relational" art practice often allude (explicitly or implicitly) to the hope that such practices may in some way contribute to the emergence of wider forms of institutionalized "participatory democracy."[7] But is there any substance to this aspiration, and justification for its assumptions and aims, beyond the wish-fulfilment of artists in search of self-justification (and funding)?

In fact there may well be. Jacques Attali famously attributes a "prophetic" function to changes in musical form and practice, positing

---

4   Plato, *Plato's The Republic* (New York: Penguin Books, 1941).
5   Marylin Butler, *Romanticism, Rebels and Reactionaries: English Literature and Its Background 1760–1830* (Oxford: Oxford University Press, 1981).
6   Barbara Taylor, *Eve and the New Jerusalem: Socialism and Feminism in the Nineteenth Century* (Cambridge MA: Harvard University Press, 1993).
7   Henry Jenkins and Nico Carpentier, "Theorizing participatory intensities," *Convergence: The International Journal of Research into New Media Technologies* 19, no. 3 (2013): pp. 265–286, https://doi.org/10.1177/1354856513482090

them as directly prefiguring wider cultural, economic and socio-political changes such as the emergence of mass consumer society (which, according to Attali, is preceded by the advent of phonography).[8] While Attali's historiography is often questionable (relying too heavily on French and German examples to make a convincingly universal case for his thesis), it is never entirely unpersuasive. Attali's basic intuition—that changes in the way that the social production of music has been organized may prefigure changing ideas about the ideal organization of society—has resonated with many readers since he first posited it in the 1970s. From another, related perspective, it is also possible to suggest that the emergence of forms of mass representational politics in the nineteenth and twentieth centuries[9] is prefigured by the rise of newly representational cultural forms, as recognizable social types (rather than allegorical or mythic figures) began to populate the fiction of playwrights and novelists from the sixteenth century onwards. From this point of view, it might well be reasonable to propose that participatory cultural forms could contribute over a very long period to the cultivation of appropriately democratic habits and expectations amongst a broader population.

At the same time, the claim that the representative forms of liberal democracy are inadequate to the task of managing a highly complex society seems to be clearly borne out by the sustained "post-democratic" crises of such societies since the 1970s, and their evident inability collectively to resolve the problem of catastrophic climate change.[10] Since the nineteenth century, and especially since the 1960s, radicals in several traditions have argued for more decentralized, more involved, more inclusive mechanisms of collective self-government. As I have argued elsewhere, one of the conditions for neoliberal hegemony since the 1970s has been the inability of mid-twentieth century democratic institutions to manage or regulate globally-networked capitalism.[11] This left a global vacuum that could have been filled by the types of intensified and participatory democracy being proposed

8   Jacques Attali, *Noise: The Political Economy of Music* (Manchester: Manchester University Press, 1985), p. 32.

9   E.P. Thompson, *The Making of the English Working Class* (London: Victor Gollancz, 1965).

10 Klein, *This Changes Everything*.

11 Gilbert, Jeremy. *Common Ground: Democracy and Collectivity in an Age of Individualism* (London: Pluto Press, 2014).

by the radical movements of the 1960s and 1970s, but was instead occupied by the power of a technocratic political class committed to implementing the neoliberal program.[12] This is one reason why struggles for commons and for participatory democracy are always likely to be deeply intertwined: both represent democratic, collectivist and egalitarian responses to the crises caused by global neoliberal hegemony.[13] So there is some basis for the hope that relatively small-scale experiments in both aesthetic practice and social organization might contribute, over the long term, to the development and popularization of participatory and egalitarian social forms. In what follows, I will consider how this process might be conceptualized at the level of aesthetic practice as such, and at the "micro-institutional" level at which commons become relatively stabilized and oriented to more or less explicit political objectives, projects, tendencies and movements.

At the level of aesthetic practice, there are many ways in which formal innovation might be considered to be in some sense prefigurative of wider social change. In particular, the capacity of artistic and expressive work to engender feelings of hope and to stimulate imaginative responses to present social conditions has long been seen as a major source of its potential political agency.[14] One way of conceptualizing this potentiality is in terms of the capacity of such practice to engender an affective experience of *possible worlds*. In his 2004 book *Les Révolutions du Capitalisme*, Maurizio Lazzarato sets out an intriguing political ontology derived from the ideas of Gottfried Leibniz, Gabriel Tarde and Gilles Deleuze. According to the terms of this ontology, politics should be understood as the process by which "possible worlds" are invented, imagined and actualized.[15] In the book Lazzarato presents this as an alternative to Marxist ideas of politics as defined by relations of antagonism, negation and contradiction, in its place positing a politics of proliferating possibilities and creative invention against the negativity of the actual and the present. Lazzarato has since abandoned this argument, arguing instead that radical politics in the twenty-first

12 Ron Formisano, *American Oligarchy: The Permanent Political Class* (Champaign: University of Illinois Press, 2017).
13 Couze Venn, *After Capital* (London and Thousand Oaks CA: SAGE Publications Ltd., 2018).
14 Ernst Bloch, *The Principle of Hope* (Cambridge MA: MIT Press, 1995).
15 Maurizio Lazzarato, *Les révolutions du capitalisme* (Paris: Les Empêcheurs de penser en rond, 2004).

century must recover the oppositional militancy and class consciousness of the classical labor and communist movements.[16] However, I
would argue that there is no necessary contradiction between a radical
anti-capitalist politics grounded in class struggle, and a political ontology that places high value on the "powers of invention"[17] that can be
exemplified by both grassroots political innovations[18] and by innovative aesthetic practice. Both approaches can be accommodated by a
perspective that is attentive both to the "molar" and macro-political
dimensions of political and aesthetic practice, and to the "molecular"
and micropolitical scales of social invention, for the analysis of which
Lazzarato's early 2000s schema is most appropriate.

From this perspective, we might describe "possible worlds" as
potential future states, actualized at the level of affect, if not at the
level of institutionalized social reality. Such possible worlds prefigure
new "distributions of the sensible"[19] (to borrow a term from Rancière),
or what we might call "affective distributions," making possible new
sensations of potentiality and possibility. We might describe this as
a process of "pre-actualization," whereby affective distributions are
enabled that have specific, utopian political implications. The promotion of affective distributions capable of pre-actualizing "commons" is
likely to involve an emphasis on one particular type of politico-affec-
tive relation that receives relatively little attention in contemporary
theoretical literature: the relation of solidarity. Solidarity can be characterized as a sense of shared interests pertaining either to relatively
homogeneous social groups or to members of heterogeneous groups
with little in common besides their shared interests.

This latter characterization is particularly important, as examples
of solidarity in action are often most striking when they pertain to
groups who clearly do not share a common cultural or social identity.
In the UK, for example, the most famous manifestations of solidarity

16 Éric Alliez and Maurizio Lazzarato, *Wars and Capital*, trans. Ames Hodges (South Pasa-
dena CA: Semiotext(e) Native Agents Series, 2016).

17 Maurizio Lazzarato, *Puissances de l'invention: la psychologie économique de Gabriel Tarde
contre l'économie politique* (Paris: Les Empêcheurs de penser en rond, 2002).

18 Marianne Maeckelbergh, *The Will of the Many: How the Alterglobalisation Movement Is
Changing the Face of Democracy,* Anthropology, Culture and Society (London and New
York: Pluto Press, 2009).

19 Jacques Rancière, *The Politics of Aesthetics: The Distribution of the Sensible*, trans. Gabriel
Rockhill (London: Bloomsbury, 2013).

in (relatively) recent political history involve productive political relationships between members of very distinct social groups. The 1976–78 "Grunwick Dispute"—a strike by mainly female South Asian workers over pay and conditions at a film-processing factory—famously saw the strikers supported by large contingents of mainly white, male trade unionists from other workplaces and trades.[20] The activities of gay and lesbian organizations in support of the 1984–85 miners' strike have even been made the subject of a popular recent feature film (*Pride*, 2014). But it is not cultural heterogeneity as such that characterizes situations of solidarity, so much as the fact that those situations are always grounded both in the shared material interests of their participants and in a "horizontal" set of relationships between them, not dependent upon shared identification with a leader, an ideology or any particular identity. I would suggest that a crucial feature of "commons" on any scale is their dependence upon relations of solidarity, and their tendency to generate, amplify and reproduce such relations. In what follows I will consider some of the ways in which interventions brought together in the *Creating Commons* project might be seen as contributing to such processes of communing, solidarity-building, world-actualization and collective empowerment, and also reflect upon what it might mean to derive more widely-applicable political strategies from their experiments.

Micro-Institution Building

Describing itself as "an international NGO that engages with citizens and civil society organisations to explore and mitigate the impacts of technology on society," Tactical Tech engages in a number of educational and artistic projects aimed at promoting awareness both of the nature of contemporary digital surveillance and of means of evading and resisting it. The activities of Tactical Tech constitute an exemplary practice of "commoning" in several senses. Firstly, in making available an important body of knowledge on an open-access basis, they produce a relationship of mutual empowerment between their

---

[20] Jack Dromey and Graham Taylor, *Grunwick: The Workers' Story* (London: Lawrence & Wishart, 2016).

own projects and an indeterminate number of users, all of whom can benefit from the wider dissemination of the knowledge and techniques that they make available. Secondly, the ongoing and interrelated nature of their multiple projects constitutes ideal examples of micro-institution building, quite distinct from the effects of discrete art interventions, installations or exhibitions. Thirdly, their projects are clearly and explicitly organized *against* the appropriation of data and the practice of unaccountable surveillance by large platform corporations. In this sense, despite their explicit "tactical" emphasis, there is no question that the overall project of Tactical Tech is characterized by a certain "strategic orientation"[21] towards active resistance to "surveillance capitalism."[22] While Tactical Tech generally frame their activities and aims in terms of a more or less liberal defense of personal data "privacy" against corporate intrusion, they also challenge capitalist power at one of its most strategically crucial sites of contemporary operation.[23]

One of the most interesting questions raised by Tactical Tech's interventions is that of their scalability and potential applicability in the wider public sphere. On the one hand, there is clearly a crucial potential role for progressive state institutions to play in the widespread promotion of techniques such as personal privacy protection and even "data detox,"[24] and this may well be considered a crucial feature of any attempt to promote a politics of commonality and "the public good" in decades to come, in every part of the world. In this sense, the project exemplifies the capacity of such "micro-institutional" interventions to experiment with forms of commoning capable of being taken up by state actors on a much large scale. On the other hand, it is arguably the limits of such interventions, precisely in their relatively weak capacity to generate stable and large-scale commons, that also demonstrates the importance of relating such interventions to wider political

21 Jeremy Gilbert, *Anticapitalism and Culture: Radical Theory and Popular Politics* (Oxford: Berg, 2008).
22 Shoshana Zuboff, *The Age of Surveillance Capitalism: The Fight for a Human Future at the New Frontier of Power* (New York: PublicAffairs, 2019).
23 Nick Couldry and Ulises Ali Mejias, *The Costs of Connection: How Data Is Colonizing Human Life and Appropriating It for Capitalism.* Culture and Economic Life (Stanford CA: Stanford University Press, 2019); Nick Srnicek, *Platform Capitalism* (Cambridge: Polity Press, 2017).
24 https://tacticaltech.org/#/projects/data-detox-kit (All URLs in this text have been last accessed October 20, 2020)

projects. Ultimately, the effectiveness of Tactical Tech is mainly confined to promoting awareness of, and enabling individuals to equip themselves with some effective tools against, specific forms of corporate exploitation.

The far more fundamental task of actually neutralizing the sources of that exploitation would clearly require political intervention on an entirely different scale. While liberal commentators such as Zuboff have recently suggested that government regulation may be sufficient to break the monopoly power of platform corporations, it seems clear enough that this is a naive assumption. The power of companies like Amazon, Google and Facebook to evade regulation is already legendary[25] and simply breaking up their monopoly status (as center-left politicians such as Elizabeth Warren have proposed[26]) would have little effect on this capacity. Only removing major platforms from the domain of capital accumulation altogether is likely to have the effect of re-orienting their administrative objectives away from intrusive-but-profitable forms of data extraction, towards the actual expression of their evident potential to function as sites of collaborative communication on multiple scales. It is unlikely that individual national governments could effect such a policy, given the inherently global nature of the major platforms, and their dependence for their full functionality on this very global nature. Only some kind of coordinated political collaboration between organizations of users, governments, and supra-governmental institutions (such as the European Union) is likely to be able to produce the effect of realizing the full potential of the platforms as commons, finally rendering obsolete the types of institutional intervention being modeled by Tactical Tech.[27] Nonetheless, the very existence of a project such as Tactical Tech can serve as an important incubator for the forms of criticality and the forms of collective power that any such project to challenge the authority of techno-capitalism would require.

---

25 Zuboff, *Age of Surveillance Capitalism*.
26 Team Warren, "Here's how we can break up Big Tech," March 8, 2019. Available at: https://medium.com/@teamwarren/heres-how-we-can-break-up-big-tech-9ad9e-0da324c
27 Jeremy Gilbert, *Twenty-First Century Socialism* (Cambridge: Polity Press, 2020); Srnicek, *Platform Capitalism*.

Connecting the Digital and Physical Commons

Furtherfield is an artist-led space and organization, founded by Ruth Catlow and Marc Garrett, that has historically taken a particular interest in facilitating public engagement with themes and questions emerging from the public deployment of new digital communications technologies, as well as a range of other sets of cultural and social issues. According to their own self-description, "Furtherfield connects people to new ideas, critical thinking and imaginative possibilities for art, technology and the world around us. Through artworks, labs and debate people from all walks of life explore today's important questions." Significantly, Furtherfield has a physical location in Finsbury Park, a well-known and much-frequented area of public space in one of the most densely-populated parts of the UK (and indeed, of Europe as a whole): central North London. As such, the project very self-consciously occupies a commons and seeks to constitute itself as a commons in that space. Its work is often characterized by a powerful emphasis on public participation, democratic knowledge-production and deliberative process. For example, the "Citizen Sci-Fi" project has invited hundreds of local citizens to participate in a collective exercise in imagining possible futures for the local community and its physical environs.

Furtherfield's work exemplifies a number of significant features of "commoning" at various scales. By both inhabiting and cultivating public space as a site of creative interrelation, Furtherfield can be seen to enact a defense of an existing commons, while actively deploying its capacity to potentiate those collectivities that come into being by sharing and using it. At the same time, projects such as "Citizen Sci-Fi" play a particularly significant role, inviting and enabling collective deliberation and imagination, while encouraging a shared and explicit orientation to the possible future of those collectivities. Crucially, this future is experienced as one that is potentially shared, and that actualizes, on a discursive-imaginative plane, a powerful sense of that shared future. This sense of a shared future is undoubtedly one of the fundamental aspects of experiences of solidarity, as is the common capacity for collective creativity and democratic decision-making.[28] We might recall here Ulrich Beck's description of the experience

---

28   Gilbert, *Common Ground.*

of cosmopolitan culture in a globalizing world as one characterized by different social groups having different pasts but shared futures. We might also recall Derrida's evocation of the "spirit" of the radical socialist tradition as characterized by a constitutive openness to the alterity of the future and its potential for "democracy to come."[29]As such, the experience of solidarity is often a positive experience of the potentially and immanently cosmopolitan nature of commons, and of the inherent openness to futurity that is their necessary feature.

Commons / Public: the Forms of Solidarity

Of course, there are forms and experiences of solidarity that are not easily describable in such utopian terms. As Prerna Singh points out in her study of the relationship between welfare policy and solidaristic social relations in India, relations of solidarity are often associated with clearly shared identities, rooted in perceptions of national, subnational, local or ethnic commonalities.[30] In all of these cases, the patterns of collective belonging and group formation that produce the solidaristic communities in question can be seen to operate according to the logic of the constitution of "peoples" described by Ernesto Laclau and Chantal Mouffe, in various texts on the logic of political identification. According to this pattern, a more or less clearly-defined identity is the condition for the circulation of solidaristic affects to a degree sufficient to sustain broad popular support for (for example) the type of social-democratic welfare policies that Singh focusses on in her study.

One way of understanding the types of collectivity that emerge under such circumstances is to see them specifically as "publics:"[31] institutionalized collectivities organized as "peoples" and sustained by, and sustaining, the success of certain kinds of state project. Antonio Negri explicitly contrasts the politics of "the public" with that of "the commons," seeing the former as expressed by the permanently

---

29 Jacques Derrida, *Specters of Marx: The State of the Debt, the Work of Mourning, and the New International*, trans. Peggy Kamuf (New York and London: Routledge, 1994).

30 Prerna Singh, *How Solidarity Works for Welfare: Subnationalism and Social Development in India*. Cambridge Studies in Comparative Politics (New York: Cambridge University Press, 2015).

31 Roland Niezen, "Gabriel Tarde's publics," *History of the Human Sciences* 27, no. 2 (2014): pp. 41–59. DOI: 10.1177/0952695114525430

compromised tradition of Western European social democracy and the latter as allied with the libertarian communist tradition with which he and his work are associated.[32] From this perspective, "the public" is indeed always bound up with national or subnational identities, identities that are inherently exclusionary, hierarchical and statist in their implications. Negri radically differentiates "the public" thus conceived from "the commons": the domain of free social creativity that exists independently of both capital and the state. This characterization derives in part from Negri's affiliation to an Italian far-left tradition that has historically seen itself in opposition as much to the politics of the socialist and social-democratic traditions as to capitalism, liberalism and conservatism.[33] From this perspective "communism" is the politics of the commons, while socialism, social democracy, liberal nationalism and Stalinist state socialism can all be seen as, in different ways, operating in the domain of "the public."

Negri's rhetorical hostility to the social democratic tradition, and to the very idea of the public sector, can be difficult to accept for readers in countries where the minimal defense of the social democratic legacy—after decades of neoliberal hegemony—has become the most urgent political task even for the radical left. But it is also possible to make use of this distinction in less sectarian ways, in order to clarify some of the issues at stake both in practices of *Creating Commons* and in any attempt to derive more sustained and scalable institutional innovations from those practices. The British political theorists Keir Milburn and Bertie Russell have recently made creative use of the "public / commons" distinction by proposing that the two distinctive domains of "public" and "commons" could be conceived as potentially *complementary* domains and fields of operation. One of the central policy mechanisms of neoliberal governance since the 1980s has been the promotion of "public / private partnerships" that see municipal and national governments entering into "partnerships" of various kinds with private sector suppliers and service providers, effectively

32 Antonio Negri, *Goodbye Mr. Socialism / Antonio Negri in Conversation with Raf Valvola Scelsi*, trans. Peter Thomas (New York and London: Seven Stories Press, 2008); Michael Hardt and Antonio Negri, *Commonwealth* (Cambridge MA: Belknap Press of Harvard University Press, 2009).
33 Negri, *Goodbye Mr. Socialism*.

privatizing significant social assets and service-delivery systems.[34] Milburn and Russell propose the "public / commons" partnership as an explicit alternative to this model and to forms of social democratic administration that seek merely to contain or replace relatively autonomous forms of social organization. For instance, there are many examples, historically and worldwide, of progressive municipal governments giving legal and financial support to autonomous housing co-operatives without seeking to take over their functions and replace them with state equivalents. From this perspective, the commons and the public might be seen as sites of forms of solidarity and democracy that are not necessarily mutually exclusive, but potentially reinforcing and even, at times, mutually constitutive.

Yet the contrast between public and commons is a potentially useful way of understanding different forms of solidarity, and thereby understanding the specificity of the commons and of political and cultural forms of commoning. Singh makes a powerful empirical case that what we might call "public solidarity," organized in terms of national and sub-national identities, plays a crucial role in enabling forms of social democratic politics that have clear benefits for populations as a whole and for the poor in particular. Conversely, we might reflect on the way that the limits of such public solidarity have been experienced in contexts where, for example, anxieties over access to public housing have become a key affective force animating the rise of right wing nationalist and racist movements.[35] We could contrast such developments with the tendency of more autonomous self-housing projects actively to reject all forms of racism and anti-immigrant discourse as a key feature of their politics, as manifested in slum-dweller movements,[36] or the radical municipal politics of the Barcelona en Comú (Barcelona in Common) movement.[37] It is this latter form of highly cosmopolitan, democratic and transversal politics that characterizes the solidarity of

34 Keir Milburn and Bertie Russell, *Public-Common Partnerships: Building New Circuits of Collective Ownership* (2019). Available at: https://www.common-wealth.co.uk
35 David Adler and Ben Ansell, "Housing and populism," *West European Politics* 43, no. 2 (2019): pp. 344–365. DOI: 10.1080/01402382.2019.1615322
36 Mike Davis, "Planet of Slums: Urban Involution and the Informal Proletariat," *New Left Review* 26 (March/April 2004): pp. 5–34.
37 Oscar Reyes, "Eight lessons from Barcelona en Comú on how to Take Back Control," (2017). Available at: https://www.opendemocracy.net/en/can-europe-make-it/eight-lessons-from-barcelona-en-com-on-how-to-take-bac

the commons, and of the types of social relation that projects engaged in *Creating Commons* on any scale seek to model and engender. But it is important to stress that despite this significant contrast, it is not necessary to see these different forms of solidarity as necessarily antagonistic to each other. Barcelona en Comú, for example, has since 2015 been actively promoting a politics of the commons from the position of having occupied the public institutions of the city government.

My purpose in making this digression into considering different modes of solidarity is ultimately to understand something about the specificity of the modes of sociality—cosmopolitan and transversal —that characterize the creation of commons. But it is also to invite reflection on what it might mean for micro-institutional projects of commons creation to build sustained relationships with public institutions and even to be treated as experimental sites at which possible models for public policy might be devised. Here, we might look to the relationship between the work of the Constant experimental artists' collective and the decidedly "public" role played by one of its key former members, Laurence Rassel, as director of the École de Recherche Graphique (ERG), a Belgian school of art and design that, while operating as a conventionally-funded, state-supported art school, has experimented with a highly democratic mode of internal organization (in line with the historical practice of various radical education institutions[38]). Here we see at work a productive network of relationships between more or less autonomous institutions and collectives— including the collective of teachers and students at ERG—and more or less state-dependent public institutions. This raises an interesting question as to how far it might be possible for projects such as Furtherfield and Tactical Tech to be seen as engaged in experiments which might be translated into more permanent institutional and pedagogic contexts, such as state schools, or projects of municipal governance.

Not only is this certainly possible; I would suggest that it is absolutely necessary *both* if such projects are not to remain merely localized distractions from the wider neoliberal and post-neoliberal degradation of our collective culture, *and* if progressive politics in the twenty-first century is to be animated by ideas and practices with a

---

38 Michael Fielding and Peter Moss, *Radical Education and the Common School: A Democratic Alternative* (London: Routledge, 2010).

real capacity to challenge that hegemony on an aesthetic and an institutional scale. In order for this to be possible, it will always be necessary for such projects to adopt the strategic orientation that I referred to above. A strategic orientation is not the same thing as a clear and defined strategy. This is not a call for a return to dogmatic schools of arts, with their manifestos, hierarchies and expulsions (well, not yet...). But a strategic orientation, a certain perspective of skepticism towards the appropriative, recuperative tendencies of advanced capitalism and a determination to evade them, is necessary if such experiments in commons-building are not merely to become part of a wider spectacle of pseudo-democratization.

Writing about the emphasis on more or less politically contentless "participation" in many strands of contemporary aesthetic practice, Claire Bishop wrote in 2012:

As this ground has shifted over the course of the twentieth century, so the identity of participants has been reimagined at each historical moment: from a crowd (1910s), to the masses (1920s), to the people (late 1960s/1970s), to the excluded (1980s), to community (1990s), to today's volunteers whose participation is continuous with a culture of reality television and social networking. From the audience's perspective, we can chart this as a shift from an audience that demands a role (expressed as hostility towards avant-garde artists who keep control of the proscenium), to an audience that enjoys its subordination to strange experiences devised for them by an artist, to an audience that is encouraged to be a co-producer of the work (and who, occasionally, can even get paid for this involvement). This could be seen as an heroic narrative of the increased activation and agency of the audience, but we might also see it as a story of our ever-increasing voluntary subordination to the artists' will, and of the commodification of human bodies in a service economy (since voluntary participation is also unpaid labour). Arguably this is a story that runs in parallel with the rocky fate of democracy itself, a term to which participation has always been wedded: from a demand for acknowledgement, to representation, to the consensual consumption of one's own image—be this in a work of art, Facebook, Flickr, or reality TV. Consider the media profile accorded to Antony Gormley's *One and Other* (2009), a project to allow members of the public to continuously occupy the empty "Fourth Plinth" of Trafalgar Square, one hour at a time for 100 days. Gormley received 34,520 applications for 2,400 places, and the activities of the plinth's occupants were continually streamed online. Although the artist referred to *One and Other* as "an open space of possibility for many to test their sense of self and how they might communicate this to a wider world", the project was described by *The Guardian*, not unfairly, as "Twitter Art". In a world where everyone can air their views to everyone we are faced not with mass empowerment but with an endless stream of egos levelled to banality. Far from being oppositional to spectacle, participation has now entirely merged with it.[39]

All of the projects that I have referred to here have as their imagined participants a quite distinctive type of digitally-enabled citizen: technologically empowered, but engaged in continuous relations with others, both face-to-face and virtually. There is every danger that in doing so, they merely provide training grounds for the subjects of the most advanced forms of digital capitalism: the ideal "networkers" that Boltanski and Chiapello already say are invoked by the management theory textbooks of the 1980s.[40] The challenge of creating commons is to avoid this fate for experimental collectivity-building in the twenty-first century, to try to engineer situations within which the modes of subjectivity and collective relationality that are enabled by them are not merely fodder for data extraction by the agencies of "surveillance capitalism," but members of "potent collectivities" engaged in strategic practices of institutional invention and world-actualization.

Informational Abundance

For such practices to be effective, there is no point denying that at times they will have to forego all of the comforts and advantages of present institutional legitimacy: even, at times, of legality under neoliberal property regimes. This is why the final project that I want to mention is of particular importance. Aaaaarg describes itself as a "content-management platform," but its major function, for the vast

39 Claire Bishop, *Artificial Hells: Participatory Art and the Politics of Spectatorship* (London: Verso, 2012), p. 277.
40 Luc Boltanski and Eve Chiapello, *The New Spirit of Capitalism*, trans. Gregory Elliott. New updated edition (London: Verso, 2018).

majority of its users, is as a straightforward pirate repository, making available a vast range of texts from the traditions of radical and critical theory, in such flagrant breach of copyright that it cannot be accessed by UK users without use of VPNs or proxy software to circumvent the prohibition on access imposed by all British ISPs. Gary Hall has argued persuasively for the importance of this type of "pirate" intervention in subverting the norms and institutional mechanisms of digital neoliberalism.[41] The observation I would like to make, however, is that in many ways, Aaaaarg carries out a function that is almost as old as the very idea of the public as such: that of the public library.

Since ancient times, the idea of the open and universal repository of knowledge has been associated with ideas of the commonality and sociality of human endeavor, and with the possibility of cultural progress. As in many other domains of cultural production, digitization and the spread of high-speed connectivity have posed major problems for market-based models, for the remuneration of producers and for the accumulation of capital from their endeavors. Most political responses to each problem have involved the heavy policing of intellectual property rights (mainly for the securing of profits, but also, occasionally, in the attempt to safeguard incomes for producers). As the very existence of Aaaaarg serves to demonstrate, however, this is unlikely to be an effective long-term solution, given the ease with which such mechanisms can be circumvented, and the strong motivation of various actors to do so. Ultimately, any effective democratic response is likely to involve some system by which producers can be supported by the public (or the commons) while making their works freely available to all: a true knowledge-commons.

In this sense, Aaaaarg is a partially prefigurative project that helps us to understand one of the central features of the commons. Commons are always characterized by shared abundance. Even when their material output is meagre, they are never organized according to a logic of scarcity, with which the logic of commodification is always deeply intertwined. Digital "commodities" create problems precisely because they are not naturally scarce. Enclosures privatize abundance while enforcing scarcity in order to create a market for commodities: that is precisely

---

41   Gary Hall, *Pirate Philosophy: For a Digital Posthumanities* (Cambridge MA: The MIT Press, 2016).

THE COMMONS, THE PUBLIC, AND THE AESTHETICS OF SOLIDARITY

their logic. By de-commodifying its contents, Aaaaarg dis-encloses it, making a commons. Its success in doing so can only be partial: Aaaaarg offers no solution to the problem of how producers are to be supported or compensated for their labor. It is unlikely that that problem can be resolved without public action on a massive scale. This is what the politics of the public-commons partnership might be able to achieve.

Looking Forwards

In November 2019, during the UK general election, the Labour Party announced a policy to nationalize and upgrade the national broadband network, offering free full-fiber connectivity to every home, business and institution in the country. The plan was met with predictable outrage by the (extremely) right-wing press and pundit class. But this is precisely the type of public action that would be required to make possible the true commoning of the digital archive, which projects like Aaaaarg seem to prefigure.

All of the projects considered here serve a function which is partially prefigurative, but also immediately political in its potentiation of small-scale collectivizing and in its cultivation of relations and experiences of solidarity. If there is an aesthetic of the commons then it is to be identified thus: it cultivates and amplifies experiences of solidarity, democracy and liberation through the potential of collectivities and the positing of hopeful possible worlds. At the same time, for interventions informed by such an aesthetic to have any real historical purchase, and to avoid becoming mere accomplices in the aestheticization of the social, they must have a certain strategic orientation that will, almost always, involve them in a relationship of creative collaboration with the public and its institutions. All of these projects are, in fact, clearly informed by such an orientation; which is precisely what differentiates them from the banality of so much relational, conceptual and participatory art. This, I think, is what it means to create commons in the twenty-first century; and that is why these projects offer powerful "resources of hope."[42]

---

42 Raymond Williams, *Resources of Hope: Culture, Democracy, Socialism* (London: Verso, 1989).

.

Judith Siegmund

Which "Aesthetics of the Commons"?

Proceeding from the concept of the commons, this contribution discusses current developments of digital activism within the framework of the arts from the perspective of aesthetic theory. It is an attempt to do justice to the observation that artists situate specific social projects in the context of artistic institutions while, at the same time, they intentionally go beyond the horizons of these institutions with their social concerns and actions. In doing so, they are less concerned with their freedom or with the freedom of art than they are with the concrete practice of "commoning," in which they directly or indirectly work on the production, organization, maintenance, and accessibility of "common-pool resources."[1] If these practices are described as aesthetic practices, this raises the question of what, exactly, is meant by the concept of the aesthetic. In what follows, two different understandings of the aesthetic in philosophy will be compared and assessed. After providing a critical representation of the *dispositif* of unlimited aesthetic freedom, I will attempt to ascertain, from the perspective of aesthetic theory, the consequences of the fact that the artistic practice of commoning can be understood as a form of agency. This agency involves giving, in one's own way, definition to something that is unavailable and turning it into something to which people can connect (paradoxically despite its general unavailability). Digital commons are ambivalent. On one hand, they are structured in a way that is entirely real, rule-based, and institutional; on the other hand, they embody utopia. Although this ambivalence is experienced both by the initiators of the archives discussed here as well as by their users, the self-empowerment of such projects—and this is my thesis—lies in their ability to organize themselves specifically and in detail while not dwelling on the representation of ambivalence as a value of its own.

---

1   See Elinor Ostrom, *Governing the Commons: The Evolution of Institutions for Collective Action* (Cambridge: Cambridge University Press, 1990).

1. Commons

The idea of the communality of the production, possession, maintenance, and use of resources —which is meant by the term "commons"—is somewhat obvious. Seen philosophically, however, the concept of the commons is rather broadly conceived and thus appears unclear: the more we examine its aspects, the blurrier and more undefinable it becomes. At the very beginning of my discussion, then, I would like to point out the contrast between the intuitive nature of the idea of the commons (the apparent ease with which this concept can be conveyed to anyone) and the fact of its conceptual vagueness. What do we mean when we use the concept of the commons?

The concept of the commons refers, *first*, to models of (collective) action that do not follow the rules of the market or the state but rather make their own rules. This is the first and most important definition of the commons; it derives from Elinor Ostrom, who calls the commons an "empirical alternative."[2] *Second*, the concept of the commons refers implicitly (and some also formulate this explicitly) to so-called "human nature." It draws a clear distinction, that is, between *homo oeconomicus* and *homo cooperativus*.[3] *Homo oeconomicus* is an invention of economics; it is entirely unsuitable as an anthropological figure of thought. Humans are not guided by considerations of utility alone but also by emotions and considerations of value; moreover, they cannot fully influence the contexts of their decisions. Fundamentally, however, it is difficult to derive much concrete information from the fact that people are social. People always relate to others in different ways—this is true. In her interpretation of Thomas Aquinas, moreover, Hannah Arendt pointed out that animals too (and not only humans) are social beings.[4] *Third*, in the concept of the commons, these human social relationships are interpreted historically from a Marxist perspective as non-alienated relations[5]—a feature which the

2   Ibid., p. 18.
3   See Stefan Reinicke and Hanna Voss, "Sozialismus ohne Klassenkampf," *taz* (July 27/28, 2019).
4   Hannah Arendt, *The Human Condition* (Chicago: University of Chicago Press, 1958), p. 24.
5   See An Architektur, "On the Commons: A Public Interview with Massimo De Angelis and Stavros Stavrides," *e-flux* 17 (2010): www.e-flux.com/journal/17/67351/on-the-commons-a-public-interview-with-massimo-de-angelis-and-stavros-stavrides (All links in this text last accessed October 20, 2020).

commons share with the conception and representation of art in twentieth-century aesthetic theory (I will examine this in greater detail below). *Fourth*, a major element of the commons is what is shared: the so-called resources. On the one hand, these resources are preexisting things that we can relate to; Elinor Ostrom called them "public goods" or "open-access resources."[6] Resources of this sort, one could argue, include air and water, which should be equally available to all human beings and to other life forms as well. On the other hand, commons are things that are created by the act through which we relate to them: "common-pool resources," in Ostrom's terms. Yochai Benkler and Felix Stalder have discussed such commons in detail.[7] According to Stalder, these relationships are not structured by money; at their heart, instead, is the idea of direct social cooperation.[8] *Fifth*, the sharing of the commons, which gives rise to them in the first place, is genuinely non-instrumental for the individual subjects involved; that is, it goes beyond the pursuit of individual interests. Thus, for instance, Elinor Ostrom took issue with Mancur Olson, who skeptically maintained that self-interested individuals would not act in support of group interests. According to Ostrom, this is more a matter of representing the inherent obstacles to commoning than it is about systematic problems that reveal the structural limits of commons-theory.[9] Common interests are therefore to be pursued, and yet—*sixth*—the creation of commons is also expected to involve autonomy (such statements are often made in the same breath).[10] *Seventh*, in sum, the commons are associated with utopia.

This utopia is often conceived in contemporary diagnostic analysis as a foil to neoliberalism, which is empirically apparent in the suffering of subjects from the capitalist enclosure of social relationships and goods. John Roberts, for instance, has written the following

---

6   Ostrom distinguishes between "resource systems" and "common-pool resources." If common pool resources are not used by anyone, then they become what she calls "open-access resources." She refers to resources that preexist us as "public goods." See Ostrom, *Governing the Commons*, p. 32.

7   Yochai Benkler, "The Political Economy of Commons," *UPGRADE* 4, no. 3 (2003): pp. 6–9; Felix Stalder, *The Digital Condition*, trans. Valentine A. Pakis (Cambridge: Polity Press, 2018), pp. 152–173.

8   Ibid., pp. 152–153.

9   Ostrom, *Governing the Commons*, pp. 5–6.

10   See John Roberts, "Art, Neoliberalism, and the Fate of the Commons," in *The Art of Direct Action*, ed. Karen van den Berg et al. (Berlin: Sternberg Press, 2019), pp. 239–257.

about socially engaged works of art: "Indeed, the erosion of democracy under neoliberalism runs in parallel with its counter-practice and counter-theoretization in contemporary art, insofar as the neoliberal destruction of the commons is the metapolitical framework through which socially engaged art organizes its noncompliant and resistive 'experiment in democracy'."[11] This notion that capitalism's enclosure of commonly shared goods represents the latter's "destruction" within the framework of the transformation of commodities was discussed by Marx as an idea that dated back to the fifteenth century and thus emerged during the early stages of industrial capitalism. The disappearance of the traditional commons (those areas of land that fell neither under the category of private property nor under government control but were rather used according to customary law by so-called freeholders) was thus part of a chapter of economic history at the very beginning of industrialization. In fifteenth-century England, the enclosure of pastures by landowners for the sake of raising sheep and thus for the textile industry was referred to as commodification (the transformation of land or other goods into a commodity). Oliver Schlaudt has made it clear that commodification consisted (and still consists) of several steps. He is thus in agreement with current theorists of the commons, who hold the view that the enclosure historicized by Marx has continued to repeat itself in capitalism as a sort of dialectical process, and that it continues to take place today.[12] Schlaudt identifies the following stages:

- Identification (itemizing, framing): The removal of a good from its context and renaming it with an economic or quantifying concept (e.g. "human capital").
- Enclosure: (a) Assigning a good a title of ownership, regardless of the owner; (b) excluding others from using it.
- Privatization: Transferring a good from public to private hands.
- Commercialization: Administering a good according to commercial principles and methods, usually with commercial intentions (efficiency, cost minimization, cost-benefit analysis, profit maximization).

11 Ibid., p. 240.
12 See footnote 5 above.

- Commodification in the strict sense: Transforming a good into a commodity (standardized, if necessary) with a market price.[13]

The sequence outlined here—conceptualization, declaration of ownership, the exclusion of others, and the transformation into a commodity—demonstrates very clearly that the process of commodification also involves linguistic, value-formational processes that create attention for the resources in question. That is, they draw linguistic attention to something material and thereby summon it into consciousness. It is now a matter of perspective whether such interpretational and ordering relations to the world (the first step in the schematic) should be regarded as an element of economic appropriation or as its opposite.[14] The latter variant opens up the space for thinking about commons as something that exists outside of the sphere of economics. On the one hand, this "exterior realm" is a possible opportunity for new enclosures, and to enclose more things has always been the aim of capital's desire in the capitalist and neoliberal system. On the other hand, it is also something that can oppose the desire of capital, because the way it is dealt with does not function according to the laws of neoclassical economics.[15] Oliver Staudt refers to the Kantian paradigm of inalienable property, which he summarizes with the idea that many things lose their particular human value when they are imagined and treated as commodities.[16]

If, as suggested, we understand commons as something outside of classical economics and as something outside of the market, then it becomes immediately apparent that the commons share with art a traditional figure of thought from the context of philosophical aesthetics (particularly twentieth-century German-language aesthetics): the definition of art in terms of its alterity—that is, in terms of its "otherness" in relation to society, the economy, and politics.

---

13 Oliver Schlaudt, *Wirtschaft im Kontext: Eine Einführung in die Philosophie der Wirtschaftswissenschaften in Zeiten des Umbruchs* (Frankfurt am Main: Vittorio Klostermann, 2016), p. 97.

14 I mean this less in a political sense than in a philosophically systematic sense. The act of naming something creates certain relations that are later understood as economic fact. Naming could also take place in a way that might lead to a different outcome.

15 Schlaudt also counts knowledge and reproductive work as areas outside of the neoclassical conception of economics.

16 Schlaudt, *Wirtschaft im Kontext*, pp. 98–99.

2. What Is Meant Here by Aesthetics?

If an aesthetic component is added to the concept of the commons, new questions arise. What is meant by an *aesthetics* of the commons? Do all sorts of commons possess aesthetic features, or just a certain type?

In the sense of aesthetic theory, the combination of words "aesthetics of the commons" implies a structural equality of aesthetics and commons that is not related to the existence of resources (objects or products) but can rather be understood as a similarity of attitude. According to Kant, the aesthetic attitude is related to the idea of aesthetic freedom. Where, then, does the idea of this aesthetic freedom come from—an idea which, for instance, can evade both the economic and political spheres? Here I will provide only a brief sketch by way of explanation: The free play of the human faculties of imagination and understanding when enacting aesthetic judgements is described by Kant in such a way that, first, it releases pleasure in the aesthetically enjoying subject and, second, its basis is that the enjoyed object (and thus also the enjoyed situation) is not perceived on the part of the subject within the framework of any set of interests. Thus, if someone has an economic interest in a work of art (for example), then he or she is no longer able to receive it aesthetically. As an interest, this economic perspective, according to Kant's *Critique of Judgement*, displaces the possibility of adopting an aesthetic attitude. To the extent that there is a market, which evaluates things according to success and money (as is the case in the artworld as well), a distinction has to be drawn between the speculative economic interest in the object and (as Kant says) the disinterested attitude toward an aesthetic object—an attitude that holds the object at a greater distance in the sense, for instance, that one cannot possess an object aesthetically in the same way that one can appropriate it economically. This defining figure of thought— the disinterestedness of the aesthetic attitude—has already been subjected to much criticism, for instance by Pierre Bourdieu, who argues that the Kantian aesthetic can historically be attributed to the interests of the bourgeoisie and that it should not be afforded the status of a universally valid (to one and all and for all times) definition of the aesthetic, as Kant maintained. Another argument against the philosophical position of the disinterested attitude is that it is a world-appropriating position that, in the name of disinterestedness toward morally dubious goods (or also toward culturally foreign objects and their mystique), "releases" the subject from responsibility. With respect to globalization, this always has something to do with economics. And thus the pleasure and freedom of one's own aesthetic judgment—represented as the free play of faculties in so-called disinterested pleasure—is that which stands in the foreground for the aesthetically judging subject. This is not a collective freedom (a freedom of the "we") but rather one of the self (a freedom of the "I"). This figure of thought has nevertheless been regarded as emancipatory—the aesthetic is not (at least not at first glance) a class privilege; rather all people without exception possess the faculties of imagination and understanding and are therefore able to make aesthetic judgments. This fact, evoked by Kant, is interpreted as a sort of equality, via which (or in a "roundabout way," one could say) it is possible to insert an imaginary "we" into the aesthetic, namely in the mode of "as-if." However, this "we" is distinguished by a commonly shared distance from the aesthetically perceived world; it is distinguished by standing back and by the ability of individuals to reflect about themselves. It is this distance and, with it, the reflexivity of aesthetic experiences and judgements that now seems to have entered a crisis. The crisis in question concerns the figure of the autonomous Western subject as a free individual in aesthetic matters. Today, such freedom is no longer the privilege of bourgeois subjects who, in contemplating the world, "achieve" reflective distance; rather, what is meant by freedom is increasingly our emotional decisions related to consumption. Here, something has shifted. An economization of art is also part of this context. The meaning of the concept of the aesthetic is a renewed matter of debate.

In sum, one could thus say that both the idea of individual freedom as well as the purely aesthetic attitude, which has historically been linked to this freedom, are unsuitable for describing the features of the aesthetics of commons. By definition, commons are resources whose use is independent of market forces. Nevertheless, the collectives that create the commons do develop rules (in the sense of their institutional rules) that limit individual freedoms. Absolute freedom is therefore not a criterion of the commons. What, then, is their genuine aesthetics? What relationship do the latter have to economics and politics, but also to ethics and critique? Under the conditions of globalization and the climate crisis, is there a new way to think about the aesthetic?

In the case of economics, it is clear to see that the aesthetic in the twentieth century is regarded as the opposite of the practical and rational, the very things with which economics has long been associated. The conflict between the obligation to pursue the rational ends of the market and the desire to adopt an aesthetic attitude (as its alternative) has been a significant figure of thought in modernity. Regardless of how they are experienced, aesthetic attitudes thus represent a space outside of the economic sphere. In the end, however, this equation of the commons and art as two phenomena exterior to economics overlooks one aspect that is essential to understanding the commons: the economic manner in which they function. In her book *Governing the Commons*, for instance, Ostrom demonstrates the great significance of functioning institutional structures to the management of what she calls "common-pool resources." With concrete examples, I would therefore like to show that aesthetic freedom alone, as a counterpart to the economic, is insufficient for defining the commons.

3. Archives and Libraries[17]

A third concept is of importance: that of the digital. The focus is on "[s]elected artistic projects of alternative resource generation" in the digital sphere. Here, it quickly becomes clear why, when contemplating the "culture of digitality," it is useful to proceed from the idea that digital commons are created in the first place by the praxis of their users. The "archives and libraries" in question all emerged from a specific application of (partially existing, partially altered, partially reprogrammed) software, which can be administered communally and easily, and which enables the communal use of digital archives of texts, images, and films. It is only through the practice of programming, collecting, and organizing that these commons emerged, though the collected (digitalized) works of course predate the archives and libraries themselves. That is, these digital commons came about by drawing upon resources that already existed independently. In that these materials or products are not interpreted or treated in commercial terms,

something new arose from gathering them together. Everyone interviewed from the project stressed that distance from the market is one
of its essential features. Keeping this distance is a goal that they set for
themselves, and it also represents a common feature of the archives
under consideration. The latter consist of UbuWeb, Memory of the
World, Monoskop, and the film database 0xDB, which runs on the
software pan.do/ra.

Although Kenneth Goldsmith, the poet who runs the avant-garde
archive UbuWeb, told Cornelia Sollfrank in a 2013 interview that he
pays no attention to copyright laws—"Copyright? What's that? Never
heard of it," he says with some pride—today one finds a standardized
answer to copyright questions on the website: "We cannot grant you
permission to reprint or quote anything since we don't own the rights
to most of it. You need to contact the artist or artists' representative
directly for permission." The growth of the size and significance of
the avant-garde archive has seemed to create increasing demands that
the managers of digital commons refuse to acknowledge, especially
regarding copyrights. Since the beginning of UbuWeb, the nature of
the internet, which was once regarded as a place of grass-roots democratic possibilities, has changed into a crowded digital space and competitive marketplace, and certainly many of the requests to use the
documents on UbuWeb for personal research are no longer based on
the idea that one can refuse to yield to market forces or that it might
be possible to create different user rules for disseminating art-histori-
cal materials. The commodification of the internet has reached a point
where it presumably seems normal to many people. One of the critical concerns of the digital commons projects mentioned above is that,
as part of their basic conceptualization, they aim to create and defend
a specific online context that opposes enclosure by those who think
and act in terms of the neoclassical market. In this context, the frequently mentioned keyword is solidarity. As a resource, knowledge
can be shared in such a way that this knowledge is not appropriated
and declared private property, as Marcell Mars, one of the operators
of Memory of the World, made clear in a statement about this public
digital library. Conversely, however, this does not mean that these
library and archival projects do not work with players who accept
copyright laws. The same is true of their collaborations with the publishing houses whose work they make available. As Dušan Barok *has*

summarized: "There are publishing houses that require me to remove their books from my archive. There are presses that silently tolerate it, and there are presses that appreciate that their books are available on Monoskop. In this regard, an interesting sort of variability has arisen that can be interpreted as a new realm with its own rules."

The idea of sharing knowledge is traditionally based on the concept of education—several of the interviewed commons activists refer to it as often as they do to the activity of preservation, which is generally the foundation of archival work (Sebastian Luetgert and Jan Gerber). Here there is a clear effort to resist the appropriation and commodification of traditionally public goods, which education and archives generally represent. Marcell Mars has stressed that the users of his library project are addressed as library users, exactly as they would be if using a normal public library. In the same way, people are granted access to books that would otherwise be unavailable to them.

In addition, Memory of the World has organized several workshops and installed its own book scanner (developed in-house), on which participants could scan books and upload them. Regarding the motive behind his "public library," Mars has cited the fact that public libraries (in Croatia) remain unable to access e-books because they cannot pay the fees attached to the leasing system that online bookstores have set up for granting access to books.

The motivation of the two directors of the film archive 0xDB (Sebastian Luetgert and Jan Gerber) is likewise linked to the fact that many films and videos today are produced without the aid of mainstream institutional support and distribution mechanisms and are thus prone to being quickly forgotten. Yet, for them, it is about more than simply collecting these works; it is also about using software that can "keyword" these independent films both visually and textually in order to influence, expand, and shift the production conditions of filmmaking. In all of these archives, the task of keywording is usually undertaken by a small group of engaged collaborators, so in this way too they resemble traditional libraries and archives. It must be stressed, however, that in many cases the selection of books and films remains a democratic choice by those who contribute something to the archive in question. In the case of the avant-garde archive UbuWeb, this is not possible; here, the idea of the commons lies in its common use of an inventory of data that is art-historically valuable. In general, it can be said that, in each project, the rules for selecting and uploading texts, images, films, and interviews follow varying ideas of sharing. Whereas Monoskop is set up as a Wiki—as an inclusive space, as Dušan Barok has called it—the scope of its content was at first limited to "arts and humanities" from Eastern Europe and later expanded to cultural phenomena from non-Western contexts. In a Wiki structure, participants can engage in mutual dialogue. On the contrary, 0xDB, according to its operators Sebastian Luetgert and Jan Gerber, is not curated at all; instead, the selection criterion in the background is a rather broad media concept that includes a wide variety of publicly available film products.

What is significant for all five projects is the technical-digital innovation that has taken place within the framework of managing the self-imposed tasks at hand. Jan Gerber, for instance, makes it clear that there are large technical differences between archiving and managing one thousand, ten thousand, or a hundred thousand films, and he admits that growth can be slow as projects advance from one level to the next. The software used by 0xDB, which is known as pan.do/ra, was developed in-house; that used by Memory of the World, which is called Let's Share Books, is a plug-in for Calibre, a freely available software for managing digital publications. For its part, Wiki is a type of software that is available as a democratic tool for the public sphere; it was designed from the very beginning with the idea of open collaboration in mind. These commons projects resemble one another in the fact that all of them, on account of the constant engagement and input of their initiators, have existed for a long time and have had to make multiple technical adjustments in response to changing online conditions. Many of them also pay for the servers that they use. Here, the keyword that sums everything up is unpaid labor, and it is presumably no coincidence that unpaid labor contributes to the formation of commons. Could this effort ever be converted into paid labor? The answer to this question depends on whether, with the financial recognition of their activities, the products themselves might make their way into the private sphere. In the context of the archive projects, payment of any sort would lead to increased copyright conflicts, which are now kept in a grey zone by the absence of money. In order to avoid self-exploitation, a different sort of financing would have to be found from that which could be provided by private enterprises. In this sense (but only in this sense), unpaid labor is likewise a resource that refuses to obey the laws of the market.

4. Digital Commons and Artistic Autonomy from the Perspective of Aesthetic Theory

Regarding the question of the aesthetics of the commons, an interesting observation that binds the five projects under consideration is that all of their founders refer to themselves as artists working in one genre or another, from visual art, poetry, and film to curatorial or other cultural activity. At this point, I should refer once again to the close connection that several of them see between the arts and the humanities. What is decisive is that the financing and dissemination of nearly all of the platforms are supported through sponsoring structures in the art world and by cultural institutions (which are themselves funded partly publicly and partly privately). "I need to play the artist's role"—this statement by Marcell Mars summarizes his (self-proclaimed) strategic perspective. All of the founders take advantage of the opportunities provided by artistic networks (digital as well as analog) to promote their own projects.

Overall, the situation looks as follows: 1) Without exception, the operators of the commons platforms discussed here are men, and nearly all of them have a background in art or at least curation. 2) According to the interviews, none of them places any special value on this background. Finally, 3) they have all used the infrastructures of artistic institutions to realize their projects, though they do not limit themselves to such institutions.

At first glance, strategies for acquiring recognition and financial means within the framework of art could be regarded theoretically as an act of instrumentalizing artistic autonomy on behalf of the artists. However, I would like to distance myself from such a representation. The concept of the autonomy of art is closely connected to art's promise of alterity (which I discussed in my second section above), according to which art must be understood as something that exists outside of the realms of politics, the economy, and society. Now, in my opinion, the practice of commoning is distinguished by the very fact that it is meant to achieve certain effects in social, political, and economic spheres, and that—at least in the example projects under consideration here—it has achieved this goal. This practice has prevented the enclosure of traditional commons (beyond the world of art), and new commons have been created on the basis of today's digital technology. These thoughts are supported, for instance, by Yochai Benkler when he speaks of "the political economy of commons."[18] This is not merely a matter of presenting model platforms through which the idea of the commons is conveyed in the mode of "as-if." Rather, it is about the professional and real acquisition, management, and communication of large data sets that are available to users and are archived by the users themselves.

The announcement of the research project *Creating Commons* at the Zurich University of the Arts emphasizes both the "symbolic function" of artistic projects, on the one hand, and "making available freely usable resources," on the other (see the project's website). To me, this formulation seems to imply a dialectical opposition. Although the projects in question function symbolically, they nevertheless also succeed in making real resources available for users beyond the context of art. Oppositional formulations of this sort, which can be read (for instance) as ambivalent or even paradoxical, ultimately refer to a concept of artistic autonomy, which, historically, has something to do with the aesthetic attitude discussed above; to the extent that, historically and theoretically, this attitude always derives from an opposition between art and reality (here, reality can be understood as a real extension of the practical possibilities of accessing the internet). In this regard, the self-perception of artistic actors also plays a role to the extent that they present themselves in interviews as people who intentionally employ the arts' claim of autonomy for their projects. However, the effect of the projects (their output, so to speak) goes far beyond the goal of earning recognition from the institutions and discourses of art. Although the figure of thought of artistic autonomy has often been interpreted by artists as their own autonomy, there is much to contradict this assumption from the theoretical side.[19] Ultimately, the figure of thought of artistic autonomy in philosophical aesthetics

---

18 Benkler, "The Political Economy of Commons."
19 See, for instance, Peter Osborne, *The Postconceptual Tradition: Critical Essays* (London: Verso, 2018), ch. 4.

is not based on the guarantee of a sort of autonomy that is made available to artists by the field of art; rather, the type of autonomy in question is related to a definition, according to which art should be regarded as a unified whole. Thinking about the autonomy of art in this way can also mean that, today, art's claim of autonomy can seem precarious (as Rancière sees it) or that the margins of this autonomous field can be understood as "frayed."[20] Even if one thinks in such a way, however, the systematic and intellectual figure of artistic autonomy ultimately remains intact—conceivable, first, as an aesthetic attitude of recipients and, second, as a self-imposed law of the field of art. In my opinion, the relationship between the inside and the outside becomes different when the autonomy of art is seen as an instrumental means of external (e.g., private sector) ambitions, such as the accumulation of capital. Recently, authors have pointed out various artistic strategies and forms of transgression.[21] This is, so to speak, a sort of delinquency (performed as transgression). First, economies transgress the boundaries of alterity by appropriating what had been conceived as "other" by actors and institutions. Thus, in connection with the integration of the arts and sciences (humanities) into the knowledge economy, Kerstin Stakemeier has referred to autonomy as a "representational leftover."[22] The sociologist Karl-Siegbert Rehbert has formulated his critique as one of the corruptibility of autonomous arts: "With cynical openness, autonomy and utility have come together to form an increasingly successful union."[23] Here, the transgression is conceived as coming from both sides. Sven Lütticken, on the contrary, has managed to derive a constructive and thoughtful perspective toward action from the very "representational leftover" of artistic autonomy: "While it is imperative to defend zones of exception to the dominant state of

20 See Theodor W. Adorno, "Art and the Arts," in *Can One Live After Auschwitz? A Philosophical Reader*, ed. Rolf Tiedemann (Palo Alto: Stanford University Press, 2003), pp. 368–390.
21 See Sven Lütticken, "To Live Inside the Law: Aesthetic Practice as Paralegal Activism," in *Funktionen der Künste: Transformatorische Potentiale künstlerischer Praktiken*, ed. Birgit Eusterschulte et al. (Stuttgart: Metzler Verlag, 2021), forthcoming.
22 Kerstin Stakemeier, "(Not) More Autonomy," in *Reproducing Autonomy: Work, Money, Crisis, and Contemporary Art*, ed. Kerstin Stakemeier and Marina Vishmidt (London: Mute, 2016), p. 28.
23 Karl-Siegbert Rehberg, "Kunstautonomie als (historische) Ausnahme und normative Leitidee," in *Autonomie der Kunst? Zur Aktualität eines gesellschaftlichen Leitbildes*, ed. Uta Karstein and Tessa Zahner (Wiesbaden: Springer, 2017), p. 55.

exception [...] it is equally necessary to descend into the forums where decisions are made on which lives count as truly human, and which will be treated as disposable biomatter."[24] Here, transgression is formulated as a task that involves, on the one hand, impeding enclosures (in the sense of economic takeovers); on the other hand, Lütticken also insists that there should be more transgressive activity within the arenas of decision-making themselves in order to oppose the biopolitical and private-sector appropriation of the world.

The following question is thus at stake: In which scenario can the narrative of artistic autonomy truly oppose its economic (and politically representative) takeover, and when is this narrative merely a "representational leftover" (or perhaps even less than that)? Because there can be so many differences of opinion about this, I suggest that we should test out the suitability of a different narrative to see whether it might better explain the assertion and reality of the aesthetics of the digital commons. This would be a narrative of artistic action and its interrelations with the effects that it causes. If the effects of poietic actions, which are undertaken in artistic institutional contexts, are related to extra-artistic social contexts (economic contexts, for instance), then it must be explained how the connection between artistic and non-artistic activities and practices should be understood.

If we proceed from the assumption that the internal motivation of artistically acting subjects can no longer be understood in terms of radical empowerment or as efforts to gain absolute mastery over practices and their contexts, then notions such as motivationality—intentionality in the sense of the importance and attention accorded to a thing or an activity—remain meaningful concepts. Rather, in order to begin something—or even to contemplate it in a non-arbitrary way—self-empowerment is necessary in the sense that it enables us to put something in a perspective that is our own or at least feels as though it is. Considered systematically, this also means that there must be a distinction between participating, without further ado, in something that exceeds and thereby legitimizes the self (as might be said, for instance, of digitalization processes or the algorithms that represent these processes to us), and intentionally attempting to do so. Of course, this does not mean that the perspective which a given subject

24 Lütticken, "To Live Inside the Law."

adopts towards his or her actions—in the development or cultivation, for instance, of digital commons—is the only norm; rather, one's own perspective is a starting point for entering an open praxis with others in the sense that the results of such activity are in principle uncertain and unavailable.[25]

An understanding of commons as "commons-based peer production" emphasizes processes of manufacturing things and thus emphasizes processes of poietic activity that embody socially shared ideas of interrelations.[26] I speak of embodiment, though this is really about digital archives; ultimately, I understand the digital commons as products that have arisen from creative activities and will continue to emerge from them. Inscribed in these products are socially shared "meanings" or ascriptions of meaning on the part of the initiators and users of the platforms. They also include the sets of rules that each of the respective projects has institutionalized to govern the organization, administration, and use of the archives and public libraries. The social significance of commons is thus closely related to the specific conditions of their creation and organization, as well as to the convictions and practices of those who organize and manage them. Their actions are significant, first because their convictions and work are valuable in their own right and, second, because they influence the way that the commons' recipients, participants, and users understand how they function. Moreover, it is productive and sustaining in any case to interpret commons as economically organized projects—indeed, as economies of their own—that are able to comment on (if not correct) the leading principles and convictions of today's (commercially-driven) economy. As Felix Stalder has noted, it is precisely the idea of intertwining different understandings and actions that might give rise to a social opportunity to recapitulate our convictions and practices in a critical manner: "The economy is not understood here as an independent realm that functions according to a different set of rules [from those governing art and culture] and with externalities, but rather as one facet of a com-

---

25 I will admit that this sounds awfully close to the ideas of Hannah Arendt, but Arendt would not have associated action so closely with production. On this issue, see Judith Siegmund, *Zweck und Zweckfreiheit: Zum Funktionswandel der Künste im 21. Jahrhundert* (Stuttgart: Metzler Verlag, 2019), p. 110–127

26 See Stalder, *The Digital Condition*, p. 152.

plex and comprehensive phenomenon with intertwining commercial, social, ethical, ecological, and cultural dimensions."[27]

Viewed philosophically, the idea that the arts are embedded in society is nothing new; it has been expressed by classical authors such as Plato and Aristotle but also by authors such as Alexander Baumgarten, G. W. F. Hegel, Konrad Fiedler, Edgar Windt, John Dewey, and Arthur Danto. Aristotle's concept of mimesis, for instance, is not just about art imitating life, as is often stated; rather, the imitative function of the theater, according to Aristotle (in the *Poetics*), operates in such a way that it surpasses the model of reality and is therefore "truer"— in the sense that its modelling comes closer to the truth—than our everyday experience, which is codetermined by contingencies, could ever be. Subjects who artistically act (and other subjects as well) are entrenched in social structures and yet, at the same time, are striving for something of their own. Purpose—understood as telos—does not entail that people must have sovereign access to certain means or that they must act alone or in a purely self-determined way. Rather, the concept of purpose also contains the idea of responsivity, which can only be fully understood in scenarios that involve interdependence.

27   Ibid., p. 154.

Care & Infrastructure

Daphne Dragona

Commoning the Commons:
Revisiting the Role of Art
in Times of Crisis

Introduction

The emergence or empowerment of the commons is often associated with periods of crisis. Different regions or countries, communities or populations have experienced the rise of the commons in times of struggle and recovery, when questions of livelihood arose anew.[1] This was the case in Britain in the 1980s, in Argentina in the early 2000s, and in Greece in the last decade, when the potential of the commons— manifested through alternatives and collective action—appeared as a response to the violence of financial capitalism. The crisis, in each of these cases, was communicated as economic and temporary. What this last decade—from 2010 until 2020—has shown, though, is that what we have been experiencing is generalized; it is a crisis "of social stability, not a simple recession,"[2] as the social bonds that keep society together have collapsed and the ecological systems upon which life depends are no longer able to support the needs of the insatiable capitalist system.[3] The present crisis is an economic, social and climate one experienced on a global scale, yet asymmetrically and differently between and within continents, countries, territories and areas. Within this crisis, new "varieties of racism" appear, and forms of

---

1   An Architektur, "On the Commons: A Public Interview with Massimo De Angelis and Stavros Stavrides," June 2010, *e-flux*, www.e-flux.com/journal/on-the-commons-a-public-interview-with-massimo-de-angelis-and-stavros-stavrides/ (accessed April 17, 2020).
2   Massimo de Angelis, "Crises, Capital and Co-optation: Does capital need a commons fix?," *The Wealth of the Commons*, http://wealthofthecommons.org/essay/crises-capital-and-co-optation-does-capital-need-commons-fix (accessed April 17, 2020).
3   Sarah Leonard and Nancy Fraser, "Capitalism's Crisis of Care," Fall 2016, *Dissent Magazine*, https://www.dissentmagazine.org/article/nancy-fraser-interview-capitalism-crisis-of-care (accessed April 17, 2020).

populism and nationalism are strengthened, making the world "inhospitable, uninhabitable and unbreathable" for many.[4]

In this period of "troubling troubled times" as Berlant[5] calls it, the role and the understanding of the commons changes. The commons, as she argues, become the *affective infrastructures* needed "to manage the unevenness, ambivalence, violence and ordinary contingency of contemporary existence." The commons—with their language and politics—are called to "re-enchant the world" as Federici[6] puts it; it is at these moments "when we feel that we are at the edge of the volcano," "in the midst of much destruction," that one realizes the need to question and oppose hegemonic worlds. The recent Coronavirus pandemic made this apparent, as it not only exposed the lacks and vulnerabilities of the health system, but also revealed the interconnection of the social, economic and climate crises and affirmed the necessity of practices and strategies of care, solidarity and reparation. But, what does the understanding of the commons as affective infrastructures or as elements that can re-enchant the world really mean? How does it differ from prior understandings of the scope and goals of the commons? Is the notion of the commons in this case enriched or unsettled in an attempt to reconstruct it,[7] or does it entail a danger of romanticization?[8] And, who are the active subjects, the commoners who build, maintain or repair these relations and bonds?

This paper revisits past and recent ways of understanding the commons, paying attention to their affective qualities and highlighting their potential to constitute active points of relation. It examines commons as infrastructures, as systems and even more as ecologies of resources, people and relations linked to the sociopolitical conditions of their time. It discusses how acting and being in common can assist in the recuperation of society's social bonds, and it specifically explores how initiatives and practices driven through art can exemplify this. Paying

4   Sindre Bangstad and Torbjørn Tumyr Nilsen, "Thoughts on the planetary: An interview with Achille Mbembe," 5 September 2019, *New Frame*, https://www.newframe.com/thoughts-on-the-planetary-an-interview-with-achille-mbembe/?fbclid=IwAR25XEG67lJNshASc_c-MWQwaqSSaPv8YgnZ72-E_xF-JE37QcMm9PZ7ea0 (assessed April 17, 2020).
5   Lauren Berlant, "The commons: Infrastructures for troubling times," *Environment and Planning D: Society and Space* 34, no. 3 (2016): pp. 393–419.
6   Sylvia Federici, *Re-enchanting the World: Feminism and the Politics of Commons* (Oakland: PM Press, 2019), p. 1.
7   Ibid., p. 110.
8   de Angelis, "Crises, Capital and Co-optation."

attention not to individual artworks but rather to ongoing collaborative projects or spaces, the paper examines practices of commoning which at the same time constitute acts of world(s)-building. Studying artistic initiatives as spaces of multiple affective encounters, it highlights how different temporalities, cultures, and forms of knowledge meet, and offer the ground for transition and transformation. Finally, and in relation to these practices, this paper discusses how new aesthetics and values are being formed, assisting relations to be built and cherished.

A Genealogy of Affective Commons

Infrastructures, Berlant clarifies, are "protocols or practices that hold the world up"; this is the case with public infrastructures like roads, bridges and schools but also with social infrastructures that might be patterns, habits or norms.[9] Infrastructures organize life, connecting parts—or keeping them separate—and allowing—or impeding—the movement of people, goods and information. They are associated with power, sovereignty and privilege, but when it comes to affective infrastructures, as Berlant argues, they hold the potential of building worlds that can accommodate difference. The commons, according to Berlant, constitute such a case; they are an "action concept acknowledging a broken world," manifesting the need and possibility for non-sovereign relationality.[10] They assist in the decolonization of the social space, and in its transformation from one "inhabited by empire, capitalism and land-right power" to one that allows difference and ambivalence.[11] As infrastructures, the commons can embrace forms of co-existence.

The reference to the potential of the commons to operate as binding elements is not unprecedented in the theory and discourse on the commons. The thinkers of Autonomist Marxism approached the commons as built and sustained by the multitude: a heterogeneous mixed body of singularities residing mostly in urban centers and engaging with affective and cognitive labor. In the *Grammar of the Multitude*,

---

9   Berlant, "The commons: Infrastructures for troubling times," pp. 393, 394, 403.
10   Ibid., p. 399.
11   Ibid., p. 397.

Virno talks about the cognitive and linguistic habits that the multitude shares, tying the many together.[12] The multitude, according to Virno, is haunted by a shared feeling of homelessness, and *language* offers as a response a sort of shelter; this is where forms of non-representative democracy, non-governmental usages and customs, and new political forms can be found. Language, thus, seems to constitute for Virno an affective infrastructure. Similarly, in *Commonwealth*, Hardt and Negri refer to the languages, as well as to the *habits, gestures, affects and codes* of the multitude, in discussing the commons as a social infra-structure.[13] They write about the "affective" and "intellectual talents," the skills and competences of the many, and their ability to form rela-tions.[14] As they specifically mention, "the common is not only the earth we share but also the languages we create, the social practices we establish, the modes of sociality that define our relationships."[15] More than ten years ago, the scholars of Autonomist Marxism turned their attention to a common wealth that not only refers to natural resources but also to cultural ones, and specifically underlined the dependence of this common wealth on affect and social relations.

In a statement similar to the one of Hardt and Negri, anti-capitalist thinkers Caffentzis and Federici emphasize that *"although we say that commons are all around us—the air we breathe and the languages we use being key examples of shared wealth—it is only through coopera-tion in the production of our life that we can create them."*[16] Linebaugh, also, writes that the commons are not just the common goods, but mostly the social practices and the establishment of relationships by its actors, the commoners,[17] and Tan discusses the "social relations" as what is central to the meaning of the commons.[18] A holistic under-standing of the commons, therefore, includes the pooled resources,

12 Paolo Virno, *A Grammar of the Multitude: For an Analysis of Contemporary Forms of Life*, trans. I. Bertolleti, J. Cascaito, A. Casson (Los Angeles and New York: Semiotext(e), 2004).
13 Michael Hardt and Antonio Negri, *Commonwealth* (Cambridge MA: Belknap Press of Har-vard University Press, 2009), p. 39.
14 Ibid., p.152.
15 Ibid., p.139.
16 George Caffentzis and Silvia Federici, "Commons Against and Beyond Capitalism," *Com-munity Development Journal* 49, Issue Supplement 1 (January 2014): p. i101.
17 Paul Linebaugh in Louis Wolscher, "The Meaning of the Commons," *An Architektur* 23 (2010): pp. 4–5.
18 Pelin Tan, "Uncommon Knowledge: A transversal dictionary," May 2014, *Eurozine*, https://www.eurozine.com/uncommon-knowledge/ (accessed April 17, 2020).

the commoners, as well as the relationships and practices[19] established between commoners and the resources. Certain questions though are left open regarding the identity of the commoners, the character of the relations being formed and the role of affect in their creation. Understanding affect as "an ability to affect and be affected,"[20] which are, in other words, the individuals involved in—and influenced by—the creation of these relations?

Federici addresses such questions and discusses issues of power and exclusion with reference to the commons. Questioning, for instance, the special emphasis that Autonomist Marxists place on people residing in urban centers and engaging with cognitive labor, Federici argues that the potential of this common concerns a minority compared to the world population; it is based on economic activities with social and ecological implications. "No common is possible unless we refuse to base our life and our reproduction on the suffering of others, unless we refuse to see ourselves as separate from them." Highlighting the necessity of the *feminist commons* as "the foundation of new forms of social reproduction," she speaks of the importance of relations of reciprocity, responsibility and respect. For her, it is more about "the commoning of the material means of reproduction" which affect the majority of the population; it is about care work mostly undertaken by women, without which everyday life runs the risk of becoming an "affective desert." The commons, thus, "represent the social relations we aim to achieve, as well as the means for their construction."[21]

Looking deeper into the question of *whose* commons are—or are not—being addressed, Harney and Moten introduced the term *undercommons* to refer to those who cannot own, possess or settle.[22] They speak of the affective differences that still need to be recognized in order to think and act differently in finding ways of being together in homelessness and in brokenness; this is, for them, the *undercommons*, and hence the infrastructure, that "we must all find our way to" as

19 An Architektur, "On the Commons: A Public Interview with Massimo De Angelis and Stavros Stavrides."
20 Brian Massumi, "Notes on the translation and acknowledgments," in Gilles Deleuze and Felix Guattari, *A Thousand Plateaus: Capitalism and Schizophrenia*, trans. and foreword Brian Massumi (Minneapolis and London: University of Minnesota Press, 2005), p. xvi.
21 Federici, *Re-enchanting the World*, pp. 95, 105, 106, 110, 112, 185.
22 Stefano Harney and Fred Moten, *The Undercommons: Fugitive Planning & Black Study* (New York: Autonomedia, 2013).

Halberstam underlines in the foreword of the book.[23] The *we* of the undercommons, as he explains, is the indigenous peoples, the black peoples, the queers and poor peoples, and the binding element—the affective infrastructure—in this case is no other but the actual *desire of tearing down walls and structures* so that it becomes possible to find one another. Like Virno, who associated the commons with a form of shelter for the multitude's shared feeling of not feeling at home, Harney and Moten speak of a commons that "give[s] refuge" and a "refuge that gives commons." In their approach, though, it is the "stolen life": the life not being acknowledged as such and left without agency, that comes to the foreground to inhabit the commons.[24]

Wishing to address the affective specificity of *who* or *what* is not being valued, Muñoz spoke of the "brown commons."[25] "Feeling brown," as Muñoz explains, is a minoritarian affect binding people, which is "partially illegible in relation to the normative affect, performed by normative citizen subjects." It is "a commons of brown people" but also of "places, feelings, sounds, animals, minerals, flora and other objects." All these different elements share a certain "organicism" and exist in relation to each other, he argued. The infrastructure in this case expands and unites heterogenous elements forming a plurality of being-in-common, a "plurality of brown commons."[26] Millner-Larsen and Butt, elaborating on the work of Muñoz, discuss a community which is "aleatory, improvisatory and essentially multiplicitous."[27] The two scholars respond directly to Berlant's call and introduce the *queer commons* as a resource that can assist in "imagining, experimenting with and enacting the improvisational infrastructures necessary for managing the unevenness of contemporary existence." The commons, Millner-Larsen and Butt argue, are in reality always queer, as they are

---

23 Jack Halberstam, "The Wild Beyond: With and For the Undercommons," in Stefano Harney and Fred Moten, *The Undercommons: Fugitive Planning & Black Study* (New York: Autonomedia, 2013), pp. 2–12.

24 Harney and Moten, *The Undercommons*, p. 28.

25 José Esteban Muñoz, "Feeling Brown, Feeling Down: Latina Affect, the Performativity of Race, and the Depressive Position," *Signs* 31, No. 3, New Feminist Theories of Visual Culture (Spring 2006): pp. 675–688

26 José Esteban Muñoz, "Preface: Fragment from the Sense of Brown Manuscript," *GLQ: A Journal of Lesbian and Gay Studies* 24. no. 4 (October 2018): pp. 395–397.

27 Nadja Millner-Larsen and Gavin Butt, "Introduction: The Queer Commons," *GLQ: A Journal of Lesbian and Studies* 24, no. 4 (October 2018): pp. 399–419.

meant to oppose classifications and standardizations behind systems and infrastructures.

Furthermore, aiming to situate the commons in relation to a world as a "messier, entangled" place, a world that is not separated in the first place,[28] different authors have written about the elements binding humans with the environment. Of high relevance are Tsing's *latent commons* opening to other species,[29] Haraway's writing on kinship,[30] and also Braidotti's emphasis on the "transversal connections among human and nonhuman agents" which led to Lindsay Weber's writing on the "post-human commons" and the primacy of interdependence.[31] The attention in all these cases is shifting towards a commons connected to "spaces for affective encounters between human and non-human others."[32] These approaches are closer to indigenous world views and the principles of relationality, reciprocal generosity and respectful care;[33] with territories being approached as living environments and not as resources. The commons understood as infrastructures between human and more-than-human entities and environments bring to the foreground a "worlding of many worlds ecologically related across their constitutive divergence"; these are, for de la Cadena,[34] the *uncommons*: "the negotiated coming together of heterogeneous worlds (and their practices)," a *pluriverse* which is inspired by the Zapatista Movement and highlights the importance of the relations between worlds.

28 Patrick Bresnihan, "The more-than-human commons: From commons to commoning," in *Space, Power and the Commons: The struggle for alternative futures*, ed. Samuel Kirwan, Leila Dawney and Julian Brigstocke (London and New York: Routledge, 2015), pp. 105–124.

29 Anna Lowenhaupt Tsing, *The Mushroom at the End of the World: On the Possibility of Life in Capitalist Ruins* (Princeton: Princeton University Press, 2015), p. 255.

30 Donna Haraway, *Staying with the Trouble: Making Kin in the Chthulucene* (Durham NC: Duke University Press, 2016).

31 Lindsay Grace Weber, "The commons," in *Posthuman Glossary*, ed. Rosi Braidotti and Maria Hlavajova (London and New York: Bloomsbury Academic, 2018), pp. 83–86.

32 Neera Singh, "Becoming a commoner: The commons as sites for affective socio-nature encounters and co-becomings," *ephemera: theory & politics in organization* 17, no. 4 (2017), pp. 751–776.

33 Simon Bignal and Daryl Rigney, "Indigeneity, Posthumanism and Nomad Though: Transforming Colonial Ecologies," in *Posthuman Ecologies: Complexity and Process after Deleuze*, ed. Rosi Braidotti and Simon Bignall (London: Rowman & Littlefield, 2019), p. 161.

34 Marisol de la Cadena and Mario Blaser, *A World of Many Worlds* (Durham NC and London: Duke University Press, 2018), p. 4.

Returning to Berlant's writing on the commons as affective infrastructures, while taking into consideration the aforementioned positions, one realizes that such an approach stands for what binds, maintains or repairs bonds among people, communities, more-than-human worlds and environments. It refers to establishing relations that are based not necessarily on similarities and commonalities, but also on *uncommonalities*,[35] on the acknowledgment of difference and interdependence. As Singh argues, the time has come to think of the commons as "affective socio-nature relations" and the practices of commoning as a means of nurturing this relationship.[36] She speaks of *affective commons* which are based on a "coming together of singularities and exceptions" and are based on the affective capacities of those involved, being able to affect others and to build generative and inclusive commoning relations. The commons in such a case, as Federici also writes, are not built by gated or exclusive communities, but rather by communities based on "a principle of cooperation, and of responsibility to each other and to the earth."[37] This is how, one could add here, the affective *under-, brown-, queer- and more-than-human* commons operate: constantly growing and forming ecologies, and systems of commons,[38] driven by shared affect and not by sameness or likeness. It needs to be highlighted, though, that the different approaches mentioned are not understood as categorizations. They do not exclude each other; on the contrary, they complement each other and to an extent overlap. They manifest that there is not one type of commoning, but rather a form of *boundary commoning* "that crosses boundaries, activates and sustains relations among commons thus giving shape to commons at larger scales...."[39] Understanding the commons as affective infrastructures, therefore, not only emphasizes the

35 Marisol de la Cadena, "Uncomming Nature," *e-flux journal, 56th Venice Biennale,* http://supercommunity.e-flux.com/texts/uncommoning-nature/ (accessed March 20, 2020).
36 Singh, "Becoming a commoner."
37 Federici, *Re-enchanting the World*, p. 110.
38 Massimo de Angelis highlights the importance of discussing the commons as systems as Caffentzis and Federici do; this allows one to study not only the internal relations but also the relations of the commons with the environment. Massimo De Angelis, "The Strategic Horizon of the Commons," in *Commoning with George Caffentzis and Sylvia Federici,* ed. Camille Barbagallo, Nicholas Beuret and David Harvie (London: Pluto Press, 2019), pp. 209-221.
39 Massimo de Angelis, *Omina Sunt Communia: On the Commons and the Transformation to Postcapitalism* (London: ZED Books), pp. 265–302.

role of social relations in building, maintaining or repairing society's broken bonds; it is also an invitation to study "ways to keep in, and with, these messed up, troubled times."[40] and it suggests a rethinking and a commoning of the notion of the commons itself.

The Role of Art in the Building of Affective Relations[41]

> *"Relation is not made up of things that are foreign but of shared knowledge."*
> Édouard Glissant, *Poetics of Relation*[42]

Understanding the commons as ecologies or systems brings to the foreground the question about the actors, the agents building and supporting the relations that hold these ecologies or systems together. The commoners are the ones that take care of natural or cultural resources, as a third paradigm of production which is beyond the state and the private sector, while at the same time, they build communities, and negotiate responsibilities and social relations.[43] Among the communities of commoners that emerged in the last 10 to 15 years, one finds a great number of artists, along with their practices, initiatives and organizations. Through projects, workshops and different types of open and participatory events, artists have engaged with the commons in relation to earth and its resources, knowledge and information, cultural and social spaces, and have raised questions over their appropriation and ownership. Based on their capacities and sensibilities,

---

40 Femke Snelting in "Affective Infrastructures: A Tableau, Altar, Scene, Diorama, or Archipelago. A conversation with Marija Bozinovska Jones, Lou Cornum, Daphne Dragona, Maya Indira Ganesh, Tung-Hui Hu, Fernanda Monteiro, Nadège, Pedro Oliveira, Femke Snelting," *transmediale journal*, Issue 3, https://transmediale.de/content/affective-infrastructures-a-tableau-altar-scene-diorama-or-archipelago

41 Singh uses the term "affective commons" to refer to socio-nature encounters and discuss the relationship of the human to the more-than-human world. The term here is used more broadly to highlight the affective qualities of the commons.

42 Édouard Glissant, *Poetics of Relation*, trans. Betsy Wing (Michigan: University of Michigan Press, 2010), p. 8.

43 Cornelia Sollfrank, "Commoning the Institution – or How to Create an Alternative (Art School) When 'There is No Alternative'," in "Revisiting Black Mountain: Cross-Disciplinary Experiments and their Potential for Democratization," ed. Dorothee Richter, Ronald Kolb, special issue, *On Curating* 43 (2019): pp. 50–53.

artists have been initiators of—or contributors to—communities, projects and spaces of the commons. With initiatives that are not items to be collected, owned or exhibited, but rather open formats of different kinds, they have challenged the values of the contemporary art world. Bringing to the foreground the possibilities of collective authorship and open distribution, they have become facilitators and mediators for the creation and maintenance of commons. When it comes to discussing the commons as "affective infrastructures," the role of artists seems to be primary and indispensable for a number of reasons.

As Rancière points out—while referring to the work of Deleuze and Guattari—"what the artist does is to weave together a new sensory fabric by wresting percepts and affects," which allows an emerging community to be together while also being apart.[44] A community, as Rancière explains, might be a dissensual community, structured by disconnection, characterized by disidentification, standing for rupture but also for anticipation. Artistic methods and affective pedagogies have the capacity, on the one hand, to inform the production of subjectivity, and on the other hand, to allow the augmentation of community, as Hickney-Moody notes.[45] They succeed in finding a fine balance between individuality and collectivity, as the importance of individual contributions is underlined in order to support and sustain the ongoing socialization of experience and knowledge.[46] Tan especially highlights the knowledge that is produced by and shared through art.[47] She describes it as an *uncommon knowledge* which is driven by affect and involves "collectivism, otherness and transversal methodologies." Art can go beyond a commons based on the homogeneity of its actors, on a sameness based on origin, gender, class, and interests. Tan's *uncommon knowledge*—like Cadena's *uncommons*

44   Jacques Rancière, "Aesthetic Separation, Aesthetic Community," in *The Emancipated Spectator*, trans. Gregory Elliott (London and Brooklyn: Verso, 2009), pp. 51–82, here pp. 56, 59.
45   Anna Hickney-Moody, "Affect as Method: Feelings, Aesthetics and Affective Pedagogy," in *Deleuze and Research Methodologies*, ed. Rebecca Coleman and Jessica Ringrose (Edinburgh: Edinburgh University Press, 2013), pp. 79–85.
46   Daphne Dragona, "Artists as the new producers of the common (?)," in *Red Art: New Utopias in Data Capitalism*, ed. Lanfranco Aceti, Julian Stallabrass, Suzanne Jaschko and Bill Balaskas, *Leonardo Electronic Almanac* 20, no. 1 (January 2014): pp. 165–173.
47   Pelin Tan, "Artistic Practices and Uncommon Knowledge" in eds. Anette Baldauf, Stefan Gruber, Moira Hille, Annette Krauss, Vladimir Miller, Mara Verlic, Hong-Kai Wang, Julia Wieger *Spaces of Commoning: Artist Research and the Utopia of the Everyday* (Berlin: Sternberg Press 2016), pp. 14–18.

that manifests the coming together of heterogeneous worlds—is based on the acknowledgment of differences and on the creation and maintenance of a ground for dialogue and co-existence. This form of knowledge which is found in art is meant to be "translocal or borderless"; it is based on situated experience, enacting otherness and operating as a political tool. This is how relations are made and emancipation as a collective process beyond homogenization becomes possible.

Art's sensibilities and pedagogies link to its methodologies and ways of organization that assist in the enforcement of relations and the building of the commons. Olga Goriunova uses the term *organizational aesthetics* to describe something which is more than a way of looking and rather "a dynamic of assembling" that can help understand a digital object, process, or body.[48] *Organizational aesthetics*, as Fuller explains,[49] are themselves assemblages, constellations, ecologies. They are live processes that can be found "in the development, movement and transformation of a loosely, precipitously or precisely assembled system of people, technologies, words, signals..." as well as "in the ethical dimensions of relations between processes, forms of access, cultures and their carriers, whether they are people, languages or technologies." Art methodologies, in other words, are based themselves on numerous relations of an affective character which hold together these assemblages. Their power lies in the possibility they have to organize and mobilize, to reinvent systems and cultures and allow these to co-create forms of life.

The potential of art to build relations, to produce knowledge, to organize and mobilize is enhanced by the practicing of care. This practicing involves, as Moebus and Harrison[50] clarify, both the logic of *caring for the common* and the *caring in common*. It concerns relationships between subjects and resources, but also the relationships between commoners themselves. Artists' initiatives might be aiming to generate and collectivize care, or they might be revealing the labor of restoration or maintenance and pay tribute to it. As Bellacasa notes,

48 Olga Goriunova, *Art Platforms and Cultural Production on the Internet* (London and New York: Routledge, 2012), pp. 3, 7.
49 Matthew Fuller, "Foreword: The telephone and its keys," in *The Social Telephony File* (Southend-on-Sea: YoHa Limited, 2010), pp. 4–9.
50 Katharina Moebus and Melissa Harrison, "Caring for the Common and Caring in Common: towards an expanded architecture/design practice," *WHO CARES?, NORDES* No. 8 (2019): pp. 1–6.

caring "is inevitably to create relation" although this might not be necessarily easy and can also prove to be subversive or unsettling.[51] Spaces *of* and *for* commoning can also be "spaces of dissensus" and "infrastructures of agency"[52] embracing and sustaining the heterogeneity of the world.

In the following, four artist-led initiatives in different parts of the world are introduced and discussed. These examples are used to present the role of art in building, sustaining but also commoning the commons in times of a prolonged and generalized crisis. Attention is given in each case to the needs or demands of the time and place the initiative responds to, to the practices and methodologies used, and to the way bonds are established within communities, and between communities and the commons.

Platohedro: living well—knowing well

Platohedro[53] is an independent space dedicated to art, technology and activism in the neighborhood of Medellin in Buenos Aires, Colombia. Situated in one of the most violent areas of the country, it was born as a response to this. It was built in 2004, addressing the need to cultivate collective work, and to empower political action and resistance to militarization.[54] The space, with its activities and communities, is described by its founders as a "desiring love and knowledge machine." Its founders, Alex Correa and Lina Mejía Álvarez, underline that love has been a driving force constructing relations "which generate tangible realities" and provoking substantial change. Love and desire are words often used to express the emphasis put on the will to live with each other differently, in common.

The common for Platohedro manifests the urge and possibility for *buen vivir* (good living) and *buen conocer* (knowing well). Life-making and knowledge-building are interconnected. *Buen vivir* is the Spanish translation of a Quechua term—the original is *Sumak Kawsay*—describing the full life in a community where humans and nature com-

51 María Puig de la Bellacasa, "'Nothing comes without its world': thinking with care," *The Sociological Review* 60, no. 2 (2012): pp. 197–216. DOI: 10.1111/j.1467-954X.2012.02070.x
52 Moebus and Harrison, "Caring for the Common and Caring in Common," pp. 2–3.
53 https://platohedro.org/ (accessed April 17, 2020).
54 Pedro Soler, "Platohedro, Mon Amour," *Multiversos* (Medellin: Especial Impresores S.A.S, 2019), pp. 20–22.

plement each other; it is about living well, living in balance, but not about living better than others or at the expense of others. *Buen conocer* refers to "open, participatory and collaborative knowledge and to the sharing of that knowledge."[55] Knowing well and knowing in common is possible for Platohedro when an assemblage of contemporary and ancestral sources, of hacktivist practices and indigenous cosmovisions come together. As Medina Cardona[56] clarifies, the fundamentals for FLOSS (Free/Libre Open Source Software) values of collaboration, cooperation and distributed coordination successfully meet and match the open communicative processes and systems of communal organization of the region, which date from pre-colonial times. Similarly, the team mixes the hacktivist English language with common local street language, building narratives that reflect and respond to needs of the area. As Travlou writes, Platohedro "merges traditional Colombian cultural values, participatory pedagogies and new media art values (Do-It-With-Others, free/libre knowledge, open source and peer-to-peer learning)," building a new cultural heritage;[57] these shared cultural values created within the communities are indispensable in order to handle differences with care and to rethink and build a good living for a post-conflict society.[58]

In an attempt to overcome the constructed divisions of class, gender and race, Platohedro addresses different target groups as audiences—including teenagers, children, people from the area—with a mix of activities of an educational, open and experimental character; they plan workshops, collective actions, public interventions, networking activities with a focus on feminist and queer perspectives as well as

55 Penny Travlou, Luciana Fleischman and Alexander Correa, "II Meeting of Cultural Commons in Medellin," (Report from the meeting which took place on 20–21 June 2019), https://archive.org/details/2019enculturalcommons2019reportfinal/mode/2up (accessed February 15, 2020).
56 Luis Fernando Medina Cardona, "The Free/Open Source Software as Hybrid Concept: Considerations from a Colombian Activist Perspective," *NMC/ Journal of the New Media Caucus* 12, no. 1 (Spring 2016), http://median.newmediacaucus.org/mestizo-technology-art-design-and-technoscience-in-latin-america/the-freeopen-source-software-as-hybrid-concept-considerations-from-a-colombian-activist-perspective/ (accessed April 19, 2020).
57 Penny Travlou, Luciana Fleischman and Alexander Correa, "Cultural Commons: (How) do we put it into practice in Medellin?," (Report of a workshop with collectives, organizations and public institutions of art and politics which took place on 20–21 June 2018, Medellin) August 2018, https://www.research.ed.ac.uk/portal/files/128601200/ENGLISH_Report_Cultural_Commons_Medellin_2.pdf (accessed April 19, 2020).
58 Ibid.

on human rights. For Platohedro, it is the groups themselves that create the space that is inter-cultural and intergenerational, as links are built not only among its members, but also with the neighborhood and the environment. A word often used that captures how communities are created and events are organized is *parchar;* this is a local expression derived from the indigenous past that means gathering, but it also refers to creating spaces of freedom and autonomy, to allowing disagreement and difference, to learn and build the commons together.[59] Platohedro is, ultimately, "the possibility of a crack" associated with the "power of open knowledge," but also with "diversity, trans, queer, all incomplete truths, relational, imperfect in process and collectively constructed."[60]

Constant: making spaces for ambiguity

Constant[61] is a non-profit association run by artists, designers, researchers and hackers, based in Brussels and active in the field of art, media and technology. It was founded in 1997 with the aim to encourage the work of artists working on audiovisual media, and to provide a ground for collaboration based on "respect for cultural differences and gender."[62] Over the years, the field of interest of Constant opened up and focused on free software, feminist and queer technologies, copyright alternatives, performative publishing, science-fiction and networked artistic work.

At the heart of Constant's practice lies the logic and the ethics of free/libre and open source software and feminist principles; this is what binds all programs literally—with reference to the technologies being used—but also symbolically—as a continuous source of inspiration. FLOSS is approached "as an ecosystem of diverse tools that come together, as a community that shares its sources where people learn from each other."[63] An example of this is the focus on multiple authorship and the practice of synchronous or asynchronous writing using

59 Ibid.
60 "Introduction, Neither Matter, nor energy, everything is information," *Multiversos* (Medellin: Especial Impresores S.A.S, 2019), p. 36.
61 constantvzw.org (accessed April 19, 2020).
62 From Constant's Statutes of Association, written in 1997 and found at: http://constant-vzw.org/site/More-about-Constant.html (accessed 19 April 2020).
63 "Ecosystems of Writing, Interview with Michael Murtaugh," 15th September 2018, *Creating Commons,* https://vimeo.com/309009024 (accessed April 19, 2020).

inexpensive tools like Raspberry Pis and pads. There, "codes, rhythms, frequencies, scripts, scores and [other] non-verbal agreements" come together and challenge each other, "stumble and collide," posing questions and problems.[64] Code for Constant is not only written collectively, but it is also performed and enacted by the people joining and deciding together their Codes of Conduct.[65] FLOSS, according to Constant member Femke Snelting, is a "feminist project" as "it talks about the right of everyone to study, to distribute, to change or use it."[66] It manifests an open and ongoing process for shared ownership, care and maintenance, which often involves more unlearning than learning and accepting to lose control.[67] Constant is especially interested in feminist and queer systems and infrastructures and in the potential they hold to common not only technology but also ways of thinking. A server, for instance, is also a thinking tool,[68] as Snelting argues, raising questions and bringing in metaphors about how relationships are created, how roles are assigned, and how services are being provided. A technological infrastructure can make space for ambiguity and difference, and allow temporalities, identities and fluidities to find their place in them. Imaginary devices can become a starting point for a critical reflection while navigating pasts, presents and futures[69] and questioning given systems of categorization and classification.

Constant addresses various groups or individuals with a broad spectrum of activities involving workshops, readings, presentations, exhibitions, residencies and other forms of exchange. The production, sharing and distribution of knowledge is of central importance for their practice, paying special attention to *who* is in the position to

64 "Call for participants: Collective Conditions," http://constantvzw.org/site/Call-for-participants-Collective-Conditions.html (accessed April 19, 2020).
65 Ibid.
66 "Femke Snelting," interview, 28 January 2017, *notamuse*, https://notamuse.de/en/interviews/femke-snelting (accessed April 19, 2020).
67 Matthew Fuller, "Interview with Femke Snelting," 2018, *Open Source Publishing*, http://osp.kitchen/api/osp.workshop.pcmmd/a29b1fc43586fcfaa181cc66cf6764bc7f8b9fe3/blob-data/fuller_Open%20Source%20Publishing%20-%20interview%20with%20Femke%20Snelting.mkd (accessed April 19, 2020).
68 "Forms of Ongoingness, Interview with Femke Snelting and spideralex," 21 November 2018, *Creating Commons*, https://vimeo.com/302087898 (accessed April 19, 2020).
69 "Mondotheque" (2016) was a project of Constant inspired by and referring to a design by Paul Otlet from 1934 for an imaginary device, a research machine that could be at the same time archive, instrument, desk, catalog and broadcasting station. "Mondotheque", http://constantvzw.org/site/-Mondotheque-.html (accessed April 19, 2020).

speak, and aiming to reorient frameworks and enrich vocabularies and languages, while looking into the relationship of technologies to geographies.[70] Similarly, in their work on archives they explore how tools, infrastructures and protocols can work *with* and *through* difference, specifically looking into how digital archives can become a site for decolonial and intersectional practice, supporting multiple imaginations. Constant likes to focus on the empowerment of *complex collectivities* that are formed when people with "radically different needs, backgrounds and agendas" come together.[71]

The way Constant engages with infrastructures and the commons brings to mind the work of Geoffrey C. Bowker and Leigh Star on *living* classifications,[72] as well as the writing of Kara Keeling on a *Queer Operating System;* that is "a system that on a society-level would facilitate and support uncommon, imaginative, unexpected, and ethical relations between and among living beings and the environment, even when they have little, and perhaps nothing, in common."[73] When technologies are queered, there is the potential for new situations beyond constructions and situations. The commons, then, are "understood as vibrant;"[74] they are continuously built and lived.

Sakiya: rewilding knowledge

Sakiya[75] is an art, science and agriculture space near Ramallah in Palestine. It is an initiative of artist Nida Sinnokrot and architect/conservationist Sahar Qawasmi, who wanted to bring together ecological and cultural practices, and to bridge past, present and future. It was founded in 2016 as a nomadic organization with an interdisciplinary and international character. The case of Sakiya is particular because it is situated in a natural and historical site in Ein Qinyya on the outskirts

---

70   *Transmarcations* is, for instance, a project experimenting with the "heres, wheres and others" discussing bodies, terrains and displacements in relation, asking who is in the position to map and from which perspective. "Transmarcations: X is not for destination," http://constantvzw.org/site/-Transmarcations-.html (accessed April 19, 2020).

71   As stated in "Call for participants: Collective Conditions."

72   Geoffrey C. Bowker and Leigh Star, *Sorting Things Out: Classification and its Consequences* (Cambridge MA and London: The MIT Press, 2000), p. 326.

73   Kara Keeling, "Queer OS," *Cinema Journal* 53, no. 2 (Winter 2014): pp. 152–157. https://muse.jhu.edu/article/535715 (accessed April 19, 2020).

74   "Ecosystems of Writing. Interview with Michael Murtaugh," 15 September 2018, *Creating Commons*, https://vimeo.com/309009024 (accessed April 19, 2020).

75   https://sakiya.org/

of Ramallah. This site is part of Area C, a zone where Palestinians have not been allowed to build for the last two decades. For this reason, the area has been rewilded and repopulated by rich and diverse vegetation.[76] Starting from the history of the site, the founders of Sakiya decided to build a context to discuss how the loss of a land is not only measured in lost territory "but also in lost tradition, lost knowledge and the loss of cooperation."[77] They wanted to study how such subsequent losses can be addressed and restored, taking into consideration "fading local traditions of self-sufficiency."[78]

Sakiya explores how a new imaginary of cooperation and "a future commons" can emerge by turning to and learning from the land, the earth and the soil.[79] An example they are specifically looking into comes from permaculture and is known as the logic of the *guild*; these are groupings of plants, trees, animals, insects, and other components that operate together and ensure their health and productivity. The logic of the guild underlines the principle of co-existence and interdependence and inspires the character of the space and its events. Sakiya invites people from different backgrounds and generations to work together, sharing their values and objectives.[80] The Sakiya community includes artists, agro-ecologists, musicians, writers, teachers and builders. Similar is the analogy found in the logic and act of rewilding; this might refer to the rewilding "of the soil from the ravages of monoculture agriculture" as well as to "the re-wilding of local knowledge cultures from encroaching neoliberalism."[81] Rewilding is embraced as a pedagogy and a wider point of departure. Wilderness is

76 Denise Helene Sumi, "Flora, Fauna and Folk Tales – A Permaculture Network: Interview with Gary Zhexi Zhang & Agnes Cameron," September 5, 2019, *Schloss–Post*, https://schloss-post.com/flora-fauna-and-folk-tales/ (accessed April 19, 2020).
77 Ibid.
78 "Award 2017 – Shortlisted: Sakiya – Art/Science/Agriculture – Nida Sinnokrot," *Visible*, https://www.visibleproject.org/blog/project/sakiya-artscienceagricultrue-ramallah-palestine/ (accessed April 19, 2020).
79 Sumi, "Flora, Fauna and Folk Tales."
80 "Getting our Hands Dirty," a conversation between Nida Sinnokrot and Nat Muller on Sakiya – Art/Science/Agriculture, *Visible*, https://www.visibleproject.org/blog/getting-our-hands-dirty-a-conversation-between-nida-sinnokrot-and-nat-muller-on-sakiya-artscience-agriculture/ (accessed April 19, 2020).
81 As stated in the announcement of the "Rewilding Pedagogy" symposium on land, topic and the commons which took place in July 2019. Information is available at the website of the organization https://sakiya.org/ (accessed February 15, 2020).

not understood as what "no longer exists"[82] but rather as what comes to the foreground to expose the potential for new spatial and social configurations, for new networks, constellations and ways of working together.

Agriculture is approached by Sakiya as a lively part of culture, of the past and present, with ways of teaching, learning and remembering that also include stories, songs and dances. Sakiya events involve symposia, exhibitions, readings, workshops on art, science and agriculture, emphasizing the importance of sharing and building knowledge together. Zhang, who was a resident at Sakiya and also part of an expedition there, highlights that it is the intertwining of the old and the new knowledge that is of great importance in the times of crisis that we find ourselves in.[83] He himself, together with his colleague Cameron, specifically explored what one could learn from the traditional, low-tech forms of the past, and experimented with the cooperative practices emerging when these are merged with methodologies from art, design and technology. For *Sakiya, the aim, in general, is to locate the* "critical, legal, literary, and aesthetic tools" that can be employed in order to interrupt the *growing monoculture of knowledge.*[84] Similar to the practice of Constant, but here strongly connected to the land, practitioners and theorists come together to discuss how the "colonial constructions of knowledge relate to contemporary questions around access to resources (file-sharing, seed banks, agricultural commons)."[85] It is within this very context that for Sakiya the commons need to be remembered. Thinking about the land and earth's ecosystems invites us to recall the importance of systems thinking, of the interdependence between the different parts and, hence, of how cultural, natural and digital commons come together and need to be seen in relation.

---

82 Edward O. Wilson, *Half-Earth: Our Planet's Fight for Life* (New York: Liveright Publishing Corporation, 2016), pp. 71, 73.

83 Sumi, "Flora, Fauna and Folk Tales."

84 As it was stated also in relation to the symposium of Sakiya "Under The Tree II – Agriculture, Private Property and the Production of Ignorance," which took place in 2018.

85 "Nida Sinnokrot's Sakiya Receives A.M. Qattan Foundation Funding," *act-MIT program in art, culture and technology*, 19 June 2018, http://act.mit.edu/news/2018/06/19/nida-sinnokrots-sakiya/ (accessed April 19, 2020).

Pirate Care: building a syllabus

Pirate Care[86] is a transnational research project initiated in 2019 by researcher Valeria Graziano, free software advocate and cultural explorer Marcell Mars and philosopher Tomislav Medak. It operates as an open network of activists, scholars and practitioners addressing the current crisis of care. The network focuses on practices being developed as responses to the broken bonds of today's society, looking into services that are indispensable for life—such as health care, education and housing—and highlighting how rights to them are being lost and how forms of solidarity are criminalized. Unlike the initiatives mentioned before, Pirate Care does not relate to a specific space or location; it is an online project, open and accessible to anyone interested in contributing to a common care infrastructure.

The project develops a methodology inspired by the old and contemporary philosophical discourse on piracy, its imaginary, manifestations and implications. This might involve references to forms of self-organization that piracy succeeds in accomplishing,[87] to the possibilities of a "life beyond the constituted order of the state,"[88] but also more particularly to piracy's associations with sharing, openness, decentralization and free access,[89] when relating it to anti-copyright initiatives in digital culture. The project is strongly linked to this latter aspect, as two of its initiators, Mars and Medak, are also the initiators of Memory of the World, an online repository of—at the time of writing—154,047 digital or digitized books supported by a community of contributors. Memory of the World, like other publicly distributed library infrastructures, was created in order to provide universal access to knowledge as a commons.[90] At its core were and are the librarians. These are the people who offer the human and labor infrastructure that is invisible, yet indispensable for the building of the commons of knowledge. They are the *custodians* who care about the infrastructure and not only

---

86 https://www.piratecare.net (accessed April 19, 2020).
87 Gabriel Kuhn, *Life Under the Jolly Roger: Reflections on Golden Age Piracy* (Oakland: PM Press, 2010).
88 Amedeo Policante, *The Pirate Myth: Genealogies of an Imperial Concept* (London and New York: Routledge, 2015), p. 215.
89 Gary Hall, *Pirate Philosophy: For a Digital Posthumanities* (Cambridge MA and London: The MIT Press, 2016).
90 Marcell Mars, "Public Library (an essay)," 27 October 2014, *Memory of the World*, https://www.memoryoftheworld.org/blog/2014/10/27/public_library_an_essay/ (accessed April 19, 2020).

rely on it, but also keep the system running.[91] Their act, according to Mars, is an act of civil disobedience filling in the gaps that institutions in crisis leave behind.[92] Moving from Memory of the World to Pirate Care, the call is again for acts of caregiving, but this time it concerns the services of welfare. Care labor is a form of labor largely underpaid or unpaid, invisibilized, feminized, racialized, and it manifests asymmetries and power relations. The project wishes to provide caregivers access to resources, knowledges, tools and technologies, to empower and collectivize care as a commons. Pirate Care, just like different forms of piracy, is not only about a form of resistance to the sovereign power, but also about exposing the different forms of violence and inequality that prevail.[93]

At the heart of the Pirate Care project lies a collaborative online *Syllabus* emphasizing the pedagogic aspect of the initiative. This *Syllabus* covers different practices of care, looking into specific topics and proposing sessions and exercises as learning materials. People who are interested can propose, write, remix the syllabus, activating and maintaining the learning process. The idea is that this syllabus can be adopted by practitioners anywhere and adapted to different contexts and needs. Workshops and events of the Pirate Care network also use it as a tool and assist in its further development and empowerment. During the COVID 19 crisis, a collective note-taking effort was initiated under the topic *Flatten the curve, grow the care*[94] aiming to respond to the need for solidarity and support initiatives for the affected groups, communities and populations. Practices, protocols and proposals were shared in multiple languages within this context.

"If," as Policante writes, "the pirate is a figure that evokes, and brings into being a gray zone between war and peace,"[95] similarly, a project like Pirate Care can research and possibly reconceive care provisions "between autonomous organizing and state institutions, between insurgent politics and commoning, and between holistic and scientific methods."[96] Such systems and infrastructures might of

---

91 "Caring for the Public Library, Interview with Marcell Mars & Tomislav Medak," *Creating Commons*, https://vimeo.com/325000943 (accessed April 19, 2020).
92 Ibid.
93 Policante, *The Pirate Myth*.
94 https://syllabus.pirate.care/topic/coronanotes/ (accessed April 19, 2020).
95 Policante, *The Pirate Myth*, p. 215.
96 https://syllabus.pirate.care/topic/piratecareintroduction/ (accessed April 19, 2020).

course be fragile, but on the other hand, following Hall, turning to piracy means not only producing new ways of thinking about the world, but also reflecting about how to undertake the role of care and act from the position that one is in this time of crisis.[97]

Conclusion

In her book *Light in the Dark*, Gloria Anzaldúa uses the Nahuatl word *nepantla* to refer to the in-between spaces that appear in transitional times.[98] These are spaces where connections can be made, scenarios can merge, and changing one's perspective and perceptions becomes possible. *Nepantlas* operate in the cracks between opposite worlds, and work as bridges enabling transformation, moving beyond binaries and divisions. Just like Berlant's commons as *affective infrastructures*[99] or Singh's *affective commons*,[100] such spaces nurture and aim for multiplicity, non-sovereignty and difference.

While, according to Anzaldúa, *nepantlas* emerge in one's mind, the different commons-based initiatives discussed above can be read as physical or digital places that create the conditions for the aforementioned transition. They are spaces where *affective encounters* become possible thanks to the *affective capacities* of the ones involved,[101] and that is the artists initiating the projects and developing the program. Artists and activists, as Anzaldúa explains, can help in the crossings and guide the transformation process;[102] they can construct alternative roads and create new topographies and geographies. Their methods and pedagogies can give birth to new associations, perceptions

---

97   In *Pirate Philosophy*, Gary Hall explores how we can produce not just new ways of thinking about the world, which is what theorists and philosophers have traditionally aspired to do, but new ways of actually being theorists and philosophers in this time of riots. This is here opened up in order to address the crisis of our times and the role of artists, activists and all actors in times of a generalized crisis.

98   Gloria E. Anzaldúa, *Light in the Dark/ Luz en lo Oscuro: Rewriting Identity, Spirituality, Reality*, ed. Analouise Keating (Durham NC and London: Duke University Press, 2015), pp. 28–29, 86–87, 107–108, 245.

99   Berlant, "The commons: Infrastructures for troubling times."

100 Singh, "Becoming a commoner."

101 Ibid. Singh argues that the affective capacities of the commoners shape affective encounters.

102 Anzaldúa, *Light in the Dark*, pp. 17, 82–83.

and habits, and invite people to reimagine common worlds.[103] This becomes possible through the attention being paid to the building and maintenance of relations—existing or needed—between individuals, communities and resources. Four specific points can be identified which support this assumption.

Firstly, all the initiatives presented take highly into consideration the role of place, which might be physical—like the violent area of Medellin and the historical site in Ein Qinyya—or digital—like local servers and online repositories. This means that the needs, references, anxieties and desires of the respective audiences or communities are taken in mind, in order to locate what can be cherished in common in the present and future. At these spaces, people from different origins, backgrounds, fields and disciplines come together, and a prerequisite for the building of the commons is a process of *dis-othering* rather than othering, adopting a term of Bonaventure here; the necessity is to find ways of being and living together despite and because of the importance and difference of differences, as he explains.[104]

Secondly, and in accordance with the first point, attention is paid to the history, culture and values of a place. Within this context, one notices how indigenous knowledge informs today's open source logic at Platohedro, how practices of permaculture influence understandings on the use of mesh networks at Sakiya, or how studying technologies together with geographies in the case of Constant can offer an understanding of privilege or exploitation. Knowledge, therefore, is situated and embodied; following Haraway, one could say that attention is given to the locality and to a vision that is partial and not universal, which is built collectively, and cannot be possessed by one.[105]

Thirdly, knowledge production in all spaces is performed and lived. It is an "active object,"[106] which escapes usual formats. It is rather a form of studying and a speculative practice, as Harney and Moten have described it with reference to their *undercommons*, referring to "what you do with other people," which might also be talking, walk-

103 Hickney-Moody, "Affect as Method: Feelings, Aesthetics and Affective Pedagogy," pp. 79–85.
104 Bonaventure Soh Bejeng Ndikung, "Dis-othering as Method: Leh Zo, A me ke nde za," eds. Lorenzo Sandoval and Benjamin Busch, TERN.1 Reader (2019). (Grey literature).
105 Donna Haraway, "Situated Knowledges: The Science Question in Feminism and the Privilege of Partial," *Feminist Studies* 14, no. 3 (Autumn 1988): pp. 575–599.
106 Ibid.

ing, but also sharing the same feelings and affects.[107] Therefore, it is not specific projects or artworks reflecting upon the commons that are the focus of interest here, but rather the sociality which is being built to be and live in common. Examples are the activities Platohedro organizes in its neighborhood, the way agriculture and its customs are embraced by Sakiya, or the way an infrastructure of Pirate Care collectively emerges.

Fourthly, this bringing together of different locations, audiences, temporalities, cultures and knowledges gives birth to ways of thinking that escape classifications, categorizations, hierarchies and binaries. This is highlighted in the character of their programs, in the ways they operate and the tools they use. These are initiatives that have a horizontal structure, aiming to enrich vocabularies, languages, indexes with opinions and voices that might not have access to their building. They involve a form of *code-switching*, a method Pedro Oliveira refers to when referring to Anzaldúa and her writing on the *nepantlas*;[108] this is a fundamental skill that allows one to cross borders, to move in-between different cultures and territories, to embrace multiplicity.

Artists, therefore, one could summarize here, play a significant role in building commons as affective infrastructures in a literal but also metaphorical sense: literally, because they create open spaces—that involve physical or digital infrastructures—where people can be and act together; metaphorically, because they build bridges between geographies, temporalities and cultures, and aim to restore affective bonds that have been broken. Within these spaces, where heterogeneity is accommodated and uncommon knowledge is embraced, unprecedented forms of assemblage become possible, while a new aesthetics also emerges. This is an aesthetics of openness and ongoingness, of transversality and multiplicity, which embraces change and social transformation. It is an aesthetics that challenges given understandings of the world,[109] and invites people to co-shape, inhabit and explore new possible visions of it.

---

107 Harney and Moten, *The Undercommons,* p. 110.
108 Pedro Oliveira in "Affective Infrastructures: A Tableau, Altar, Scene, Diorama, or Archipelago."
109 This is how artist Tania Bruguera understands aesthetics, highlighting the role of ethics in it. https://www.taniabruguera.com/cms/931-0-Interview + with + Tania + Bruguera.htm (accessed February 15, 2020).

The commons built, maintained and cared for at these spaces are commons that are affective, living, and ongoing. Their foundational quality, returning to Berlant, is a non-sovereign relationality understood as the possibility of being in common without having to belong or to identify with others, of being receptive to ambivalence and fluctuation.[110] The commons, within this context, are always a starting point;[111] they relate to a feeling of what is to come[112] and they change once they expand and multiply. The meaning of the word *commons* similarly changes. While it might still refer to cultural, natural or digital resources and to the relations needed for their creation and maintenance, it also specifically underlines the affective character of acts of commoning, and it points to their potential to build and support multiple worlds, acknowledging their difference and interdependence.

---

110 Berlant, "The commons: Infrastructures for troubling times," p. 392.
111 de la Cadena and Blaser, *A World of Many Worlds*, p. 19.
112 Harney and Moten, *The Undercommons*, p. 98.

Magdalena Tyżlik-Carver

In Search of Common Forms and Curatorial Epistemologies

On the Exhibition *OPEN SCORES:*
How to Program the Commons

Curation and exhibitions have been dominant methods for displaying objects and making art public. Yet, they have also been part of
a much wider expansion of public space into the digital domain and
its subsequent incorporation into digital infrastructures, which reach
simultaneously across art, and life. Beyond the practice of care and
maintenance that is curating, which in the words of Beatrice von Bismarck is defined as "techniques" that "allow an exhibition to come
into the world,"[1] curating is an event of knowledge-making, a construction of meaning that is visualized in the form of an exhibition
and regularly referred to as "the curatorial."[2] This implied knowledge
is embodied in the selection of objects for display, and in processes
of creating displays, and where an exhibition becomes a temporary
location for meaning making, a moment for disrupting knowledge in
order to invent it.[3]

OPEN SCORES: How to Program the Commons is an exhibition that
opens up to data as objects of curatorial concern in order to reveal
artistic production as careful creation and capture of practices, people
and things as commons. If the curatorial, as Irit Rogoff and Jean-Paul
Martinon argue, is an event of knowledge that "explores all that takes
place on the stage set-up, both intentionally and unintentionally, by

1   Beatrice Bismarck and Irit Rogoff, "Curating/Curatorial," in *Cultures of the Curatorial*, ed.
    Beatrice von Bismarck, Jörn Schafaff, and Thomas Weski (Berlin: Sternberg Press, 2012),
    p. 24.
2   Beatrice von Bismarck, Jörn Schafaff, and Thomas Weski, eds., *Cultures of the Curatorial*
    (Berlin: Sternberg Press, 2012); Jean-Paul Martinon, ed., *The Curatorial: A Philosophy of
    Curating* (London and New York: Bloomsbury Academic, 2013).
3   Jean-Paul Martinon, "Theses in Philosophy of Curating," in Martinon, *The Curatorial: A
    Philosophy of Curating*, p. 30.

the curator,"[4] how do intentional and not, acts of curating influence what we know about the world? My intention in this chapter is to think with *OPEN SCORES*'s capacity to disrupt epistemological terrains of curatorial knowledge and curating, and of data and its science, while accounting for the main subject of the exhibition: the commons. The exhibition's curatorial method of commissioning and exhibiting scores is an experiment in curating that makes public how artistic and collaborative practices work with data, and how data are the very material for an aesthetics of commons.

In this discussion of the exhibition *OPEN SCORES: How to Program the Commons*, I start with the suggestion to consider an exhibition as a format for collecting and presenting data. Curators have been dealing with data for some time: harvesting, cleaning, filtering, analyzing and displaying data. Writing, liking, blogging, reposting, commenting. Organizing data in tables, storing them on servers and clouds, displaying them via different media forms, making them public, making them secure, optimizing. These are the contemporary techniques of curating in art institutions, on online platforms, or in research institutes, which are performed by curators, human and nonhuman, whose objects of care are data. What, then, is the curatorial knowledge generated in this way and how to articulate it if its focus is as much on data as it is on art objects and artistic practices presented in the exhibition? An answer to this question becomes possible when an exhibition usually understood as static display of objects is apprehended as a curatorial event that is a process of locating objects in the space of the gallery and the time of the exhibition in order to encourage "another way of thinking and sensing the world."[5]

The fact that art, like life-forms, is becoming data and curating that data is a curatorial concern is no surprise. The reason for this is not just that so many artists work with computers, which only deal with data and language, but because data has become the basic material with which worlds are built. In an environment where computation increasingly frames how we live, work, imagine and love, data are common in that they are continually generated, captured, recorded

---

4   Ibid., p. ix.
5   Jean-Paul Martinon and Irit Rogoff, "Preface," in *The Curatorial: A Philosophy of Curating*, ed. Jean-Paul Martinon (London, New York: Bloomsbury Publishing, 2013), x.

and mediated into different forms. Data as a material and fabric of everyday life are big,[6] and small,[7] and open,[8] and compromised.[9] Even if data are regularly considered scientifically objective they are not raw,[10] and they are "connected to the world in a variety of contexts that exist 'beyond' the realm of traditional data science."[11] While the world's industries and other organizations are focused on capturing and processing data, artists use them as a material to model and visualize, an object to be made, a subject to be discovered, medium to be explored and shared. The question of how to include artistic data practices in the exhibition is not only concerned with how to present and display them. Such a study has to account for the fact that the object to be curated is regularly complimented with its data, its subjects are posthuman,[12] and their location also computational.[13] How this information becomes part of curatorial knowledge through an exhibition is the main focus of this chapter.

6   danah boyd and Kate Crawford, "Six Provocations for Big Data" (A Decade in Internet Time: Symposium on the Dynamics of the Internet and Society, Oxford Internet Institute, 2011), http://papers.ssrn.com/sol3/papers.cfm?abstract_id = 1926431; Rob Kitchin, *The Data Revolution: Big Data, Open Data, Data Infrastructures and Their Consequences* (SAGE Publications Ltd, 2014); Kate Crawford, "The Anxieties of Big Data," *The New Inquiry* (blog), May 30, 2014, https://thenewinquiry.com/the-anxieties-of-big-data/ (accessed April 11, 2020)

7   Kitchin, *The Data Revolution*; L. Blackman, "Social Media and the Politics of Small Data: Post Publication Peer Review and Academic Value," *Theory, Culture & Society*, June 17, 2015, https://doi.org/10.1177/0263276415590002

8   Kitchin, *The Data Revolution*; "Open Data," *Creative Commons* (blog), accessed April 11, 2020, https://creativecommons.org/about/program-areas/open-data/; "What Is Open Data?," (accessed April 11, 2020), https://opendatahandbook.org/guide/en/what-is-open-data/ (accessed April 11, 2020)

9   Ganaele Langlois, Joanna Redden, and Greg Elmer, eds., *Compromised Data: From Social Media to Big Data* (New York, NY; London: Bloomsbury Academic, an imprint of Bloomsbury Publishing, Inc, 2015).

10   Lisa Gitelman, ed., *"Raw Data" Is an Oxymoron* (Cambridge, MA and London: The MIT Press, 2013).

11   Andrew Iliadis and Federica Russo, "Critical Data Studies: An Introduction," *Big Data & Society* 3, no. 2 (December 2016): 205395171667423, https://doi.org/10.1177/2053951716674238

12   Magdalena Tyżlik-Carver, "Posthuman Curating and Its Biopolitical Executions: The Case of Curating Content," in *Executing Practices*, ed. Helen Pritchard, Eric Snodgrass, and Magdalena Tyżlik-Carver (Open Humanities Press, 2018), pp. 171–89; Magda Tyżlik-Carver, "| Curator | Curating | the Curatorial | Not-Just-Art Curating," *Springerin*, no. 1, The Post-Curatorial Turn (2017), https://www.springerin.at/en/2017/1/kuratorin-kuratieren-das-kuratorische-nicht-nur-kunst-kuratieren/ (accessed October 22, 2020)

13   Magdalena Tyżlik-Carver, "Curating in/as Common/s. Posthuman Curating and Computational Cultures" (PhD, Aarhus, Aarhus University, 2016).

From Score to Data

OPEN SCORES: How to Program the Commons is an exhibition curated by artists, educators and researchers (Cornelia Sollfrank, Shusha Niederberger and Felix Stalder), and was presented at the panke.gallery in Berlin in autumn 2019. This exhibition is part of the multiyear research program *Creating Commons* (2017-2020)[14], which explores practices that open the space between art and commons, and presents artistic projects that "envision a (post-)digital culture in which notions of collaboration, free access to knowledge, sustainable use of shared resources and data privacy are central."[15] The hypothesis of the research project is that art and commons can offer new theoretical and aesthetic models that point beyond the commercialization of culture and the project showcases how artists are involved in practices of making commons.

The title *OPEN SCORES: How to Program the Commons* refers to the digital context in which these practices take place, and acknowledges an artistic tradition of scores and score-making that is well known in the history of art. Specifically, the exhibition refers to open source as a form of property relation and access that has been part of Free/Libre Open Source Software (FLOSS) culture, and it suggests that practices of commoning might be a matter of algorithmic operations that can be inscribed into code. The use of score as the chosen form through which each artistic project is represented in the exhibition credits Fluxus scores as objects and performances, and can be seen as a set of "intermedia"[16] practices that link to data and data capture practices. Scores exhibited in the exhibition are discrete representations which translate collaborative processes into data and information, thus making them accessible beyond the conditions in which each project originated.

For Fluxus artists in the sixties, score was the main format for experimenting across different art media. Anna Dezeuze maps the rich genealogy of Fluxus works onto a progressive development from inde-

---

14 Available at: http://creatingcommons.zhdk.ch (accessed October 22, 2020).
15 *Creating Commons*, "Open Scores: How to Program the Commons. #exhibition Guide" (Berlin: panke.gallery; Zurich: ZHdK, 2019), http://creatingcommons.zhdk.ch/wp-content/uploads/2020/01/openScores_exhibitionguide.pdf (last accessed October 22, 2020).
16 Dick Higgins, "Intermedia," *Leonardo* 34, no. 1 (2001): pp. 49–54.

terminacy to the Do-It-Yourself aesthetics, and argues that the study of scores as objects and independently of the way they had been performed brings out "the radical questioning of authorship and spectator participation."[17] Dezeuze discusses Fluxus adoption of the score—a set of printed instructions—as an art form, drawing particular attention to how time and duration structured an event as a raw material for making poetry, music or dance; whatever happens within this time, and the nature of such an event is, according to Simone Forti, "left completely up to the choice of the performer."[18] The use of chance and choice informed the events as independent of author's subjective influence, leaving it open to the reader. *The Anthology of Chance Operations*, published by LaMonte Young and Jackson MacLow in 1963, is a collection of scores that capture abstraction and its performative quality through "...concept art anti-art indeterminacy improvisation meaningless work natural disasters plans of action stories diagrams Music poetry essays dance constructions mathematics compositions,"[19] all recorded on pages in the collection.

The curator Carlos Basualdo refers, however, to the double purpose of a score: "that of performing a certain action and that of producing a physical record of an abstract quality or quantity."[20] This definition of score can be applied to Fluxus scores too, where abstraction and action are always entangled and the hierarchy between object and performance is problematized. The Fluxus score is a formal approach to frame events, unpredictabilities, chances, actions, indeterminations and improvisations in an attempt to open them up. As works published in *The Anthology of Chance Operations* and other Fluxus publications show, scores organize artistic events into propositions that can be performed but they also exist as visual objects representing instructions often printed on index-sized cards for easy storage, circulation and display. These are forms of abstraction that visualize information into notational forms "employed as a means to fracture

17 Anna Dezeuze, "Origins of the Fluxus Score: From Indeterminacy to the 'Do-It-Yourself' Artwork," *Performance Research* 7, no. 3 (January 2002): pp. 78-94, here p. 79, https://doi.org/10.1080/13528165.2002.10871876

18 Ibid., p. 81.

19 La Monte Young, ed., *An Anthology of Chance Operations*, First Edition (New York: La Monte Young & Jackson Mac Low, 1963).

20 Carlos Basualdo, "In Terms of Performance: Score," 2016, http://intermsofperformance. site (accessed October 22, 2020)

the homogeneity of time in order to organize it according to the com-
poser's intentions."[21] Composers associated with Fluxus such as Earle
Brown, Christian Wolff and John Cage developed experimental music
and sound notations, the best known of which is Cage's score *4'33''*.
Others include La Monte Young's and Yoko Ono's word scores, and
Simone Forti's dance constructions, which translated task-based stage
directions from theatre and dance into minimal scores. They all demonstrate how Fluxus scores formalize a set of attitudes that intensify
the tension between action and object by involving time, duration and
chance as formal features in the work.

This heterogeneous quality of the score has been described as "intermedia" by one of the co-founders of Fluxus, Dick Higgins, in his article
from 1965. Intermedia refers to the location "between media," which
is where, according to Higgins, most of the best work was being produced at the time.[22] For Higgins the historical separation of art forms
from forms of life, which he argues started in the Renaissance with the
separation between media, was concretized in the concept of a pure
medium.[23] It is this "essentially mechanistic approach" that had been
rejected by Fluxus artists, and Dadaists before them, to "open up aesthetically rewarding possibilities" that arise from operating between
art media and life media. The intermedia character of the score suggests occupying a space between forms, but it may also be seen to
locate the human body as a material object in motion and between
forms.

The root of the word *score* in the Indo-European word *sker* means
"to cut" and it also connotes "notions of creating a notch and keeping
a tally."[24] Florian Cramer offers a similar interpretation of Emmet Williams' *Counting Songs* (1962) when he defines this score as "a simple
data-mining algorithm" because of its pragmatic use by the artist to
obtain, as Williams says quoted by Cramer, "an exact head count
to make sure that the management [of the festival venues] wasn't
cheating us."[25] Ready-made or found objects, which to Higgins were

21 Ibid.
22 Dick Higgins, "Intermedia," *Leonardo* 34, no. 1 (2001): pp. 49–54.
23 Anna Shechtman, "The Medium Concept," *Representations* 150, no. 1 (May 8, 2020):
    pp. 61–90, https://doi.org/10.1525/rep.2020.150.1.61
24 Basualdo, "In Terms of Performance: Score."
25 Florian Cramer, "Crapularity Hermeneutics: Interpretation as the Blind Spot of Analytics,
    Artificial Intelligence, and Other Algorithmic Producers of the Postapocalyptic Present,"

examples of intermedium because they did not "conform to the pure medium," are today most commonly found in databases that capture bodies as they perform online. As bodies become data there is an urgent need to imagine aesthetic possibilities for bodies and with bodies while accounting for abstract locations such as databases and datasets, which register bodies as numbers and represent them visually in spreadsheets. Score as an account of something that is being counted helps to reflect on the intermedium as a de facto location for data capture. At the same time, it reveals the difference between score and data as the relation between action and abstraction; either counting takes place each time to keep track of objects and people, or it captures bodies into stats and statistics once and for all. As a curatorial method, commissioning scores offers another form of knowledge-making with art and data where scores capture what is between media: between information and the movement of bodies. The exhibition is not an exercise of visualizing data as extracted from bodies and their environments but a rehearsal of possible transformations of life as commons, where data escapes the reductive function of database logic for which what counts is a number.

Commons: Affective Politics and its Imaginaries

Any discussion of commons and its aesthetics has to acknowledge the close relations between commons and reproductive labor, and how commons have been made operative for capitalism and neo-liberalism through different forms of enclosures.[26] Practices of data extraction enclose data as part of a digital economy where data is the basis of ideology of datafication, which reproduces subjects through surveillance.[27] OPEN SCORES: How to Program the Commons introduces other subjects of data that make difference. Departing from exploitative forms of labor such as digital and free labor, these data subjects

in *Pattern Discrimination.*, ed. Clemens Apprich, Wendy Hui Kyong Chung and Florian Cramer (Lüneburg: meson press, 2018), p. 25.

26 George Caffentzis, "The Future of 'The Commons': Neoliberalism's 'Plan B' or the Original Disaccumulation of Capital?," *New Formations. Imperial Ecologies* 69, no. 1 (Summer 2010): pp. 23–41, https://doi.org/10.3898/NEWF.69.01.2010

27 Shoshana Zuboff, *The Age of Surveillance Capitalism: The Fight for a Human Future at the New Frontier of Power* (London: Profile Books, 2019).

reproduce collaboration and commoning through artistic scores. The exhibition, while presenting art projects, is clearly engaged in a politics of commons dedicated to care and reproduction of free subjects through artistic collaborations and production of tools and objects.

Feminist scholars for years have addressed capitalist exploitation through the question of reproductive work showing capitalism to be a dominant force that turns the bodies of people, animals and earth into productive machines and factories. For example, Salma James and Mariarosa Dalla Costa, and Sylvia Federici recognize how capitalist forms of production changed how social life is organized and reproduced.[28] James and Costa claim that "the separation of man from woman became a capitalist division,"[29] leading to externalization of housework from paid work. While communities are subverted and their members separated through systems of production into waged and unwaged labor, housework is transformed into "a natural attribute" instead of being "recognized as a social contract."[30] Second-wave feminists, especially those associated with Wages against/for Housework and Lotta Feminista recognize how female roles embodied in the subject of a housewife have sustained this division of labor for capitalist growth. The call for wages introduced housework and home as a practice and place of struggle against the exploitation of reproductive labor and ideological manipulations that hide the fact that housework is "the only condition under which you [women] are allowed to live" in capitalism.[31] These theories and histories of labor and exploitation situate the source of gendered labor divisions in patriarchy and accumulation. They also show how reproductive labor is crucial to sustaining capitalism by producing its workforce and the so-called *natural resources* of commons that enter productive economy as capitalist subjects and objects to be exploited.

More recent scholarly critique of science and technology trace genealogies of contemporary surveillance technologies in the slave trade,[32]

28 Mariarosa Dalla Costa and Selma James, *The Power of Women & the Subversion of Community*, 3rd ed. (Wages for Housework, 1975); Silvia Federici, *Wages against Housework* (Bristol: Falling Wall Press, 1975).
29 Costa and James, *The Power of Women & the Subversion of Community*, p. 51.
30 Federici, *Wages against Housework*, p. 2.
31 Ibid.
32 Simone Browne, *Dark Matters: On the Surveillance of Blackness* (Durham NC: Duke University Press Books, 2015).

showing how algorithmic operations within supposedly neutral search engines and data classification systems reproduce racism and formalize gender stereotypes back into everyday life.[33] Search terms that return results objectifying women of color, applications that recognize Asian faces as squinting or winking, or soap dispensers unable to distinguish skin other than white are all examples of racist technologies. As Ruha Benjamin argues "so much of what is routine, reasonable, intuitive, and codified reproduces unjust social arrangements, without ever burning a cross to shine light on the problem."[34] As different forms of oppression are encoded into "unjust systems," automation continues to be offered as the solution to the human bias that, it is believed, can be overcome with calculations and data-based modelling and predictions.

With these different critical approaches to studies of science, technology and design, the question of digital commons or any commons to be programmed should also be a question for the potential of commons beyond the programmatic logic that accompanies *"techno quo"* and tech-solutionism.[35] Questions of justice are also important to the projects included in the exhibition even if they mostly come from a European and Western context. There is an urgent need to keep asking about the ethics of the commons: what is the common form of social relations produced as the result of an algorithm or a score? To whom are commons available? Who and what is defined as resources and who as community? The reproductive labor of technological commons involves the work of re-imagining social relations reorganized through capitalism and injecting care necessary to maintain life worth living. Artistic projects presented in the exhibition offer answers to some of these questions.

As Peter Linebaugh argues, "labor is important to commoning but commoning is also conducted through labor with other resources; it does not make division between 'labor' and 'natural resources'."[36]

33 Safiya Noble, *Algorithms of Oppression: How Search Engines Reinforce Racism* (New York: New York University Press, 2018); Ruha Benjamin, ed., *Captivating Technology: Race, Carceral Technoscience, and Liberatory Imagination in Everyday Life* (Durham NC: Duke University Press, 2019).

34 Ruha Benjamin, *Race after Technology: Abolitionist Tools for the New Jim Code* (Cambridge: Polity Press, 2019).

35 Benjamin, *Captivating Technology*, p. 12.

36 Peter Linebaugh, "Some Principles of the Commons," *Counter Punch*, January 8, 2010, http://www.counterpunch.org/linebaugh01082010.html (accessed October 23, 2020).

Commoning as a practice of commons is not a means to an end, but rather it focuses on the practice and means of living where subsistence is the source of and for the community.[37] The projects presented as part of *OPEN SCORES* offer, through aesthetic means, an opportunity to inquire into contemporary forms of subsistence *with* digital technologies. Through re-imagining them into a score, the value of reproduction and sustenance is shown to be part of labor of maintenance and care for and with bodies rather than extraction of the value they generate as data. The exhibition makes visible how data is common and it also demonstrates that it can be captured and shared in other ways than enclosing logic of datasets, databases and surveillance.

Commissioning Data: Commissioning Common Forms

In their essay "On Misanthropy," Alexander Galloway and Eugene Thacker suggest that the care etymologically present in curating refers to the "presentation of the static," which they define as "collecting, archiving, cataloguing and preserving, in a context that is both institutional and architectural."[38] This form of curating requires what they call "historical stillness" as the condition of care. Care is defined as control executed on immobilized objects. It is clear what such an immobilized object could be and examples of such conventional curatorial forms include: a painting hanging on the gallery wall, a display cabinet in the museum, or a public sculpture in the city square. One of the main conditions of care is the capture and representation of the object to the public.

Does the *OPEN SCORES* exhibition make its materials historically immobile and would it be a problem to do so? The curators do ask for a score that distils experience into a set of instructions that can lead "to a realization of an intended action." For the curators the score functions as both a kind of algorithm to count and number projects for the exhibition, while it is also "an interface between a human actor and an object/material/machine."[39] The artists respond by delivering

---

37 Maria Mies and Vandana Shiva, *Ecofeminism* (London: Zed Books, 1993).

38 Alexander R. Galloway and Eugene Thacker, "On Misanthropy," in *Curating Immateriality: The Work of the Curator in the Age of Network Systems*, ed. Joasia Krysa (Brooklyn: Autonomedia, 2006), p. 166.

39 *Creating Commons*, "Open Scores: How to Program the Commons. #exhibition Guide."

a series of notations, drawings, diagrams, booklets, stickers, manuals, questions, comic books, instructions; these are all objects that gather different ways of working together and recording this process while making things and relations of different kinds. The act of capture in the form of a drawing or a manual *mobilizes* possible future executions of the score, while illustrating figurations and re-figuring relations that can be created.

For example, in *Score #4*, Laurence Rassel offers a series of five diagrams that represent the process of directing an institution. (She is director of l'École de Recherche Graphique in Brussels.) Rassel's ambition is for a *good enough institution*, which is defined, after the French researcher and psychologist Philippe Kinoo,[40] by its ability to "recognize its mistakes, analyze them and correct them."[41] This definition serves as a method for managing an institution and helps to generate a set of drawings that represent and map "the balance, the compromises, the limits we have to accept, to negotiate, to experience in order to work collectively and with care in the framework of an institution and maybe achieve a *good enough* direction position."[42] Each diagram in the work consists of a drawing and a question, or a description of a situation, or a method to follow. Together they point to hesitations and models that drive a process of instituting and that mobilize drawing and writing together to work out principles that can help an institution "recognize its limits and accept them, as best they can."

The diagrams define these limits by combining the complexity of the task of directing an institution with simplicity of design, keeping within Cartesian space of X and Y axes and using classical geometric shapes of circles, squares and lines. Laws/rules and values are mapped onto relations between symbolic, real and imaginary, and the limits of the institution are inscribed into the space that has been imagined and framed. This is localized practice where commoning is about instituting, understood as a process where it is possible

---

40 Philippe Kinoo, "Autorités, pouvoirs, décisions, responsabilités dans une institution," in *Qu'est-ce qui fait autorité dans les institutions médico-sociales?*, ed. Muriel Meynckens-Fourez and Christine Vander Borght (Toulouse: Édition ERES, 2007), pp. 55–70, https://www.cairn.info/qu-est-ce-qui-fait-autorite-dans-les-institutions--9782749208343-page-55.htm.

41 *Creating Commons*, "Open Scores: How to Program the Commons. #exhibition Guide," p. 2.

42 Ibid.

"to work below the ideal of the model."[43] The diagrams are abstractions of how to achieve this by framing institution not as a thing but a process that operates as much conceptually as it is material. *Score #4* maps an institution that is not imagined but a real existing space, geographically located in Brussels and dedicated to teaching art and design. Diagrammatic models of this score conceptualize specific relations and scenarios that have taken place or might occur. Rather than offering a universal formula the score captures a process of working towards a good enough institution as a series of diagrams, which are abstract representations of the school figuring out and accepting its limits.

One might ask if curatorial gesture of requesting translation of commons into a score or an algorithm to be displayed in the exhibition, might be considered overtly ambitious, futile or naive? Anyone who engages in labor that makes commons knows that copy&paste commons or some conditional statements of '*if [...] then commons*' do not exist. The decades-long history of the World Wide Web proves that neither freedom nor care nor love have ever been automated. However, by commissioning a score for the good-enough institution to be part of the exhibition, the curators open an inquiry into conditions for different forms of instituting and commoning. While the score is a static object that records abstract qualities it also captures the performative potential that can be realized as care taken in achieving a good-enough institution.

Mapping Common Territories

Historically, commons were associated with common land. *Magna Carta* (1215) and the *Charter of the Forest* (1217) were the two important legal documents that defined use and users of commons in medieval England. Peter Linebaugh traces historical commons such as wooded pastures and he describes the distribution of access and use of wooded commons:

43 Kinoo, "Autorités, pouvoirs, décisions, responsabilités dans une institution."

Wooded pasture: same land for trees and grazing animals. Wooded commons: owned by one person, but used by others, the commoners. Usually the soil belonged to the lord while grazing belonged to the commoners, and the trees to either – timber to the lord, and wood to commoners.[44]

The importance of woods and trees to the medieval economy as the source of energy and subsistence is at the center of common laws protected by the two charters and it was the reclamation of woods for the use by free men that the two documents protected while also restricting the amount of land that could be enclosed by the monarch. These legal documents had defined and legislated a particular kind of life and living on common land, but the laws governing the use of commons had been customary before the woods were enclosed as royal forests. If *Magna Carta* confirmed the freedoms of barons and lords, protecting them from the influence of the king, the *Charter of the Forest* complemented this by safeguarding practical changes to the use of common land. As Linebaugh claims, "[t]he message of the two charters (…) is plain: political and legal rights can exist only on an economic foundation."[45]

Contemporary communities depend on economic foundations such as the infrastructures accessible to them. Today infrastructures are increasingly computational and communities need the protected right to digital networks just as much as to public transport, education or space. *Score #6 Community Servers: Bringing Community Networks to the Ground* is a booklet offering a set of methods and notations for DIY projects for network-based communication between local neighborhoods. The project NetHood was initiated by Panayotis Antoniadis, as a non-profit organization in Zurich dedicated to planting "seeds of collective awareness, critical listening, long-term thinking, social learning and reflective action toward sustainable social life."[46] The score in the exhibition is a record of community mapping skills and resources necessary to create neighborhood networked commons.

The NetHood booklet opens practices of commons to the forms of knowledge-making today, injecting data with practices of care for

---

44 Peter Linebaugh, *The Magna Carta Manifesto: Liberties and Commons for All*, (Berkeley: University of California Press, 2008), p. 33.
45 Ibid., p. 6.
46 "NetHood," http://nethood.org/projects/ (accessed April 17, 2020).

creation and sharing of socio-technical knowledge among neighbors and neighborhoods. NetHood infrastructure includes building tools for Community Networks while looking for "common understanding and language toward the vision of Community Server."[47] The process involves developing technical infrastructure as part of design by a community in the physical space of neighborhood for its local application. The participatory co-design process which is part of the Net-Hood building methodology creates commons as a hybrid space that connects the physical and digital realized by hosting alternative Community Server and its maintenance by the community. The booklet for design of Community Networks records the process as an archive of tools and resources, while a score model invites to improvise and build nethoods together as part of DIY spirit.

Technical Images: Diagrams and Grids

If the exhibition helps to chart commons as abstract territories defined by their communities, and infrastructures, the scores are offered as an invitation to execute such different commons here or elsewhere, now and with others. While the projects are concerned with institutions, developing public platforms, and ways of social organizing through collaborations dedicated to creating and maintaining alternatives, the collection of these projects as scores represents commons in their multitudes of forms and their value is captured as a possibility for their reproduction by others and at other times. Becoming part of commons, is a struggle for self-representation and the projects in the exhibition address it as an intervention into a form.

The grid is a common format for organizing and reproducing data, for example in tables and spreadsheets, and extracting knowledge from elements distributed in this way. It is a standard also used in graphic design to arrange text, images and other graphical elements on a webpage. The design of webpages in the nineties was practically based on tables, and today grid is a dominant visual way to organize

---

47 Payanotis Antoniadis, "Community Servers: Bringing Community Networks to the Ground" (Zurich: NetHood, n.d.), p. 5, http://creatingcommons.zhdk.ch/wp-content/uploads/2020/03/6-nethood-methodology-booklet.pdf (accessed April 17, 2020).

images on Instagram and similar platforms. The grid has a much longer history as an efficient method for organizing ancient cities.[48] Symbolically, a grid can be associated with its definition as "a prominent piece of visual iconography,"[49] whose meaning today refers to "not only the structural laws and principles behind physical appearance, but the *process* of rational thinking itself."[50] Jack H. Williamson links the modern conception of a grid to analytical geometry, whose foundations were laid out in the seventeenth century by René Descartes, who emphasized the structural and rational meaning of the grid. For Descartes a problem, visually understood in terms of a field, was to be divided into its smallest components. This abstraction of knowledge was based on a mental process of mapping what is known into geometric values by defining "the position of coordinates and axes – conceived as numerical quantities – on a plane in space."[51] According to Williamson, the Cartesian grid emphasized the interchangeable relation between the world (Nature) and what is known about it (Reason). The grid, claims Williamson, achieved its highest development in modernism where, drawing on concept of universal continuum in physics, it became "synonymous with the continuum itself."[52]

With the *Score #3 How to use GRIDr as an exhibition tool for Youtube-Videos* we enter the space of a grid as a durational practice of arranging digital files and creating collection of smaller collections. Here, a continuum is organized along time and space with GRIDr, an open online platform to curate online exhibitions of YouTube videos using a grid pattern. As with Fluxus scores, time here becomes a structural feature that emphasizes the performativity of this platform. Developed by network art curator Robert Sakrowski and artist Jonas Lund, GRIDr provides a virtual space to lay out YouTube videos and display them as compositions of 2x2, 3x3 or 4x4 video grids. GRIDr combines the graphical organization of the webpage with the sociality and aesthetic formats developed for the YouTube platform as anyone

48 Dan Stanislawski, "The Origin and Spread of the Grid-Pattern Town," *Geographical Review* 36, no. 1 (1946): pp. 105–120, https://doi.org/10.2307/211076

49 Jack H. Williamson, "The Grid: History, Use, and Meaning," *Design Issues* 3, no. 2 (1986): pp. 15-30, here p. 15, https://doi.org/10.2307/1511481

50 Ibid., p. 20.

51 Ibid., p. 20.

52 Ibid., p. 22.

and at any time can curate their grid on the platform with videos uploaded on YouTube.

The experience of curating on GRIDr involves performing actions that are normally captured and executed by algorithms as part of platform infrastructure. However, on GRIDr things shift slightly so the platform becomes an *experience* of organizing data. Using the grid as a form of algorithmic abstraction the GRIDr application reproduces conditions for automated curating as a visualization technique that allows the user to coordinate space visually on a monitor. In GRIDr the plane is constricted to four, nine or sixteen videos yet the space that it maps is much more expansive and necessarily time-based. The curatorial decisions of selecting and ordering videos on the website are exercises in abstractions executed by the human curator, who retrospectively defines and discovers patterns when choosing videos and when deciding on their order. Such grid-based display is what Vilém Flusser would call technical images that "appear to be on the same level of reality as their significance."[53] They restructure reality into a "global image scenario" as a form of technical hallucination.[54] Curating videos on GRIDr reveals a grid as a technical image while offering the potential to recover it from claims to objectivity. GRIDr helps to reflect on how abstraction organizes knowledge and how the subjective view is never out of the picture, even if executed by algorithmic operation.

Conceptualization of grids as technical images gives a critical shape to the idea that knowledge is constructed and that technical images "are products of applied scientific texts,"[55] and that today such texts are often replaced by data. If data are representations of facts, and collections of information captured as sets of numbers, the question is what then is excluded from such forms of representations and what is not counted. This question enquires about compositional elements of the image more broadly, which always includes positive and negative spaces, where the first refers to the subject of the image and the latter defines the space surrounding it; relation between the two influences aesthetic potential of the image. In case of GRIDr, negative space is framed as a grid and while exposing gaps it activates another level

53 Vilém Flusser, *Towards a Philosophy of Photography* (London: Reaktion Books, 2000), p. 15.
54 Ibid., p. 9.
55 Ibid., p.14.

of images coded into autonomous collections outside of their original context.

Negative space in technical image represents commons that are spaces, objects, times and practices some of which are not yet enclosed and captured; commons cannot be seen but they are made and it is through this making that one can experience and feel commons. Negative space as commons is depicted in *Score #1 for Artworld Commoning*, a diagram made by Furtherfield, a London-based organization currently housed in Finsbury Park. The score is based on the Decentralized Autonomous Organisation With Others (DAOWO) and it is part of a much longer project of re-imagining art worlds, which started over twenty years ago, when the mainstream art scene in Great Britain was dominated by the YBA (Young British Artists). Over the years Furtherfield have engaged their punk spirit into a networked collaboration with projects such as Furthernoise, Visitors' Studio, and DIWO (Do It With Others) E-Mail Art exhibition, which aimed to "highlight the already thriving imagination of those who use social networks and digital networks on the Internet as a form of distribution."[56] Furtherfield continuously re-invents the territory in which it operates, and DAOWO is a composite of these reinventions and their histories, which encompasses relations between art, technology and commons. Visualized as a Venn diagram, DAOWO illustrates how these three areas are superimposed to create "connected communities with a sense of: agency, imagination and alliances."[57] The diagram contains the complexity of contemporary network systems that act on many fronts simultaneously while being committed to marking possible and probable engagements between artists, technologists and publics. The diagram does not limit being in common by defining two possible outcomes but it is a continuous becoming driven by desire and commitment to create decentralized organization with others.

When reading *Score #1* as a technical image that defines commons as negative space, it is important to consider the apparatus that created this image, which here is not a product of applied scientific texts, but the result of artistic practices, engagements with communities and the self-design of digital tools and spaces that have been part of Further-

---

56   Furtherfield, in *Creating Commons* 2019, #1
57   Furtherfield, "DAO Practices Booklet," 2019, p. 2.

field's activities over many years. The DAOWO diagram abstracts this rich history of practice to offer a method for self-analysis that can be used by artists, commoners and decentralizers (technologists invested in distributed technologies). It defines six attitudes that can be simultaneously attempted by an infinite number of players who can "join, learn and perform a piece of artworld commoning."[58] DAOWO imagines a space and traces it by locating and charting rituals, data management practices and artistic projects, also described as "trans-local seeing rooms," all in order to intercept the problems that exist in the spaces between art, technology and people. This diagram is deductive in that it maps art, tech and people as separate. At the same, time it points to DAOWO as a specific construction, a composite that results from merging these three independent fields, superimposing relations between them and charting space for new formations to emerge.

While diagrams and grids are examples of abstract forms through which information is visualized, they also map commons as an apparatus of collective efforts needed to generate data on social media platforms and to build any kind of community. What is normally part of processing information on YouTube becomes an aesthetic arrangement of patterns on the GRIDr platform. Decades-long practices and experiences of working with art, technology and different communities are re-imagined into a diagram accompanied by a set of possible interpretations and a guide to create one's own DAOWO score. Knowledge is reproduced and shared, scores are collected and displayed, and commons is revealed as abundance of creation in artistic spaces and on social media platforms.

Movements: Border Crossing, Metamorphosis

Scores in the exhibition exemplify different forms of thinking with commons, where keeping a score refers to *accounting for* another kind of reason. Rather than enumeration it is about performing change. *Score #5 Against Immunisation: Boxing as a Technique for Commoning* is a calendar of counterintuitive forms of collaboration in which bodies are involved. Time and space organize collage representations of bodies

58   Ibid.

boxing, transversing boundaries and crossing them with bodies. This score refers to commons where collaborations take the forms of "difficult conversations," "painful compromises," and "unavoidable conflicts" that mobilize bodies. Here collaborations are fluid, bodies are active, and accommodating touch, proximity and power. The calendar frames time and by accounting for it, defines change as contagion where permeability happens through touch of fists, hitting, sweating, attacking, working with bodies to cross borders between them. Engaging bodies in motion is a way to practice commons. *Against Immunisation* is presented as a state of pandemic that absorbs rather than protects one body from another, where the state of protection inevitably always renders bodies as a possible threat. In the current pandemic times, when immunization is needed, *Score #5* reminds about death not as a state of exception but rather as a common state, and shows the change that is needed if our desire is to live in common.

Score #2 How to be a feminist hacker is a transformation guide in the form of a sticker zine that visualizes the process of metamorphosis into a feminist hacker. Eleven stickers are each dedicated to specific actions, which include finding out about your own priorities, finding like-minded people to make a community with, dancing together, coding by yourself and debugging with others, giving birth to people and ideas, fighting about stuff in the community; and being friends and finding space to start a lab. This work is created by the collective and feminist hackspace Mz* Baltazar's Laboratory and is accompanied by the story of how this transformation takes place in a lab where open source technology is used in the space for feminist artists, including transgender women and nonconforming people. This score is about becoming another subject and building another culture and technology to break through existing norms that traditionally rule in technology labs and tech communities. This is a guide to create different common norms and change culture by inviting community to make a common space through values of open source and equal access to technology, to learn from each other and do technology together. This is a room of one's own, a safer space to become a feminist hacker.

These scores record movement by arranging it in a calendar format organizing time and bodies in motion, and between moments that mark change. Movement and time are components of duration and they encourage to be performed as social practice of being with other bodies, and re-creating community as feminist technological space. The two scores encompass difference as non-normative space and action. Boxing body accounts for its own vulnerability and that of others, while feminist body is performance of the self in a category of one's own making within spaces and networks that facilitate it. Score records what is needed for this change and the change itself is an act of marking these moments as commons that support change. The exhibition accounts for these commons as difference-performing change.

Queering User Guides

Commons as a challenge to normative spaces and subjects are enacted with other scores collected and displayed in the exhibition. *Collaboration Guidelines* is *Score #11*, developed by Michael Murtaugh, Femke Snelting and Peter Westenberg, members of Constant in Brussels. This score is a curious installation of cushions that look like keyboard keys, paper print-outs of rules, and LED displays of collaboration guidelines as they are re-written collaboratively online. In the exhibition this space is a comfortable one to relax at and reflect and discuss issues such as conflict, consent and authorship among others, which often are experienced through their violations. Here and now, rules, modes and expectations can be continuously discussed, changed and edited in an open guidelines document stored on the Constant server.[59] These guidelines in progress are defined through conversations and are co-written by users. In contrast to the computer keyboard letters, the cushions are embroidered with keywords such as "doubt," "joy," "support," "magic," "tension," "dis/agree," "change," "generous," marking their importance to this process. The environment of this score, constructed for the exhibition and online, reflects its own material dependence on bodies, human and nonhuman that support it. Commoning here takes place through set up of infrastructures and it points to desired attitudes as collectively listed into user documents.

The online version of this user guide takes the form of a "bug report," which is traditionally a technical document describing a soft-

[59] https://pad.constantvzw.org/p/guidelines.questions (accessed April 17, 2020).

ware problem, usually written by a tester or a community of users. But as Jara Rocha claims, a bug report is "a performative document that in itself is always already activating a change in the environment it inhabits."[60] She points out that the act of writing such a report is "one of the key performative devices in software development."[61] In the case of *Collaboration Guidelines*, the bugs that are reported include inequality, injustice, privilege and ableism, and the act of setting guidelines together is performative of the politics of commons. The document imagines users as collaborators in an environment that can accommodate them whoever they are and however able they are, and the score is about deconstructing collective conditions that trigger injustices that prevent collaboration.

The format of the manual in *Score #15, Zen and the art of making tech work for you. Practical guidance for women and trans*activists, human rights defenders and technologists*, is another example of appropriating a technical document to support a community. The manual published with the wiki, a collaborative digital writing and editing tool, introduces collaboration as a form of crafting "appropriate online presences" and maintaining collaboration as safe practice.[62] The question of crafting directs attention to techniques and tools, showing how they are interlinked with what collaboration is possible. The manual is about material conditions necessary to ensure safety for women, activists and non-conforming people. This practice envisions responsibility as matter of building and sharing tools which support safety of their users. The manual is an inventory of what is needed to craft safe collaborative spaces and it reimagines such a list as a toolbox for creating Zen, a meditation practice that aims at understanding the nature of mind and things, and expressing it through daily practice that benefits others. This spiritual reference in the score title poetically complements the practicality of the manual and tools described in the list, proposing that commoning is about reflecting its values through practice. Meditation is part of crafting commons.

60 Jara Rocha, "Depths and Densities: A Bugged Report," *Transmediale Journal*, no. 3, Affective Infrastructures (September 23, 2019), https://transmediale.de/content/depths-and-densities-a-bugged-report (accessed April 17, 2020).
61 Ibid.
62 *Creating Commons*, "Open Scores: How to Program the Commons. #exhibition Guide," p. 4.

Rather than a guideline or a manual, *Score #7 QomMo(a/w)nin?!...* contributes two tree diagrams of commons as *qommons* to map affects and capture relations around collaborative practices. *Score #7*, the work of Zeljko Blace, a curator and instigator of the sport-culture-activism projects qSPORT/QueerSport.info in Croatia and ccSPORT. link in Berlin, questions and reveals in/exclusions that are present in various projects across art, culture and sport. Commoning and qom-moning are charted across different axes including, among others, those of values, time, participation, and proximity. This is common-ing as a form of complaint and queer moaning suspended between "being worn down" and a refusal accompanied by "a sense of opti-mism about how things could happen differently."[63] The contradiction of openness and opacity accommodates values that queer the idea of commons by taking into account positions of people who are vulner-able and at the same time are involved in collaboration. This diagram also exists in pseudocode on GitLab so it can be read as an attempt to generate data values and code defining "(non) obvious limitations and frustrations by queer and questioning people." Here too the dia-grams define a space that stays open to online intervention on GitLab and etherpad, embodying the dynamic of collaborative presentation, performing, selecting and competing online.

But what is the context of this QomMo(a/w)ning?!... What is the territory that is marked by the two diagrams' mind-maps? Abstraction here works through language mapping commons and qommons but also it is a coding exercise that reflects frustrations and acknowledges regimes that while being positive for some might be problematic for others. The diagrams are open and unfinished, suggesting that also commonning and qommoning is always under construction, at times failing. The work focuses on values of opacity for qommoning, defined into different categories such as informative (partial information pres-ent), representational (selected information serve as symbolic/for-mal gesture), revealing (some things can be observed and justified), insightful (most can be accessed in informative way), inspirational (all data shared, relations explicit and analyzed together), indoctrinative

---

63   Sarah Ahmed, "Complaint as Diversity Work," *Feministkilljoys* (blog), November 10, 2017, https://feministkilljoys.com/2017/11/10/complaint-as-diversity-work/

(full transparency abused against vulnerable). Others are still to be developed.

All these examples of scores as queering commons recognize inaccuracies and failures as productive moments in which relations can be made otherwise, on which basis they point to the expansion of the idea of commons. They suggest that commoning is a craft that requires commitment to change and difference that is realized in practice.

Digital Bodies: Objects and Archives

Crafting commons is about sustaining diversity of practices, cultures and things and about creating conditions for commoning. In digital environments this also means accounting for material relations with digital things, be it data or other digital objects such as platforms and code, by inquiring into how what is considered part of commons is made into commons, in other words at what point it becomes a common resource? At the core of these questions is the issue of labor and its role in the process of commoning, which also involves creating things and making and maintaining knowledge through craft.

Another example of how relations with digital objects are reconfigured is the *Score #13* by Sebastian Luetgert and Jan Gerber, the creators of the pan.do/ra video archive network, the 0xDB film database and other projects that address questions of intellectual property and piracy. Entitled *Get Into the Car / Get out of the Car* this score takes the form of 25-minute film that is described as a "semi-automatic edit of almost 300 film clips in which someone either says 'Get in the car' or 'Get out of the car'."[64] This is a film as digital object, which can be also defined as a technical image in that it is the result of data processing apparatus, an online archive with its interface and categories and other functions. With the use of full text search in time-based annotations, almost 100 years of moving images were processed over five days to make the film in which multiple characters from different films perform the score of getting in or out of the car. This score is simulta-

---

64 *Creating Commons*, "Open Scores: How to Program the Commons. #exhibition Guide," p. 3.

neously a recording of algorithmic process, data visualization, and an intervention into a formal structure of the aesthetic object that is film.

Film traditionally defines a cultural form and artistic format for communicating stories with moving images and sound. It also refers to a set of practices of film production and distribution involving people, from film crew to audiences, materials including celluloid and digital film, techniques such as editing, and analogue and digital technologies. *Score #13* represents a transformation from film as moving image to film as data. Once included into an online movie archive, it is recorded digitally, which means that it becomes a dataset of frames, texts, timelines, annotations, and other metadata including subtitles and other information. Film as a database is a collection of even more data which then can be manipulated and reorganized to create another film and another dataset, for example according to the scored instructions to get in and out of the car. The status of the film as a technical image is clear, especially when looking at the online interface of the archive 0xdb.org, where films are presented as moving image and as timeline of data defined by its abstract colors, lines and shapes. Film as data becomes a different kind of storyline, which is dependent on algorithmic processing becoming part of a craft of film-making.

How data affect the making of this film can be seen when watching *Score #13*, in which fragments of films last only a few seconds and progress one after another, suspending the storyline and expanding the duration of the score being performed. Peer-to-peer sharing technologies such as BitTorrent are crucial to creating the film archive, which remains in the shadows of intellectual property laws and outside of traditional film distribution frameworks. With Pan.do/ra, a free and open source media archiving platform, it is possible to manage huge collections of films and video as digital objects. However, how film affects the database is more opaque. The film *Score #13* is a method for sharing the database within a community that comes together as users of the online archive and as audience of the screenings organized in publicly available spaces in Berlin. Commoning here is an affective process in which people actively produce value for the archive through performing a community that exists temporarily in conditions different to exclusive access to films and its data, and in spaces other than cinema halls. The film is experienced as a different object and in different environments, where it can be shared as a copy and as a viewing experience.

Digital archives and libraries exist in opposition to restrictions that are put on digital practices, as their primary function is to support file sharing. Dušan Barok in *Score #12 Inverse Reader* emphasizes how libraries are spaces that support "amateur librarianship, scholar-led publishing, the politics of search, pirate care, critical pedagogy, self-education" and create communities around these libraries. *Score #14* is a repertorium of the *Scrolled Score*, a collection compiled by Marcell Mars and Tomislav Medak of the Memory of the World shadow library. *Scrolled Score* created from a query "score" is also a set of instructions how to download and install Calibre, software for reading and organizing books and texts. *Score #9 Temporary Library for Creating Commons* is co-curated by exhibition curators with Alessandro Ludovico, and consists of a list of titles put together as the basis for the physical collection of books for the exhibition, now housed permanently in the ZHdK library. *Score #10* is an extension of Aaaaarg and The Public School, combining radical self-education and an online library collection into an open mic Internet radio station. The instruction for this score invites people to read aloud the last page they read silently and to record it so it becomes part of the *Last Pages – an Iteration of Very Public Radio*. This archive remains open as part of the *Creating Commons* website, thus making a space for this practice to continue. In all these different examples of sharing in shadow libraries, files are exchanged and the ways of being together are sustained by a commitment to collective learning and to the generosity of these practices and tools. As objects and subjects become data, data too become materially located within practices and sites of exchange.

Curating Epistemologies

The variety of scores displayed in the exhibition communicates the abundance of commons. The exhibition visualizes that not only are commons possible, but that they exist. The exhibition exposes that commons are not heroic and grandiose but daily, and at times uneventful moments of being and becoming together. Commons are dependent on infrastructures and collaborative conditions and the scores in the exhibition represent how such conditions can be negotiated by the community.

That digital participation is regularly pre-defined and a non-negotiable set of conditions which accommodate data capture and extraction and where creative possibilities are instrumentalized is not only common but increasingly naturalized. Curators of the show are well aware of the unequal arrangement of relations online and they comment on it in their own contribution to the exhibition, the *Score #16 Too long, don't read – just accept*. The title of the score is a typical response to terms of use that users are presented with and have to accept before being able to participate on platforms such as Facebook, Google, YouTube and many others. The curators playfully recreate similar environment in the exhibition where visitors automatically agree to all the terms of use upon the entry to the show. *Score #16* replaces the usual curatorial statement that normally introduces audience to the exhibition theme and to the artworks on display, with a set of partly absurd rules prescribing how to engage with the show. This performative curatorial gesture invokes gallery goers as internet users and it refers to the familiar process of saying yes to whatever when online. The *Score #16* is shorter, however, than typical Terms of Use agreement, and with its humorous tone it mocks the legal language of such documents. The function of this score in the exhibition is to suggest that an exhibition like commons is a set of relations and form of participating that could be otherwise. And it locates commons as a daily choice against enclosure, which requires labor, self-education and commitment to collaborative practice of building common infrastructures and conditions that distribute and negotiate agency away from service provision and towards a practice of being and becoming in common.

The final score in the exhibition, *Score #17 Proposition: Let's Make a Salad*, is another contribution by curators. This is a homage to Alison Knowles, who originally performed the score at the Fluxus concert at ICA in London in 1962. Performed by the curators during the first night of the *OPEN SCORES* exhibition this score is a provocation to consider making a salad to be a new commons, similarly to the way in which Cage declared the salad score to be "New Music." The invitation to make a salad might be trivial but its performance in the exhibition together with the performative gesture of *Score #16*, is done for a reason. There is a curatorial commitment to create exhibition as form of commons by breaking from the constraints that define elements of the exhibition, and by inciting suspicion and hesitation about forms of participation that are increasingly limited.

In digital spaces or in exhibitions, roles are pre-defined and forms of engagement set at the entry and curatorial responsibility becomes that of introducing a critical edge into common activities. Curating is "a practice on the edge," which "precariously balances between the struggle over and appropriation of commons."[65] And this curatorial edge is represented in the show as a gap, negative space between the convivial event of making and sharing a salad with the visitors and the terms of use for the exhibition *OPEN SCORES* that are accepted upon entry. However, the curators do not offer a choice between accepting terms of use or eating a salad but they construct a temporal situation for disrupting such a choice. The exhibition is a moment of sensing the edge where curating and the knowledge it engenders define conditions for curating commons as continuous struggle between commons and its enclosure; between presenting art objects or their exhibition; between presenting data and the database. This struggle is central to curating and curatorial knowledge, while it also contributes to understanding how data when engaged in these artistic projects is refigured into commons.

In conclusion, let me go back to Galloway and Thacker's essay where they invite us to "imagine an art exhibit of computer virus."[66] This invitation is a helpful provocation to the reader and the curator to think about caring for objects and things that are not, by their nature, still or immobile. To ask for a score which on the one hand is a graphical representation of action while containing its infinite possibilities of performance shows how the form of capture *is* a curatorial concern in *OPEN SCORES*. Rather than presenting stillness, the exhibition is a call to action. The curatorial method of building a collection of scores based on specific practices is an experiment in translations: from practice into instructions, from events and labor into forms and objects such as diagrams and databases, which register past actions while opening them up to possible future collaborative and creative reinterpretation. If

---

65   Magdalena Tyżlik-Carver, "Interfacing the Commons. Curatorial System as a Form of Production on the Edge," *A Peer-Reviewed Journal about: Public Interfaces* 1, no. 1 (January 31, 2011): pp. 16–17.
66   Galloway and Thacker, "On Misanthropy," pp. 153

commoning is not one practice but many varied and intensely oblique relations that can materialize in many forms, the curatorial provocation is a particular kind of test whether each project can be turned into a standard form that could be easily scored and redistributed, repeated and recycled while reflecting their different struggles for values through their diverse practices of reproducing what, how and with whom it can be shared. *OPEN SCORES: How to Program the Commons* archives such practices, and by doing so actively opens the possibility for reproduction of many different commons in future practices. Not through exact copy but in many common mutations.

Gary Hall

Postdigital Politics

PART 1
ON THE COMMONS AND THE CRISIS OF
REPRESENTATIVE DEMOCRACY

What Does Postdigital Mean and Why Is It Important?

I want to begin with a proposition. A lot of work in the arts, humanities and social sciences of late has been taken up with the commons. It's a fascination that is only likely to increase following the coronavirus pandemic that began in late 2019, early 2020. Over the next few years attention will understandably be paid to the manner in which communities all over the world spontaneously self-organized to fill the gaps in care left by the market and the state. Communities did so by collectively providing those in need with critical resources. Everything from information and accommodation, through medical supplies, to emergency childcare, financial aid packages, even company during periods of lockdown and quarantine, be it by telephone or video call.[1]

The commons, put simply, can be understood as non-proprietary shared spaces and resources—both material and immaterial—along with the collective social processes that are necessary for commoners to produce, manage and maintain them and themselves as a community. My proposition, then, is this: if we want to help transform society by actually creating such commons, we need to work, act and think very differently from the ways in which most of us do now. And I include in this "us" many of those who are well known in the fields

---

1   For more details, see "Flatten the Curve, Build the Care": http://syllabus.pirate.care/topic/coronanotes/. This is part of the Pirate.Care.Syllabus collective response to the coronavirus crisis offered by my colleagues Valeria Graziano, Tomislav Medak, Marcell Mars, Maddalena Fragnito and others: https://syllabus.pirate.care (all links in this text have last been accessed October 21, 2020).

of art and culture for writing about community, collectivity and the commons. I'm thinking here not just of authors who address the issue from within the liberal philosophical tradition of Garrett Hardin, Elinor Ostrom and Yochai Benkler. I also have in mind radical theorists and philosophers such as Isabelle Stengers, Donna Haraway, Michael Hardt and Antonio Negri.[2]

How can we do this? How can we act differently with a view to transforming society through the creation of more commons-oriented ways of being and doing? Like the last group of writers on the commons I mentioned, a lot of those I work with, as well as being media artists, activists or practitioners, identify as being radical theorists. However, we're theorists who are also exploring ways of reimagining theory and what it means to be a theorist. We're doing so by challenging some of the taken-for-granted categories and frameworks concerning what critical theory is considered to be, especially the highly individualistic, liberal-humanist model that's performed by most theorists and philosophers today, regardless of whether they're Marxists, post-Marxists, feminists, new materialists, posthumanists or accelerationists.[3] Instead, we're endeavoring to work, act and think in terms of the commons by experimenting with the invention of what can be called—rather teasingly, I'll admit—"anti-bourgeois theory."[4] This is theory that is:

1) *more consistent with the kind of progressive politics many of us in the arts, humanities and social sciences espouse.*

---

2   If the liberal approach focuses on the normative frameworks and principles of governance and self-organization that best allow a shared pool of spaces and resources to be managed and maintained as a specific property regime, radical theory is less concerned with associating the commons with things—land, sea, water, air, music files, digital books, software, code—and more with the social relations of commoning; with constructing the commons on the basis of shared political activities, practices and principles. For a recent account of the differences between liberal philosophy and radical theory with regard to the commons, see Marek Korczysnki and Andreas Wittel, "The Workplace Commons: Towards Understanding Commoning Within Work Relations," *Sociology* 54, no. 4 (2020): pp. 711–726.

3   Duncan Bell is just one of many political theorists to have developed an argument to this effect. See his "What is Liberalism?," *Political Theory* 42, no. 6 (2014): pp. 682–715, here p. 689; citing Thomas Nagel, "Rawls and Liberalism," in *The Cambridge Companion to Rawls*, ed. Samuel Freeman (Cambridge: Cambridge University Press, 2003), p. 62.

4   For more, see Gary Hall, "Anti-Bourgeois Theory," *Media Theory* 3, no. 2 (December 2019): pp. 1–26, http://journalcontent.mediatheoryjournal.org/index.php/mt/article/view/91.

It is important to be aware that neoliberalism is not directly opposed to liberalism. It is rather a version of it, as its name suggests, the wider historical tradition of liberalism having provided the discursive framework of modern capitalism. The singularized neoliberal *homo oeconomicus* is not necessarily always struggling *against* the liberal-humanist rights and values that the vast majority of theorists continue to adhere to in practice, then. Consequently, while most theorists position themselves as being politically on the left, many end up operating as rampantly competitive, proprietorial individuals nonetheless. Driven by a goal-fixated instrumentalism, what's important to them are the number of books published, grants captured, keynote lectures given, followers acquired, or likes and retweets gained. (Elsewhere I've associated this behavior with being a "micro-entrepreneur of the self."[5])

2) *in tune with the changing political zeitgeist, especially the shift from representative to direct forms of democracy.*

In the UK this shift can be traced at least as far back as the horizontal groundswell against the "old politics" of the liberal and neoliberal establishments that was such a prominent feature of the 2014 Scottish independence referendum. More recently, it's been apparent in the decentralized manner in which the Extinction Rebellion movement operates. It's not just a progressive phenomenon, though. The move to more direct forms of democracy is apparent in the UK Brexit party's rapid rise to a position of political influence under the leadership of Nigel Farage, prior to the December 2019 general election. In large part this rise was achieved through the adoption of the digitally savvy electoral strategy of the Five Star Movement (M5S) in Italy. Both used data gathered from the online activity of their members to help shape party direction and policy.

3) *a more appropriate mode of engagement for today's postdigital world than are printed and closed-access books and journal articles.*

---

5   Gary Hall, *The Uberfication of the University* (Minneapolis: University of Minnesota Press, 2016).

We arguably find ourselves in the midst of a fourth great transformation in communications technology. Crudely put, if the first transformation involved the development of speech and language, the second writing, and the third print, the fourth entails the change from analogue to digital that is associated with the emergence of Facebook, Google and Twitter. In fact, it can be said that we are already living in a postdigital era, if we take this term to name "a technical condition that … is constituted by the naturalization of pervasive and connected computing processes … in everyday life," to the extent that "digitality is now inextractable from the way we live while its form, functions and effects are no longer necessarily perceptible."[6] Historically, such transformations have often been followed by social and political upheaval and unrest, even war. The development of printing was at the heart of the Protestant Reformation in sixteenth century Europe, for example, resulting in the breaking of the religious monopoly of the Catholic Church. A key figure was Martin Luther with his Ninety-five Theses. However, although many book historians regard print as having subsequently led to the Renaissance, the Enlightenment and the development of modern science and democracy, we need to remember print has its dark side, too. Given the anti-Semitic attack at a synagogue in the East German town of Halle in October 2019, it's worth recalling that shortly before his death in 1546 Luther published a pamphlet called "Warning Against the Jews." Nor was this a one-off. "We are at fault for not slaying them," Luther proclaimed in an earlier 65,000-word treatise titled "On the Jews and Their Lies." The latter text was exhibited publicly in the 1930s during the Nuremberg Rallies.

We're all probably going to be long gone before anyone knows if we're currently living through a period of change as profound as the Reformation—although some have heralded the Sars-CoV-2 outbreak, to give the virus its proper name, as a sign that we are. This is because of the high degree of interconnectivity of global capitalism in terms of travel, trade, tourism, migration, the labor market and supply chains, all of which depend on postdigital information processing. Together with the associated destruction of biodiversity accelerated by the climate emergency and human population growth, such interconnectiv-

---

6   Maik Fielitz and Nick Thurston, *Post-digital Cultures of the Far Right: Online Actions and Offline Consequences in Europe and the US* (Bielefeld: transcript Verlag, 2018).

ity is held as having created the conditions for new, infectious, zoonotic diseases such as Sars, bird flu and Covid-19 to cross over from wildlife to humans as a result of their greater proximity to one another. Nevertheless, it's important to make an effort to come to terms with the shift from analog to postdigital, not least for political reasons, as the above examples drawn from German history suggest.

Of course it's questionable to what extent the traditional political division between left and right is still applicable. The situation is complicated today by the fact that this division has been overlaid, at the very least, by that between populist nativism and elitist cosmopolitanism. It's going to be interesting to see what changes there are to the public mood in this respect post-coronavirus. Will the backlash against the liberal establishment continue, or will it be replaced by a newfound respect for scientists and journalists, and for institutions such as the NHS and BBC in the UK? Retaining the left/right political distinction for the time being, however, we can say that it's mainly those on the populist authoritarian right who, to date, have realized the possibilities created by the new communication technologies. It's as if they've read their Gramsci and figured out that if you want to change politics, you need to begin by changing culture. To return to an international frame for a moment, recent years have provided us with examples such as: Donald Trump, who's been called a Twitter genius and the first meme president of the United States; Jair Bolsonaro, the first president of Brazil elected using the Internet, Google's YouTube especially, as his main means of communication; and the UK's Vote Leave campaign's sophisticated exploitation of Facebook data to intervene in the 2016 EU referendum, as revealed by the Cambridge Analytica scandal. What the actors behind these developments have done is create a new model of political communication by seizing on the opportunities created by the fourth great transformation in media technology to precipitate the cultural crisis in representative politics.

For populist politicians this new model has two very important characteristics. The first is that it allows those who don't already have control over their state media (à la Jarosław Kaczynski in Poland and Viktor Orbán in Hungary) to sidestep the old, established forms of political communication that rely on the major newspapers and influential TV and radio programs. They have thus avoided being held to account by journalists, even when they have fabricated, lied, doctored videos and rebranded fake "fact-checking" websites. Consider the boycotting by Boris Johnson's government of leading BBC news programs —until the need to keep the population informed about Covid-19 made such a stance untenable, that is.

The second important feature of this new model is that it nonetheless provides populists with a means of overcoming the apparent disconnect between professional politicians and "the people." The nativist right has overcome this disconnect by using the repetition of slogans—most famously "Make America Great Again" and "Take Back Control"—to link the grievances of a number of different sections of society. They include a sense of abandonment and betrayal by elites, resentment against women, Muslims and immigrants, and the general lack of control over their lives felt by many of those living through late-stage capitalism, coupled to an anxiety about the future. By articulating such sentiments with a nationalist pride, populist politicians have been able to create chains of equivalence across those parts of the population that have been adversely affected by the results of neoliberal globalization.[7] In this way the radical right have managed to mainstream their ideas by tapping into those affective forces—those drives, desires, fantasies and resentments—that motivate people to become part of a group such as, precisely, " the people," and form the basis of collective forms of identification.

Reactionary authoritarians have been aided and abetted in the creation of this new model of political communication by Silicon Valley companies. The latter are aware it's not logical reasoning and verified information and evidence but extreme displays of emotion that keep audiences hooked, and so drive their profits by maximizing attention. Not only do Twitter, Facebook and YouTube render indistinct the difference between making carefully thought-out comments on the current issues of the day, and hastily announcing one's unconsidered feelings about them, they actively amplify and reward expressions of anger, hatred, insecurity and shame, since contributions to these platforms don't need to be true to get a reaction and go viral, just hugely captivating.

All of which goes some way toward explaining how small numbers of people have been able to use communication technologies to move

---

7   For more in this context, see Chantal Mouffe, *For A Left Populism* (London: Verso, 2019).

large numbers of others in the direction of nativist forms of populism characterized by an emphasis on authority, group insecurity and an exclusionary nationalist pride. The emphasis on hyper-emotionalism has played straight into the hands of the reactionary right, which defines itself negatively against those it considers "the other." Hence the rise in sexism, racism and white supremacism we've experienced in recent times, both online and off, together with the presentation of the coronavirus as a "wartime" (Johnson) or "invisible enemy" (Trump), and description of it as the "Chinese disease" (Trump again). Indeed, those on the anti-liberal right have been so successful in making their ideas acceptable—many produce brilliant viral videos and memes, often containing language and images that are full of humor, irony and ambiguity—that they can be said to have completely transformed the political landscape. As a result, we find ourselves living in a "post-truth" world of "alternative facts," deep fakes," Holocaust deniers, climate breakdown deniers, pandemic minimizers and people who are anti-immigration and anti-LGBT + rights too.

Granted, the left has its own affective-emotional themes and tropes. Yet whereas the right *has* succeeded in using affect as a mobilizing political force, the left has been conspicuously bad at turning its representations into actions that are compelling enough to make different people, especially those in the mainstream of society, want to constitute themselves as a group around issues such as community and the commons. On the contrary, research shows that far right parties in Europe have tripled their share of the vote in the last three decades, with one in six choosing them at the polls.[8] Don't get me wrong: the left has its memes. Witness the one-time popularity of the "Oh, Jeremy Corbyn" chant in the UK. The pink pussy hats, *Handmaid's Tale*-style cloaks and "Un Violador en Tu Camino" (A Rapist in Your Path) performance piece adopted by various groups of feminist protestors around the world are also worth mentioning in this context. Still, there's arguably been no really successful progressive equivalent of the kind of forceful play found on "White Boy Internet" platforms such as 4chan,

8   Matthijis Rooduijn, Stijn van Kessel, Caterina Froio, Andrea Pirro, Sarah de Lange, Daphne Halikiopoulou, Paul Lewis, Cas Mudde and Paul Taggart, *The PopuList 2.0: An Overview of Populist, Far Right, Far Left and Eurosceptic Parties in Europe* (2020): www.popu-list.org

8chan and Reddit.[9] The democratic left has been conspicuously lacking in such politically effective "meme magic." And perhaps this is not surprising. Generally speaking, the left is less concerned about the kind of extremes of emotion that drive the reactionary right, and more about social justice, hospitality and mutual aid. Besides, societies are so diverse, pluralistic and fragmented these days it's far easier to unite people around what they are *not* than around what they *are*.

PART 2:
INFRARED

"Fuck Business"

How, then, are those of us who are on the left to challenge this takeover by the populist authoritarian right? Can we employ communication technologies for more progressive purposes that *are* attuned to today's rapidly changing political landscape?

As we've seen, over the decades the left has found it difficult to devise collective forms of identification that are able to successfully counter the two main kinds of neoliberalism dominant in much of the West: the global neoliberalism of Barak Obama, David Cameron, Angela Merkel, Emmanuel Macron and Joe Biden, which depends on a rule of law-based system of economic governance; and the libertarian neoliberalism associated with Donald Trump and Boris Johnson that wants to destroy this rules-based system, as embodied by the EU, in order to generate new, disruptive business opportunities free from regulation. Johnson's "fuck business" here means fuck the existing business.[10] Of late, however, there have been signs that a practical and relevant left alternative, capable of capitalizing on the possibilities created by the fourth great transformation in media technologies to shift toward more direct forms of democracy, may (just *may*) be beginning to emerge. As reasons for optimism we can point to phe-

---

9   Luke Winkie, "I Was a Teenage 4chan Troll – Until I Learned to Change My Ways," *Daily Dot*, August 26, 2015: https://www.dailydot.com/via/4chan-troll-white-boy-internet-sexism/

10   "Fuck business" was an aside made by Boris Johnson at a 2018 private reception. See Robert Shrimsley, "Boris Johnson's Brexit Explosion Ruins Tory Business Credentials," *Financial Times*, June 25, 2018: https://www.ft.com/content/8075e68c-7857-11e8-8e67-1e1a0846c475

nomena such as the grassroots upsurge against the political establish-ment associated with Alexandria Ocasio-Cortez in the US and her use of social media, the rise of the platform cooperativism movement,[11] and calls for the monopolies of Google and Facebook to be broken up and for people and communities to control their own data. The latter idea is being explored in Barcelona by housing-activist-turned-city-mayor Ada Colau.[12]

It's with this kind of emphasis on engaging with postdigital tech-nologies for purposes grounded in principles of social responsibility, solidarity and mutual care coupled to the collective redistribution of knowledge and resources that my collaborators and I align ourselves. And since a number of us are theorists, as I say, one of the issues we're interested in as part of this is reimagining theory in the aftermath of the digital. In this respect, a question we're raising with our work is: might exploring new modes of authorship, ownership and reproduc-tion that are more in tune with this fourth great transformation in com-munications technology have the potential to lead to non-neoliberal — but also (and this is extremely important) non-liberal—ways of being and doing as theorists? Ways that are more consistent with the kind of progressive politics many radical theorists advocate, in their writings on community, collectivity and the commons especially?

Over the last twenty years we've been involved in a number of bottom-up projects for the production and sharing of free resources, infrastructure and knowledge (objects). To briefly take my own trajec-tory as an example: in 1999 Dave Boothroyd and I launched *Culture Machine*, one of the first open access journals of critical and cultural theory.[13] In 2008 *Culture Machine* became a founder member of Open Humanities Press (OHP).[14] Directed by myself and two colleagues based in Australia, Sigi Jöttkandt and David Ottina, this initiative involves multiple semi-autonomous, self-organizing groups around the world, all of them operating in a non-rivalrous fashion to make works of contemporary theory available on a non-profit, free/gratis open access basis using Creative Commons licenses. Open Humanities Press currently has twenty-one journals, forty plus books distributed

11 https://platform.coop
12 https://decodeproject.eu
13 http://www.culturemachine.net/
14 http://openhumanitiespress.org

across nine book series, as well as experimental, *libre* texts such as those in its Liquid Books and Living Books About Life series.

OHP in turn became a founder member of the Radical Open Access Collective, a community of international presses, journals and other projects formed after the 2015 Radical Open Access conference.[15] Now consisting of over sixty members, this collective seeks to build a progressive alternative ecosystem for publishing in the humanities and social sciences, based on experimenting with a diversity of non-profit, independent and scholar-led approaches.

Meanwhile, in the Centre for Postdigital Cultures (CPC) at Coventry University, we're working on reinventing knowledge infrastructures, especially those involved in the production and sharing of theory.[16] Since its launch in 2018, the CPC has brought together many people involved in such "aesthetic" practices. They include myself and Janneke Adema from OHP; and Samuel Moore, who works with us as part of the Radical Open Access Collective.

The latest of these initiatives is the Community-led Open Publication Infrastructures for Monographs (COPIM) project, which emerged in 2019 out of a consortium of six open access presses called ScholarLed.[17] An international partnership involving universities and libraries as well as infrastructure and technology providers, COPIM is designed to realign open access book publishing by moving it away from the surveillance capitalism model of competing commercial service providers. Its aim is to respond to the fact that companies such as Elsevier and Springer are increasingly looking to monetize not just academic content, but the "entire knowledge production work flow, from article submissions, to metrics to reputation management and global rankings" and the related data extraction.[18] COPIM represents an alternative, more horizontal and collaborative, knowledge-sharing approach. Here the scholarly community collectively manages infrastructures and social systems for the common good in such a fashion as to enable a diversity of initiatives—including small, non-profit,

15 http://radicaloa.disruptivemedia.org.uk
16 https://www.coventry.ac.uk/research/areas-of-research/postdigital-cultures
17 https://scholarled.org
18 Leslie Chan, "Platform Capitalism and the Governance of Knowledge Infrastructure," Digital Initiative Symposium, University of San Diego, April 29–30, 2019: https://zenodo.org/record/2656601#.XNCUS-FR1Ta,%20consultado%206%20de%20mayo%20de%202019

independent and scholar-led presses —to become part of the publishing ecosystem.[19]

How To Be An Anti-Bourgeois Theorist

Hopefully, the activities I have described go some way toward explaining how and why my collaborators and I are trying to operate differently to the individualistic, liberal humanist ways of working and acting traditionally associated with being a theorist in the fields of art and culture, especially of the "star" variety. There are a number of further dimensions to this mode of practicing commons-oriented, anti-liberal, anti-neoliberal, anti-bourgeois theory (ABT) we're experimenting with. I don't have space to go into any of the related projects in depth. Besides, engaging with these ventures in their contextual site-specificity is actually the most interesting way to understand and experience them. But I would like to quickly sketch a few here, albeit more in the spirit of an artist's talk than a full-blown philosophical argument.

ABT Is Post-literary

In the era of YouTube, Instagram and Zoom, "Gutenbergian" media technologies such as the written and printed text are no longer the natural or normative means by which knowledge is necessarily generated and research communicated. Accordingly, while my collaborators and I still publish conventional print books and journal articles, our theory might not necessarily take the form of a piece of writing at all. We are increasingly involved in opening knowledge and research up to being not just postdigital, but post-grammatological or post-literary too.

We're doing this by creating, publishing and sharing work in the form of films, videos and virtual, augmented and immersive media environments. Take Oliver Lerone Schultz et al.'s collectively produced *after.video*. Published by OHP in 2016, this is a collection of annotated digital video essays that explore the future for theory after both books *and* video.[20] It does so in two different instantiations: a freely available online version; and an offline version produced as

19 https://copim.pubpub.org
20 Oliver Lerone Schultz, Adnan Hadzi, Pablo de Soto and Laila Shereen Sakr, eds., *after. video* (London: Open Humanities Press, 2016): http://www.openhumanitiespress.org/books/titles/after-video

a distinct physical object in its own right: namely, an assembly-on-demand video book stored on a Raspberry Pi computer and packaged in a VHS case. *after.video* is therefore both an analogue and digital object manifested, in a scholarly gesture, as a "video book."

after.video also points to another way in which my collaborators and I are endeavoring to open theory to being post-grammatological: this is through the reinvention of hardware, software and network infrastructures. Included in this reinvention are facilities concerned with the production and circulation of research on a radical open access basis: books and journals, for example, as with Open Humanities Press and COPIM. But we are involved in cultural/artistic projects that operate at a larger scale, too, such as museums, galleries and archives.

Let me provide an example of one such initiative that can be copied and reproduced relatively easily. Mandela27 is a website and digital platform created in 2014 by Jacqueline Cawston and her partners for the Robben Island Museum in South Africa.[21] Included in the project is a hybrid physical/digital DIY Exhibition of the prison cell in which Nelson Mandela was held for the majority of his 27 years on the island. The exhibition consists of a few pieces of standard wood and plywood, arranged to form the exact dimensions of the space, together with a bucket, blanket, bench, plate and cup—the items the prisoners were allowed to have with them in their cells. The wood frame is also used to hold ten specially designed posters addressing topics such as colonialism and apartheid, along with a number of screens linked to the digital platform and its content. The latter features an interactive cultural map of Europe and South Africa, a 360-degree experience of the prison, images from the UWC Robben Island Museum Archives, video interviews with a former political prisoner and a prison guard, a crowdsourced timeline and a digital game about life in Robben Island Prison. The original Mandela27 DIY Exhibition has toured South Africa, the UK and Europe and has been visited by over 170,000 people.[22] However, Cawston and her colleagues also put together a kit containing details of how to construct the DIY Exhibition, and made it available on an open access basis, along with the contents of the digital platform and

21 https://www.mandela27.com
22 A video of one of the exhibitions, held at the Delft Civic Centre, Cape Town in 2015, is available here: https://livecoventryac-my.sharepoint.com/:v:/g/personal/aa5237_coventry_ac_uk/ESeaLQJJuftMoMU9yWu1D80BgE_u5nVCUMlbMf7OzHrlsQ?e = agTufF

the ten posters.[23] Because the physical materials are extremely low cost (all that's needed really is some wood, a bucket and a blanket), this means any school or community can create their own pop-up version of the Mandela27 DIY Exhibition easily and cheaply—they don't need to travel to a traditional bricks-and-mortar museum or art gallery to experience it.

What *after.video* and the Mandela27 DIY Exhibition both show is that, as far as we are concerned, postdigital culture does not necessarily come *after* the digital in any simple temporal sense. Open access and the postdigital are not *just* to be associated with online communication technologies and the "digital commons," for instance. It's important they are understood as being potentially physical, offline and analogue—as well as hybrid combinations thereof —too.

ABT Is Low Key

Another dimension of our anti-bourgeois mode of theory is apparent from the way in which, although my collaborators and I may identify as radical theorists, we don't always function as virtuoso individual authors. In keeping with this notion, we often refuse to occupy center stage, preferring to operate in a more low-key, at times anonymous manner as part of collectives and communities of thinking and doing, such as the Radical Open Access Collective and WeMake. The latter is a makerspace fablab in Milan, with whom our fellow members of the Centre for Postdigital Cultures at Coventry, Valeria Graziano and Maddalena Fragnito, have been investigating the relationship between open technologies and healthcare.[24]

ABT Builds, Develops, Maintains and Repairs

In fact, our activities as theorists frequently don't involve *authoring* at all. Along with affective labor such as supporting, encouraging and inspiring, they can on occasion involve operating in the background to build, develop, maintain and repair more than actually *author*—as with the work of another collaborator as system administrator for the

---

23   https://www.mandela27.com/assets/downloads/Mandela27%20DIY%20Exhibition%20-%20Building%20Instructions.pdf
24   http://wemake.cc. See also Valeria Graziano, Zoe Romano, Serena Cangiano, Maddalena Fragnito, Francesca Bria, *Rebelling With Care: Exploring Open Technologies for Commoning Healthcare* (Milan: WeMake, 2019): http://wemake.cc/digitalsocial/cure-ribelli/

file-sharing shadow libraries Aaaaarg and UbuWeb. This is because we see theory not just as a means of imagining our ways of being in the world differently. It is a means of *enacting* them differently too.

ABT Is Performative and Pre-figurative

Many of our projects are similarly *performative*, in the sense that they're concerned not only with representing the world, but also with *intra-acting with* it in order to make things happen. Some have referred to this kind of approach as hacking the situation or context.[25] However, our theory-performances can also be understood in terms of the pre-figurative practices Graziano has written about: of "being the change we want to see."[26]

As I say, this often involves us in experimenting with the form of scholarly communications in the shape of books and journals, and also lectures, seminars, conferences, even the very gestures of reading and writing.[27] When Clare Birchall, Joanna Zylinska and I wanted to explore the theory of books being liquid and living, for instance (rather than finished and frozen or dead), we didn't just write about it. We actually made some liquid and living books that could be continually rewritten and republished: two series' worth, in fact.[28]

Other projects we are engaged in concentrate on pre-figuratively reinventing the museum, gallery, archive, library or university in a postdigital context. Public Library: Memory of the World, for example, launched by Marcell Mars and Tomislav Medak in 2012, is an "artist-run" online shadow or pirate library that contains more than 150,000 titles that it makes sure remain widely accessible without charge and without any other restrictions, including those associated with copy-

---

25   Mark Amerika, *remixthecontext* (New York: Routledge, 2018).

26   Valeria Graziano, "Prefigurative Practices: Raw Materials for a Political Positioning of Art, Leaving the Avant-garde," in Lilia Mestre and Elke Van Campenhout, eds., *Turn, Turtle! Reenacting The Institute* (Berlin: Live Art Development Agency & Alexander Verlag, 2016).

27   For the latter, see Janneke Adema and Kamila Kuc *Unruly Gestures* (2015): http://www.cultureunbound.ep.liu.se/v11/a11/unruly_gestures.mp4; and Janneke Adema and Kamila Kuc, "Unruly Gestures: Seven Cine-Paragraphs on Reading/Writing Practices in our Post-Digital Condition," *Culture Unbound: Journal of Current Cultural Research* 11, no. 1 (2019): pp. 190–208, http://www.cultureunbound.ep.liu.se/article.asp?DOI = 10.3384/cu.2000.1525.201911119

28   Clare Birchall and Gary Hall, eds., *Liquid Books* (London: Open Humanities Press, 2008): http://liquidbooks.pbwiki.com; and Clare Birchall, Gary Hall, and Joanna Zylinska, eds., *Living Books About Life* (London: Open Humanities Press, 2016): http://www.living-booksaboutlife.org

right law.[29] It consists of a network of private libraries that, although independent and maintained locally by a community of "amateur librarians," are connected with the project's server through the "let's share books" software developed by Mars. The software allows people to search all the collections in Memory of the World, *d*iscover a title they want and import it directly to their own virtual library that, like the others, is organized using a version of the Calibre open source software for managing digital books.

Given the controversial and potentially transgressive nature of Memory of the World, *it's* perhaps important to say a little more about why, as anti-bourgeois theorists, we're interested in piracy. Quite simply it's because one thing even the left finds it hard to question these days is the idea of private property. Yet it's private property that helps to construct and shape our subjectivities as both possessive individuals and members of the bourgeoisie. Piracy thus provides my collaborators and I with one starting point from which to develop an affirmative critique of private property and bourgeois subjectivity that is designed to help us be more consistent with the kind of radical politics many theorists espouse (but don't necessarily perform themselves) when writing about the commons.

Having said that, Memory of the World, like a number of our other projects, does not, as Sollfrank points out, itself constitute a "commons in the strict sense of involving not only a non-market exchange of goods but also a community of commoners who negotiate the terms of use among themselves" as equals in a voluntary, unforced, non-hierarchical fashion. That, in her words, "would require collective, formalized, and transparent types of organization." It would also require governance, including the establishment of rules for resolving conflicts between individuals, the community and society at large, and the agreeing of sanctions for those commoners who do not comply. Moreover, most of the books that are made publicly accessible by Memory of the World are "privately owned and therefore cannot simply be transferred to become commons resources." As Sollfrank suggests, such projects are perhaps best understood instead as a "preliminary stage" in which commoning is performed in an emergent,

---

29 Marcell Mars and Tomislav Medak, Public Library: *Memory of the World*: https://www. memoryoftheworld.org/blog/2015/05/27/repertorium_public_library/

participative manner. They are moving us toward a horizon of "*culture as a commons*," while at the same time providing us with the kind of "experimental zone needed to unlearn copyright and relearn new ways of cultural production and dissemination beyond the property regime."[30]

Certainly, one of the shared aims of our pre-figurative projects is to disarticulate the existing playing field and its manufactured common sense of what it means today to be a theorist, a philosopher, an academic, an artist or a political activist. They seek to foster instead a variety of antagonistic spaces both *inside* and *outside* of states and capital—spaces that contribute to the development of institutions and environments that are able to counter the hegemony of the traditional, liberal, public institutions such as the university on the one hand, and private, for-profit companies such as Elsevier, LinkedIn and Academia.edu on the other. This is the reason for our interest in the commons and commoning. *Creating Common*s is one way we have chosen to describe our work producing, managing and maintaining such alternative, emergent spaces that are neither simply liberal nor neoliberal, public nor private. The fact of the matter is, "coming prior to adequate legislation, we currently lack even a vocabulary to talk about" the commons in this sense, as the philosopher Roberto Esposito acknowledges. "It is something largely unknown, and even refractory, to our conceptual categories." (And that includes communism, I would add.) Nevertheless, as Esposito insists, the struggle for an alternative "must start precisely by breaking the vise grip between public and private … by seeking instead to expand the space of the common."[31]

The coronavirus event, with the huge systemic shock and suspension of *business as usual* it has delivered, provides us with a significant strategic opportunity to do just this. After all, Covid-19 has made it clear that, as the climate emergency develops and we continue to face health crises and other disasters, neither (globalist nor libertarian) neoliberalism nor a highly individualistic liberal humanism is going to

30 Cornelia Sollfrank, "The Surplus of Copying—How Shadow Libraries and Pirate Archives Contribute to the Creation of Cultural Memory and the Commons," in Michael Kargl and Franz Thalmair, eds., *originalcopy: Post-digital Strategies of Appropriatio*n (Berlin: de Gruyter, 2019).
31 Roberto Esposito, "Community, Immunity, Biopolitics," *Angelaki* 18, no. 3 (2013): pp. 83–90, here p. 89.

be fit for purpose. Now more than ever it is important to experiment with ways of working, acting and thinking that are different to both. For us, this is precisely what an (symbolic/functional) entity such as the Centre for Postdigital Cultures, or indeed a university, is for. One of the purposes of a university is to create a space where society's common sense ideas can be examined and interrogated, and to act as a testing ground for the development of new knowledges, new subjectivities, new practices and new social relations of the kind we are going to need in the future, but which are often hard—although not impossible—to explore elsewhere.

We're Not Necessarily Going Back To Arguing From Evidence, So Deal With It

Although I can understand the temptation to do so, we should take care when it comes to understanding such enterprises as "aesthetic practices," no matter how much they may occupy the intersection between the commons and art, and for all art is another field with the potential to create such a space where new realities can tested and constructed. To be sure, we need to interrogate the manner in which art and culture in the twentieth century became, as intellectual historian François Cusset puts it, "on the one hand, the most thriving industry of the new capitalism, if not its laboratory of ideas; and, on the other, a collection of devices and situations that were mostly disconnected from the social and political field, a kind of refuge cut off from the exterior world."[32] But this should only encourage us to ask: even if our commons-supporting projects *can* be perceived as expanding conceptions of aesthetics, so that the two discourses (i.e. the commons and aesthetics) come into close contact and can potentially create something new, might there still be something conservative about interpreting the likes of *after.video* and Memory of the World primarily in artistic terms? Isn't there a danger in doing so of going along too much with the belief that the right is interested in politics and power, while what the left cares about is art and (self-)expression?

Nor is this an issue that can be resolved by "challenging established notions of contemporary aesthetic practice" through the adoption of the kind of "truth and evidence" approach that has been proposed

---

[32] François Cusset, *How The World Swung To the Right: Fifty Years of Counterrevolutions* (Los Angeles: Semiotext(e), 2018), pp. 20–21.

as a means for artists to resist post-truth politics.[33] Media artist and activist David Garcia offers as an example the "Evidentiary Realism" of Lawrence Abu Hansen, Trevor Paglen, Lev Manovich and !Mediengruppe Bitnik.[34] The "gold standard" of Evidentiary Realism as far as Garcia is concerned, however, are the investigations into cases of state violence and human rights violations conducted by the Forensic Architecture art and knowledge research agency at Goldsmiths, University of London. Yet when it comes to engaging with postdigital political issues such a pro-evidence, pro-data stance is not without difficulties of its own.

In response to a question as to whether "identifying their outputs as art might ... 'take the edge off the truth he is trying to show'," Garcia quotes Eyal Weizman, director of Forensic Architecture, countering as follows:

> Think about it. When the most important piece of evidence coming from battle fields world wide are video graphic. You need video makers to make sense of it ... indeed aesthetic sensibilities. The sensibilities of an architect an artist or a film maker are very useful in figuring out what has taken place.[35]

Weizman is surely missing the point here, though. The problem is not whether Forensic Architecture needs to include aesthetic sensibilities in their truth-seeking investigations—and let's not forget their public art installations and exhibitions, which are arguably what they are best known for nowadays. The problem is that in positioning what they do in terms of art and aesthetics, Forensic Architecture get all the advantages that accrue from that, in terms of being nominated for the 2018 Turner Prize and so on. However, they get the disadvantages too. Not least among the latter is that Forensic Architecture's projects are indeed vulnerable to being considered *just art*. Nowhere is this danger more apparent than in the main example Garcia gives of "the

33 http://creativecommons.zhdk.ch/about/; Tatiana Bazzichelli, "Truth-Tellers: The Impact of Speaking Out," 10th event of the Disruption Network Lab, Studio 1, Berlin, November 25–26, 2016: https://www.disruptionlab.org/truth-tellers
34 David Garcia, "Beyond the Evidence," *New Tactical Research*, September 25, 2019: http://new-tactical-research.co.uk/blog/beyond-the-evidence-2/
35 Eyal Weizman quoted in Garcia, "Beyond the Evidence:." (Punctuation as in Garcia's original post.)

role Evidentiary Realism can play in countering politically motivated obfuscation": Forensic Architecture's report to the parliamentary commission investigating the role of a state intelligence agent in the 2006 murder of Halit Yozgat in an internet café in Kassel, Germany. The day before they were due to submit this report Germany's Christian Democratic Party (CDU) published a counter-report. The aim was to "de-legitimize" Forensic Architecture's findings on the grounds that it was the "work of artists" and, accordingly, "should not be taken seriously as evidence." And, to be sure, the risk of de-legitimation is very real for *aesthetic practices and sensibilities*, no matter how much they may show truth to power, nor how reflexive their relationship may be to the complex systems we inhabit. This is one of the reasons the projects of my collaborators and I constitute a plurality of forms of intervention that are responding to specific issues across a number of different sites: forms of intervention associated not *just* with aesthetics and with the practices of artists, or even theorists, but also (where appropriate) with those working in the fields of activism, education, business, politics, technology or the media.

A further concern with Evidentiary Realism's pro-data approach relates to the way in which the liberal establishment has found the politics of figures such as Trump and Johnson difficult to deal with on the basis of the agreed facts. Now there is a perfectly good explanation for this difficulty: it's because these right-wing populists are not actually operating on the level of consistent, reasoned argument. Consider Trump's description of first the climate crisis and then the coronavirus as a "hoax"—hardly an evidence-based response to the science and data on his part. Nevertheless, it's a situation a lot of commentators still find hard to accept. Instead, they continue to insist that the anti-liberal right can be contested on a truth-seeking level. Witness the spectacle of Alan Rusbridger, ex-editor-in-chief of *The Guardian*, arguing that the way to counter Johnson's evasions and lies is with good, responsible, "independent and decently crafted" journalism, in which the "lines between truth and falsehood; facts and propaganda; openness and stealth; accountability and impunity; clarity and confusion; news and opinion" are retained rather than blurred.[36] The trouble is,

---

36 Alan Rusbridger, "The Election in the Media: Against Evasion and Lies, Good Journalism is All We Have," *The Observer*, December 15, 2019, p. 47.

the roots of the current cultural crisis in democracy lie much earlier than the rise to power of the likes of Johnson and Trump: they stretch back, through the failure of the political class to hold those responsible for the financial crisis of 2008 to account, at least as far as the refusal to heed the 2003 protests against the invasion of Iraq. Both events left large numbers of people feeling they could no longer rely on professional politicians, the liberal establishment, or the state to arrive at the correct decisions based on the evidence.

It's this collapse of confidence in the processes of representative democracy and its valuing of truth and justice that the nativist right has capitalized on. They have thus been quite prepared to undermine any attempts to question their authority that privilege facts over opinion. This includes those that have come from the direction of *good journalism*—or indeed science, the media, academia and the judiciary. One way populists and their supporters have done so is by dismissing such challenges as hailing from the very partisan, city-dwelling liberal elite they denounce as being the "enemy of the people"; a people for whom they of course are speaking. Another is to undermine the veracity of the challenge by producing "alternative facts." As late as February 26, 2020 Trump was claiming the total number of Covid-19 cases in the US would be "close to zero." "On February 28, Trump said that coronavirus will 'disappear' like a 'miracle'."[37] He then predicted that the forthcoming spring weather would kill it off and prevent its spread. It's an attitude that led to an astonishing sluggishness to mobilize against Covid-19 on the part of his administration. While its effectiveness with regard to the coronavirus outbreak is certainly questionable—witness the reaction to Trump's April 23 suggestion that injecting disinfectant could kill it—the general strategy behind producing alternative facts is not so much to offer a counter-truth or even disinformation. It's to spread confusion in order to convey the overall message that no truth can be believed. (That Trump subsequently claimed he knew about the threat posed by the virus very early on but deliberately lied about it to prevent creating panic among the American people only adds to the confusion.) In the words of Hannah Arendt: "If everybody always

---

37   Katelyn Burns, "Trump's 7 Worst Statements on the Coronavirus Outbreak," *Vox*, March 13, 2020: https://www.vox.com/policy-and-politics/2020/3/13/21176535/trumps-worst-statements-coronavirus

lies to you, the consequence is not that you believe the lies, but rather that nobody believes anything any longer."[38] Or as journalist Kai Strittmatter put it recently with regard to authoritarian leaders in both China and the West: "If you're a liar and a cheat, there's no way for you to win in a world that is repelled by these things, a world that differentiates between truth and lies." What you need to do is "make everyone else a liar and a cheat, too. Then you will at least be *their* liar."[39] Indeed, it can be argued that the reason many people vote for such populist politicians is not because they actually believe their lies, or because they are necessarily right-wing nativists. It's because they know doing so is the best way to get back at a cosmopolitan liberal establishment that has ignored them for so long.

Of course, it's not an either/or (more of a Deleuze-and-Guattarian "'and… and… and'").[40] Anti-fake digital literacy initiatives, such as that set up in Finland to teach people "how to counter false information designed to sow division" by recognizing and adopting a critical attitude to fake news, are incredibly valuable.[41] This is especially the case in a time and space of contagion when rumors are rife (e.g. that Sars-CoV-2 was engineered in a lab by Bill Gates so he could profit from a vaccine, or by the Chinese government as a bioweapon). Also important are the projects and investigations of Forensic Architecture and others associated with the Evidentiary Realism movement in art. I'm thinking in particular of the former's reconstruction of the events of August 1, 2014, when Israel launched 2,000 bombs, rockets and shells against the Palestinian city of Rafah. Forensic Architecture's investigation contributed to a subsequent change in policy on the part of the Israeli government and military: namely, the withdrawal of the "Hannibal Directive," whereby the Israeli army was authorized to kill any of its soldiers taken prisoner "with maximum available

---

38 Hanna Arendt, in Roger Errera, "Hannah Arendt: From an Interview," *The New York Review of Books*, October 26, 1978.

39 Kai Strittmatter, *We Have Been Harmonised: Life In China's Surveillance State* (Exeter: Old Street Publishing, 2019), p. 18.

40 Gilles Deleuze and Félix Guattari, *A Thousand Plateaus: Capitalism and Schizophrenia* (London: Athlone, 1988), p. 25.

41 Eliza Mackintosh, "Finland is Winning the War on Fake News. What It's Learned May Be Crucial to Western Democracy," *CNN*, May 2019: https://edition.cnn.com/interactive/2019/05/europe/finland-fake-news-intl/

firepower," rather than risk them being used as hostages.[42] Still, the above concerns go some way toward articulating why, in the present postdigital conjuncture, many of my collaborators and I have taken the decision not to focus on resisting the hyper-emotionalism of post-truth politics by opposing it with empirically-based evidence presented aesthetically. When it comes to our anti-bourgeois theory-performances, we are more interested in tapping into some of the left's own affective-emotional themes and tropes—encapsulated by words such as "commons," "community," and "collective"—order to help create specific institutional and infrastructural projects that are capable of acting as a political force.

One of the motivations behind our production of free, radical open access or "pirate" knowledge objects and resources is to encourage other initiatives and movements around the world by showing what can be achieved—how things might look if the transformed habits of being and doing I'm talking about were accepted. Another is to make it possible for *chains of equivalence* to be established between our projects and a diversity of other struggles locally, nationally and internationally. In addition to those I drew attention to earlier (municipal socialism etc.), these struggles include those for a four-day working week, Green New Deal, Unconditional Basic Income and Flat-Pack Democracy.[43] There are also those featured in our Pirate Care project, the last of our initiatives I'm going to mention.

We use the term "pirate care" to refer to two processes that are particularly prevalent today. First, to the way in which basic requirements for care of a kind that were once regarded as essential to society—such as public libraries, which in the US are now not allowed to buy digital books[44]—have been driven towards illegality thanks to the commercialization of social services. Second, we use pirate care to refer to those "technologically-enabled care networks" that have sprung up

42 Forensic Architecture, The Bombing of Rafah, July 31, 2015: https://forensic-architecture.org/investigation/the-bombing-of-rafah. For more, see Eyal Weizman, "Hannibal in Rafah," *Forensic Architecture: Violence at the Threshold of Detectability* (New York: ZONE, 2018).

43 "Flatpack Democracy 2.0 – How the Independents for Frome Triggered a British and Global Wave of Community Empowerment," *The Alternative UK*, October 3, 2019: https://www.thealternative.org.uk/dailyalternative/2019/10/7/flatpack-democracy-two-zero

44 Marcell Mars, "Public Library," interviewed by Cornelia Sollfrank, *artwarez*, Berlin, February 1, 2013: http://artwarez.org/projects/GWYDH/mars.html

"in opposition to this drive toward illegality" around a range of issues, from housing and healthcare provision to education and income support.[45] Some of these networks deliberately run the risk of being considered illegal. To confine myself to those that took part in our 2019 Pirate Care conference, I can mention in this context: *SeaWatch*, which tries to save as many people as possible from drowning in the Mediterranean, in defiance of European border policy which criminalizes both migrants and rescuers;[46] and the Docs Not Cops campaign group of healthcare workers in the UK, who refuse to enforce immigration checks and charges on patients.[47] Other such "pirate" networks have decided to operate in the "narrow grey zones" of ambiguity "left open between different technologies, institutions and laws" in order to expound care as a collective political practice:

> In Italy, groups of parents without recourse to public childcare are organizing their own pirate kindergartens (Soprasotto), reviving a feminist tradition first experimented with in the 1970s. In Spain, the feminist collective GynePunk developed a biolab toolkit for emergency gynecological care, to allow all those excluded from the reproductive medical services—such as trans or queer women, drug users and sex workers—to perform basic checks on their own bodily fluids.[48]

Part of the idea behind the pirate care project is to offer these practices "some degree of protection by means of visibility."[49]

It's Not a Bug, It's a Feature

I would like to end by bringing us back once again to the commons. Notwithstanding our endeavors to establish chains of equivalence between our anti-bourgeois theory-performances and a diversity of other struggles, it's important for this network of networks to remain multi-polar, antagonistic and, to a certain extent, *messy*. Contrary to

---

45 https://www.coventry.ac.uk/research/about-us/research-news/2019/pirate-care/
46 https://sea-watch.org/en/
47 http://www.docsnotcops.co.uk
48 https://www.coventry.ac.uk/research/about-us/research-news/2019/pirate-care/
49 Valeria Graziano, Marcell Mars and Tomislav Medak, "Pirate Care: Against the Crisis," Kunsthalle Wien, March–May, 2020: https://kunsthallewien.at/en/pirate-care-gegen-die-krise/

the impression sometimes given in writing on the commons, achieving a unity, harmony or "oneness" is not what creating commons is actually about, regardless of whether it's the natural, social, civil, cultural, knowledge or intellectual commons that's being referring to. There is no common understanding of the commons. The open access, Creative Commons, free software, open source, copyfarleft and anti-copyright pro-piracy movements all have very different and conflicting conceptions of the commons, for instance.[50]

That said, we have learnt from political theorist Chantal Mouffe that the making of a decision in such an undecidable terrain—the refusal, in this case, to take the commons as a *given* and decide what it is in advance of intellectual questioning—is actually what politics is. Just as Facebook has data points that it uses to target ads at its users, so the left has data or datum points of its own; and often these *givens* take the form of the very affective-emotional fantasies and desires that constitute the basis of collective forms of left identification.[51] Does saying the kind of words that underpin most accounts of the commons—democracy, human, freedom, sharing, cooperation—not produce something of a dopamine rush in us?

My collaborators and I are aware that challenging petrified positions around community, collectivity and the commons (and around our ideas of writing, the book, the author, the seminar, university, library, museum, art gallery, copyright, private property and so on) is difficult. The tendency is to lapse back into what seems self-evident, taken-for-granted, common sense—for all one may be aware that doing so maintains the bourgeois, liberal humanist status quo, as Gramsci makes clear. Retaining a degree of multi-polarity and antagonism is therefore important. Such diversality ensures no single project, platform or conception of the commons becomes *the one to rule them all*. At the same time, it provides affective drives and resentments with a means of expressing themselves that helps avoid the kind of conflict between essentialist, non-negotiable identities and values that, as we've seen, has led to the rise of the populist right in so many countries around the world. This is why it's crucial to keep the question of how to create

50   See Gary Hall, *Pirate Philosophy* (Cambridge MA: MIT Press, 2016).
51   Caitlin Dewey, "98 Personal Data Points That Facebook Uses to Target Ads to You," *Washington Post*, August 19, 2016.

non-proprietary shared spaces and resources, along with the collective social processes that are necessary to manage and maintain them, radically open. Doing so enables the collaborative means of creating commons that we're engaged in to *remain political*, now and in the future.

Affect & Organization

Ines Kleesattel

Situated Aesthetics
for Relational Critique

On Messy Entanglements from Maintenance Art
to Feminist Server Art

If studying infrastructure implies "surfacing invisible work," as Susan Leigh Star tells us, it invokes political aesthetics.[1] Political aesthetics occur as a "redistribution of the sensible," in other words as a dissensus and expansion of the "common *aisthesis*,"[2] i.e. an anti-hierarchical shift of the visible, audible, perceivable, of what is relevant enough to matter existentially. But since all kinds of infrastructures involve service, maintenance and care labor, materialities *situated* in space and time, and a backgrounded environment usually taken for granted,[3] their study can more precisely be understood as a concern of *feminist* aesthetics in particular.

In the following, I will discuss the aesthetics of "infrastructuring," i.e. of careful practices with and within infrastructures. For this I will primarily refer to what I call the "Feminist Server Art" of Constant, a Brussels-based association for art and media, which devotes itself to (more-than-)digital technologies at the intersection of feminism, collective practice and open culture. Like all infrastructure, a Feminist Server is "fundamentally and always a relation, not a thing."[4] And even if occasionally in Constant's practice a material technical object

1 Susan Leigh Star, "The Ethnography of Infrastructure," *American Behavioral Scientist* 43, no. 3 (1999): pp. 377–391, here p. 385.
2 See Jacques Rancière, *The Politics of Aesthetics: The Distribution of the Sensible* (London: Continuum 2004); and Jacques Rancière, "Ten Theses on Politics," *Theory and Event* 5, no. 3 (2001).
3 See Ara Wilson, "The Infrastructure of Intimacy," *Signs: Journal of Women in Culture and Society* 41, no. 2 (2016): pp. 247–280.
4 Susan Leigh Star and Karen Ruhleder, "Steps towards an Ecology of Infrastructure," *Proceedings of the 1994 ACM Conference on Computer Supported Cooperative Work*, 1994, pp. 253–264, here p. 253; avilable at https://www.dourish.com/classes/readings/Star-Ruhleder-EcologyOfInf-CSCW94.pdf (all URLs in this text have been last accessed October 20, 2020)

can be located that goes by the name of a Feminist Server, this refers to much more than only the actual hardware and software. The FS is SF, so to speak, with Haraway:

> SF: science fiction, speculative fabulation, string figures, speculative femi-
> nism, science fact, so far. [...] Science fact and speculative fabulation
> need each other, and both need speculative feminism. [...] SF is a method
> of tracing, of following a thread in the dark, in a dangerous true tale of
> adventure, [... it is] passing on and receiving, making and unmaking,
> picking up threads and dropping them. SF is practice and process; it is
> becoming-with each other in surprising relays.[5]

Constant's thinking and doing of the Feminist Server as infrastructuring deals with technology as relation in a materialist as well as speculative way. Thereby the aesthetics of infrastructuring, as developed in
Feminist Server Art, are not only apt to adequately meet our troubled
techno-present, but moreover challenge the art theoretical assumptions of Relational Aesthetics, Institutional Critique, and their incom-
patibility. Through a discussion of Constant's Feminist Server Art and
with the help of Donna Haraway's theory of situatedness and relation,
I propose to rethink Relational Aesthetics as a difference-oriented *Situated Aesthetics* that articulates a non-separabilist and messily entangled Relational Critique.

But before I come to Constant's Feminist Server and how its Situated
Aesthetics give heightened relevance to both artistic critique and digital
commoning, let me elaborate on some art historical contexts. After all,
art that surfaces the hitherto invisible labor of service, care, and maintenance has half a century of history in feminist Institutional Critique.

Maintenance Art:
Institutional Critique and Relational Aesthetics

Institutional Critique has a not specifically feminist, but broader art
historical sense, denoting artistic practices since the 1960s (mainly in

---

5   Donna Haraway, *Staying with the Trouble: Making Kin in the Chthulucene* (Durham NC
     and London: Duke University Press, 2016), p. 3.

Europe and the US) which have deviated from an author- and work/object-centered understanding of art and instead deal with the art "institution" in a context-reflexive and site-specific manner. ("Institution" meaning the overall conditions of producing, distributing and perceiving the field of "art" in general and within specific social places in particular). Since artist Andrea Fraser coined the term in 1985, it has been used to cover a wide range of artists such as Michael Asher, Daniel Buren, Marcel Broodthaers, Hans Haacke, Martha Rosler, Fred Wilson, Maria Eichhorn, Renée Green, Fraser herself, and many more—all of whom focus certain structures and logics of the art institution critically. ("Critique" meaning "'exposing,' 'reflecting,' or 'revealing'" its material and ideological conditions, immanent power relations, and implicit inclusions or exclusions.)[6] There have been suggestions to distinguish different phases or generations of Institutional Critique: a first one in the 1960s and 1970s, in which the bourgeois conditions of art spaces were addressed in a more conceptual way from a somewhat *distanced* point of view (such as by Asher or Haacke); a second phase from the 1980s onwards, in which artists questioned the art institution from within, taking into account their *own entanglements and ambivalences*—at times leading to an aporetically paralyzing critique of critique (not least in Fraser herself); and a third generation, in which critical art practices merge collaboratively with other socio-political and activist practices and thus "don't exhaust themselves inside" the art field but rather *extend* their influences and effects *transversally* beyond art towards other fields of life, culture and politics.[7]

Regarding the diversity of positions and practices covered by the name of Institutional Critique as well as their discontinuities and multi-strandedness, it has also been pointed out, however, that it is neither useful nor possible to write a three-phase linear history of it.[8] And this brings me back to its feminist strand: because regarding feminist art practices, Institutional Critique is pursued transversally from the

6 Andrea Fraser, "From the Critique of Institutions to an Institution of Critique," *Artforum* 44 (September 2005): pp. 278–283, here p. 280.
7 Brian Holmes, "Extradisciplinary Investigations: Towards a New Critique of Institutions," in *Art and Contemporary Critical Practice: Reinventing Institutional Critique*, ed. Gerald Raunig and Gene Ray (London: MayFlyBooks, 2009), pp. 53–61, here p. 58.
8 See Raunig and Ray, *Art and Contemporary Critical Practice*; as well as Sabeth Buchman, "Kritik der Institutionen und/oder Institutionskritik? (Neu-)Betrachtungen eines historischen Dilemmas," *Bildpunkt. Zeitschrift der IG Bildende Kunst* (Autumn 2006): pp. 22–23.

very beginning. In the early 1970s they already engage in what Gerald Raunig later calls for in the context of neo-liberal assertions of an end to criticality—namely for "practices that conduct radical social criticism, yet which do not fancy themselves in an imagined distance to institutions; at the same time, practices that are self-critical and yet do not cling to their own involvement, their complicity, their imprisoned existence in the art field."[9] And while Fraser's art- and self-centered examinations of the art institution, its economic interests, and her own involvements in them lead her (in the aftermath of 2008's financial crisis) to state resignedly "that most forms of engagement with the art world have become so fraught with conflict for [her] that they are almost unbearable,"[10] decades earlier second wave feminists articulated with their art practices less fatalistic critiques. For artists like Mierle Laderman Ukeles, Mary Kelly, Adrian Piper, and many more, it was an inevitable prerequisite that doing art implied struggling with not only art institutional conditions, but also with patriarchal and racist divisions of cultural production at large. Of course, a "complicity" with the predominantly white male institution was maybe not so much their concern, but staying "outside" any longer was certainly not an option either. Thus, they engaged in ambivalent entanglements, worked within infrastructures—those of the art institutions and those of everyday life—and strove to transform that which seemed to be both problematic and desirable.

In her *Manifesto for Maintenance Art 1969!* Ukeles sets out the blatantly hierarchical and gendered difference in the valuation of productive-creative and reproductive-sustaining cultural work.

Two basic systems: Development and Maintenance. The sourball of every revolution: after the revolution, who's going to pick up the garbage on Monday morning?
Development: pure individual creation; the new; change; progress; advance; excitement; flight or fleeing.

9 Gerald Raunig, "Instituent Practices: Fleeing, Instituting, Transforming," in Raunig and Ray, *Art and Contemporary Critical Practice*, pp. 3–11, here p. 10.
10 Andrea Fraser, "There's no place like home," *Whitney Biennial 2012*, exhib. cat., ed. Elisabeth Sussman and Jay Sanders (New York: Whitney Museum of American Art, 2012), pp. 28–33, here p. 28; available at https://monoskop.org/images/c/c4/Fraser_Andrea_2012_Theres_No_Place_Like_Home.pdf

Maintenance: keep the dust off the pure individual creation; preserve the new; sustain the change; protect progress; defend and prolong the advance; renew the excitement; repeat the flight; show your work—show it again keep the contemporary art museum groovy keep the home fires burning [...].[11]

Ukeles then provocatively declares her entire everyday work to be "Maintenance Art," explaining:

I am an artist. I am a woman. I am a wife. I am a mother. (Random order).

I do a hell of a lot of washing, cleaning, cooking, renewing, supporting, preserving, etc. Also, (up to now separately) I "do"Art.

Now, I will simply do these maintenance everyday things, and flush them up to consciousness, exhibit them, as Art. I will live in the museum and I customarily do at home with my husband and my baby, for the duration of the exhibition. (Right? or if you don't want me around at night I would come in every day) and do all these things as public Art activities: I will sweep and wax the floors, dust everything, wash the walls [...,] cook, invite people to eat, make agglomerations and dispositions of all functional refuse.[12]

Following this manifesto, from 1970 onwards Ukeles intervenes in the institutionally taken-for-granted, by doing art that merges artistic creation with repetitive maintenance work. In several museums, she carries out cleaning and security tasks (sweeping stairs, dusting, or opening and locking buildings) herself or transfers them from service staff to curatorial staff (actually a quite logical move, after all "curating" stems from the Latin *curare*, to care for). Photo series entitled *Private Performances of Personal Maintenance as Art* moreover show her at home, brushing teeth, mopping floors and sorting socks. And she meticulously kept logs in tabular form providing information about all her activities between personal hygiene, childcare and exhibition organization. Ukeles thus simultaneously criticizes *and* adopts the

---

11 Mierle Laderman Ukeles, *Manifesto for Maintenance Art 1969!*, pp. 1–2; available at https://www.queensmuseum.org/wp-content/uploads/2016/04/Ukeles_MANIFESTO.pdf
12 Ibid., p. 3.

autonomous aesthetics of modernist abstraction (which is not least characteristic of the male-dominated Minimal Art and Concept Art of the time). Combining mundane care work with an aesthetic formalism remote from everyday life, she fosters ambivalent political aesthetics: her Maintenance Art surfaces usually invisible infrastructures of care which are a precondition for any "pure" artistic creation—and thereby problematizes the art institutional ideology of autonomy, while, provocatively and sometimes playfully, extending the aesthetic freedom from purpose to non-artistic areas of life. Its feminist Institutional Critique is thus transversal from the outset, since it subjects not only the art institution to critical reflection, but gender-specific work conditions in a broader sense, too. And in doing so, Ukeles' art evidently feeds on everyday knowledge gathered in various social fields by the political environment of contemporary feminist debates and emancipatory movements.

Remembering Ukeles' Maintenance Art, it seems rather startling that Nicolas Bourriaud, in 1998, claimed Relational Art had no art historical predecessors. His conception of Relational Aesthetics refers to artistic practices of the 1990s that deal with "the whole of human relations and their social context," by neither producing delimitable objects, nor representing or symbolizing, but rather creating situations of communality and thus actually being "ways of living [...] within the existing real."[13] Absurdly, despite leaning on artists whose work involves aspects of affective and service work as well as an awareness of hierarchies within the valuation of different types of cultural work,[14] Bourriaud's theory advocates a homogenizing, universalist understanding of social relationality. This Relational Aesthetics promotes a harmonist communality opposed to dissenting politics and critical analysis—which in turn leads to its refutation by proponents of Institutional Critique:

---

13 Nicolas Bourriaud, *Relational Aesthetics* (Dijon: Les presses du réel, 2002), pp. 113, 13.

14 Among the artists Bourriaud promotes are Christine Hill, whose art mimics classical feminized service labors, Félix Gonzáles-Torres, whose aesthetics builds on gay counterculture, and Rirkrit Tiravanija, who works with different culinary customs within the globalized urban culture of New York. For a more detailed discussion of the latter (as well as Bourriaud's shortening of relationality), see Christoph Brunner and Ines Kleesattel, "An Aesthetics of the Earth: Reframing Relational Aesthetics considering Postcolonial Ecologies," *Proceedings of the European Society for Aesthetics* 11, ed. Connell Vaughan and Iris Vidmar Jovanović (2019): pp. 106–126; available at http://www.eurosa.org/wp-content/uploads/ESA-Proc-11-2019-Brunner-Kleesattel-2019.pdf

The proposal for a Relational Aesthetics that is about, "learning to inhabit the world in a better way," seems to avoid both the element of authority inscribed within the figure of the revealer, deconstructor, liberator, and thus presumes to create "open ended" contexts for self determination that are seemingly freed from the restrictions of the state, and capitalist structures. They do not treat the institution as a privileged location [... and] avoid the predicament of being forced to take a stance on the institution's role, while working almost exclusively within them.[15]

Beyond Bourriaud, however, Relational Aesthetics must not at all be understood as difference-blind and uncritical. Not only does Félix Guattari's ecosophy (which is an important theoretical reference for Bourriaud) suggest conceiving aesthetic relationality as anti-capitalist, critical and differentiating processes of emergence;[16] Ukeles' Maintenance Art also proves how Institutional Critique and Relational Art can very well converge.

On my way to the Feminist Server, I take this art historical detour through Institutional Critique and Relational Aesthetics because their contrasting—as unfortunate as it is needless —already points to a pseudo-aporia that has recently become an issue for the *concept of the commons*. Discussing affective infrastructures within relations of material inequality, Lauren Berlant, for example, is very skeptical about the term. Whereas affirming it in an all-too-positive way runs the risk of covering over "the very complexity of social jockeying," Berlant suggests reconsidering the commons as an *action concept*, allowing us "to view what's broken in sociality"; "to dishabituate through unlearning" instead of adapting seamlessly to this brokenness, and to aspire to create transformative infrastructures "using the spaces of alterity within ambivalence."[17] As an artistic practice dealing with infrastructures of care and social relations beyond myths of

15 Walead Beshty, "Neo-Avantgarde and Service Industry. Notes on the Brave New World of Relational Aesthetics," *Texte zur Kunst* 59 (2005); available at https://www.texte-zurkunst.de/59/neo-avantgarde-and-service-industry/; see also Helena Reckitt, "Forgotten Relations: Feminist Artists and Relational Aesthetics," in *Politics in a Glass Case: Feminism, Exhibition Cultures and Curatorial Transgressions*, ed. Angela Dimitrakaki and Lara Perry (Liverpool: Liverpool University Press, 2013), pp. 131–156.

16 See Félix Guattari, *Chaosmosis : An Ethico-Aesthetic Paradigm* (Indianapolis: Indiana University Press, 1995).

17 Lauren Berlant, "The commons: Infrastructures for troubling times," *Environment and Planning D: Society and Space* 34, no. 3 (2016): pp. 393–419, here pp. 395 and 399.

individualist creation, Ukeles' Maintenance Art indicates Relational Aesthetics which are highly ambivalent. Her work is to be understood as a Relational Art which *critically* exposes institutional infrastructures while, at the same time, fostering a "learning to inhabit the world in a better way"[18] through an unlearning of disdain for maintenance work and other idealist exclusions of cultural production. Ukeles' Relational/Institutional Critique thereby not just site-specific (explicitly located in a specific social place), but moreover *situated* in the feminist sense of Donna Haraway.

I speak of *Situated Aesthetics* to emphasize that an aesthetic relationality which critically matters is one of *differentiation*, of partial connections, and an ongoing precarious commoning. Ukeles' Maintenance Art already hints at such Situated Aesthetics in a twofold way: it is conditioned by the situatedness of non-autonomous cultural care work and it engenders a materialist situating of that artistic cultural production which claims to be free from mundane constraints and messes. Being nurtured by 30 years of rich experience with feminist struggle, thinking and speculating (and having Haraway as a godmother in a way), more recent Feminist Server Art, as practiced by Constant, presents an even more complex case of Situated Aesthetics.

I would like to clarify the term "feminist"—feminist as in the Feminist Server and feminist as in Haraway's theory of Situated Knowledges. Opposing ideals of epistemic neutrality and universality, Haraway argues for a feminist science practice which "offers a more adequate, richer, better account of a world, in order to live in it well and in critical, reflexive relation to our own as well as others' practices of domination and the unequal parts of privilege and oppression that make up all positions."[19] Such an epistemically and ethically "better" account of the world would need to be based on "a view from a body" instead of on phantasms of a god-like "view from above, from nowhere, from simplicity,"[20] meaning on material entanglements, partial perspectives, and specific locations in time and space differentially relating to other bodies. Precisely, a better account of the world would need to be *situated*. Calling such a situated account feminist is not

18 Bourriaud, *Relational Aesthetics*, p. 13.
19 Donna Haraway, "Situated Knowledges: The Science Question in Feminism and the Privilege of Partial Perspective," *Feminist Studies* 14, no. 3 (1988): pp. 575–599, here p. 579.
20 Ibid., p. 589.

mere polemics against a patriarchal establishment (in the arts or in science). Rather, it proactively affirms a situatedness which some bodies are less able to dissociate themselves from than others, because they permanently *get* situated, through dominant attributions and markings, that frequently point to their restrictions. While the conditionality of male-white, non-disabled bodies and their influence on perception was made invisible for centuries, women, queers, Crips,[21] and people of color fought hard to participate actively (not just as objects) in science and cultural production despite their marked bodies. The notion of "feminist" is to be read against this historical background. In Situated Knowledges as in a Situated Aesthetics, it might act as an intersectional cipher indicating that conditionality and entanglement, positionality and partiality do not prevent a "more adequate, richer and better account of the world," but in fact make it possible.

Feminist Server Art:
Situated Aesthetics within More-Than-Digital Ecologies

Constant is a non-profit association run by artists, hackers, designers and other researchers in various collaborative constellations since 1997, creating "situations that engage with challenges of contemporary techno-life."[22] They are based in Brussels, but host and organize such situations in different locations, also internationally, often together with other artist groups and media networks. Working with digital technologies, audiovisual media, Free Software, Copyleft, networked design, collective writing, experimental publishing, and diverse forms of sociomaterial more-than-human relating, they understand technology "as being embedded in practices of maintenance, of care, of resources, of shorter and longer time frames." For Constant technologies (in a more-than-digital-sense) clearly are "about relations with things we would like to relate to, but also things we don't want to be related to."[23]

---

21 For the term "Crip" see: https://www.wright.edu/event/sex-disability-conference/crip-theory
22 Constant, http://constantvzw.org/site/More-about-Constant.html
23 Femke Snelting (with Spideralex) interviewed by Cornelia Sollfrank, "Forms of Ongoing-ness," Basel 2018; http://creatingcommons.zhdk.ch/forms-of-ongoingness/; transcript of the interview, pp. 4, 7.

Encouraging a critical, yet fearless and active approach to technology, texts published online by current and former Constant members and collaborators analyze the complex effects digital technologies have on our lives and on broader ecologies. Obtaining a deeper insight into Constant's numerous activities, however—into how they actually *do* the relations that technologies are about, and into the specific aesthetic practices coming into play in the "temporary research labs" and "otherwise-disciplined situations" called "worksessions"[24]—proves to be not too easy for someone who has not attended any of them herself. For many years now, Constant has not arranged representative events for a merely receiving audience. Instead, they issue invitations to worksessions with a limited number of participants, and they produce publications linked to these, developed through collective writing and editing processes—publications which are more experimental workbooks than classic documentaries, sometimes also including codes and digital tools for collective production. Furthermore, they host a multi-layered website that hardly provides quick overviews and ready-to-consume documentation: http://constantvzw.org/. If one takes the effort to dive into the complexly interwoven interlinkings and subpages (fig. 1), one will find a vast amount of all the material Constant and their collaborators have worked with and on over the years—published under the *Free Art License* for further use, learning, processing, modification and distribution.

Constant's online presence is openly not so much about representation as it is about infrastructures of collective creation and cultural commoning, attaching more importance to shared use value and experimentation with Open Culture content, form and means of production than to proprietorial authorship or the satisfaction of an audience remaining in a passivizing sender-receiver dichotomy. Such an approach resonates strongly with Walter Benjamin, who famously tied artistic and political quality to an "organizing function" and "exemplary character" of cultural production, and the criteria that the appa-

---

24 Constant, http://constantvzw.org/site/Call-for-participants-Collective-Conditions. html?lang = en; see also Constant's definition: "Worksessions are intensive transdisciplinary situations to which participants from all over the world contribute. Every six months Constant opens such a temporary research lab; a collective working environment where different types of expertise come into contact with each other. During work sessions we develop ideas and prototypes that in the long-term lead to publications, projects and new proposals." https://constantvzw.org/wefts/worksessions.en.html

ratus of production was "improved" in order to be more capable of turning audiences into collaborators.[25] Working in such participatory, open-ended modes certainly not mean that no preparation would be required, or that there would not be very different roles and positions within the situations hosted by Constant. But it does mean that events like the multidisciplinary symposium *Are You Being Served?* cannot be understood as a fulminant endpoint or climax of only previous research and production. Rather, such meetings are tentative manifestations within an ongoing process of Situated Aesthetics, evolving from relational trajectories as well as giving rise to further ones. The Feminist Server is just one (and immanently more than one) manifestation of Constant's longstanding Relational Critique of techno-infrastructuring. Also, strictly speaking, it is not Constant's own Feminist Server at all, because in keeping with their non-proprietary production logic, the Feminist Server's inceptions and expansions reach out in various directions far beyond Constant.

But in any case, it was Constant who organized *Are You Being Served?* in 2013 as a four-day gathering of artists, activists and other researchers dedicated "to a feminist review of mesh-, cloud-, autonomous, and DIY servers." In workshops, screenings, performances, lectures and discussions they question server-client relationships, taking the material and social implications of ubiquitous connectivity into account. Leading questions were: What is "commonly understood by terms such as server, service and hosting"? How to change violent gender stereotypes within IT environments? And how to "make current networking technologies into hospitable habitats for critique, as space for artists and solidarity, teaching and learning"?[26]

For the occasion, Constant "asked the help of a group of friends as 'hosts' to welcome and accommodate participants, integrating this 'service' into the spirit and intention of the work session."[27] There were hosting scores for the locals from Brussels who accommodated

25 Walter Benjamin, "The Author as Producer," *New Left Review* 1, no. 62 (1970): pp. 83–96.
26 Constant, https://vj14.constantvzw.org/r/about.html and https://areyoubeingserved.constantvzw.org/Introduction.xhtml; see also the book version: Anne Laforet, Marloes de Valk, Madeleine Aktypi, An Mertens, Femke Snelting, Michaela Lakova and Reni Hofmüller, *Are you Being Served? (notebooks)* (Brussels: Constant, 2015), https://areyoubeingserved.constantvzw.org/AreYouBeingServed.pdf
27 For the crucial concept of "hospitality" see Constant, https://constantvzw.org/wefts/collectivehospitality.en.html

the participants from elsewhere, as well as visiting scores for the lat-ter—since "accommodation service is a matter of protocol."[28] During the four days, among many other things, there were talks and discus-sions on the rhetoric of Open Source, on cyber harassment, on the ethics of forking code, or on Google inventing its own filiation of the "Fathers of the Internet." There was a workshop for hacking smart-phones and running them completely Open Source: "In reality, this is impossible. You can't read the source code of everything that is on your phone." But anyway: "After a full day of work, two of the fif-teen participants managed to install a more or less working system."[29] There was a performative exercise "for 32 people and 32 props" enti-tled *Home is a Server*, enacting the different tasks a server is given to publish a recipe on a wiki—"mimicking computer functioning through human energy and towards a human goal (eating the pancake instead of just publishing its recipe online)"[30] (figs. 2a and 2b). The collective preparation of meals and a careful design of the material work situa-tion played a significant role overall (fig. 3), whereby protocols and scores were repeatedly used in order to dishabituate traditional divi-sions of labor.

Moreover, there was the *Feminist Server Summit*, a daylong meet-ing of various DIY and independent server projects who narrated the "biographies" of their servers and discussed obstacles and potentials of Feminist Server practices. One of the servers presented was Amaya, who was already "dead" at the time in 2013. She had been activated and maintained by the Samedies, a group of women aligned with Free Software, some of whom got involved with Constant later, and some of whom had already been brooding over ideas for Feminist Servers since 2002. Together the Samedies appropriated and transformed a discarded network computer. Making the machine run as Amaya took two years of intense collective learning "about command line, domain name servers and Apache configuration files" as well as "decon-structing the patriarchal vocabulary of 'client' and 'server'."[31] In 2007

28 See Constant, https://areyoubeingserved.constantvzw.org/Tableau_Vivant.xhtml (my translation).
29 Gijs De Heij and Constant, https://areyoubeingserved.constantvzw.org/Freedphone.xhtml
30 Constant, https://areyoubeingserved.constantvzw.org/Home_server.xhtml
31 Femke Snelting on Amaya, http://www.newcriticals.com/exquisite-corpse/page-8. Thanks a lot to Femke Snelting for her time and willingness to deepen the narration on Amaya in particular and the Feminist Server(s) in general!

Amaya (who her facilitators thought of "as feminine, but [who] is trans")[32] went online to host projects of feminist non-profit organizations, while her* human maintenance team struggled with conflicting interests between pragmatic administration and political speculation. Tensions, ambivalences and immanent differences are uncomfortable and messy—and precisely therefore crucial for a Feminist Server Art whose Situated Aesthetics are not based on a "view from above, from nowhere, from simplicity" but rather on perspectival partialities, heterogeneously situated in time and space. After Amaya had over several years been situationally cared for through collective efforts, as creative as they were tiring, to use "the spaces of alterity within ambivalence," her services finally shut down in 2012. Younger sisters* of Amaya, however, some of whom were also present at the summit, are still actively struggling and well alive on the web—Anarcha, for example (fig. 4), a Feminist Server named after a nineteenth century African-American slave girl who was at the time subjected to brutal gynecological experiments.[33]

Amaya also has an afterlife in the *Feminist Server Manifesto*, which has been articulated subsequent to the summit (amongst others through the *Ministry of Hacking* at the *Steirischer Herbst* 2014). The Manifesto states currently:

A Feminist Server…
- Is a situated technology. She has a sense of context and considers herself to be part of an ecology of practices
- Is run for and by a community that cares enough for her in order to make her exist
- Builds on the materiality of software, hardware and the bodies gathered around it
- Opens herself to expose processes, tools, sources, habits, patterns
- Does not strive for seamlessness. Talk of transparency too often signals that something is being made invisible
- Avoids efficiency, ease-of-use, scalability and immediacy because they can be traps

32 Juliane De Moerlooze, https://areyoubeingserved.constantvzw.org/Summit.xhtml
33 See http://anarchaserver.org/

- Knows that networking is actually an awkward, promiscuous and parasitic practice
- Is autonomous in the sense that she decides for her own dependencies
- Radically questions the conditions for serving and service; experiments with changing client-server relations where she can
- Treats network technology as part of a social reality
- Wants networks to be mutable and read-write accessible
- Does not confuse safety with security
- Takes the risk of exposing her insecurity
- Tries hard not to apologize when she is sometimes not available[34]

Clearly, the Feminist Server is not just another network device with better technical capacities. More radical and molecularly revolutionary, she is rather a different—i.e. critically relational—thinking and doing of network technology. "Molecular revolution," says Guattari, "is something that I feel, that I live, in meetings, in institutions, in affects, and also through some reflections."[35]

The manifesto's Feminist Server trying "hard not to apologize when she is sometimes not available" can easily be understood in a metaphorical sense, referring to human maintenance workers within more-than-digital infrastructures. But more than this, the Feminist Server is entangled in a material-semiotic "ecology of practices" with interrelated dimensions of actual hardware and software, common infrastructures, limited resources, care- and service labors, more-than-human poetics and speculative fabulations. Considering Star's argument, that infrastructure only becomes visible when it stops functioning too well, might shift the emphasis to Constant's "radical choice to work with free software and take the consequences of that."[36] Nevertheless, the Feminist Server processes her (specifically situated and sometimes annoyingly situating) techno-material dimensions as Relational Critique transversally. Expecting servers to be permanently available and the data and services hosted by them unfailingly accessible has its costs—costs which are paid by different human and more-than-human

34 https://areyoubeingserved.constantvzw.org/Summit_afterlife.xhtml or https://esc.mur.at/de/node/1234 or https://pad.constantvzw.org/p/feministserver
35 Félix Guattari and Suely Rolnik, *Molecular Revolution in Brazil* (Los Angeles: Semiotext(e), 2007), p. 457.
36 Snelting, "Forms of Ongoingness," transcript p. 3.

earthly agents in unequally shared parts. Expectations of ubiquitous accessibility are molecularly embedded within an aesthetico-ethical culture of patriarchal-colonial mastery. The Feminist Server dissents from this culture of mastery: she troubles its persistence by irritating our expectations towards technological ecologies, by dishabituating how we (who?) are being served, and at what costs (for whom?). At all the different dimensions at which "Home is a Server," the Feminist Server tries to decolonize master-servant dichotomies, much as literary scholar Julietta Singh recommends saying: "We must begin to exile ourselves from feeling comfortable at home (which so often involves opaque forms of mastery), turning instead towards forms of queer dispossession that reach for different ways of inhabiting our scholarly domains."[37]

The Feminist Server is a relational critic—situated, not distant, engaged in better accounts of technology, not so much mastering it, rather relating with it. One of her crucial aesthetic conducts is introducing images and imaginations, concepts and vocabularies, habits and dishabituations, that suggest technology to be not "so much about control and separation and segmentation," as Constant member Femke Snelting says, but rather about ambivalent interdependencies and ecological ongoingness.[38] Hence, the Feminist Server's situated aesthetics are more-than-human and more-than-digital in Guattari's ecosophical sense: "Without a change in mentalities, without entry into a postmedia era, there can be no enduring hold over the environment. Yet, without modifications to the social and material environment, there can be no change in mentalities."[39] Within such an ecology of practices the Feminist Server might occasionally manifest as a material object—like Amaya's now shutdown computer hardware, which the Samedies used to call "the pizza-box" (fig. 5). Yet the Feminist Server always remains messily and delimitedly enmeshed, transcending any reductionist here-and-now of the one separable object through her Situated Aesthetics. She is multiple Feminist Servers, entangled in ecologies of resources and care, ambivalent commoning and not yet actualized

---

37 Julietta Singh, *Unthinking Mastery: Dehumanism and Decolonial Entanglements* (Durham NC and London: Duke University Press, 2018), p. 8.
38 Snelting, "Forms of Ongoingness," transcript p. 9.
39 Félix Guattari, "Remaking Social Practices," in *The Guattari Reader*, ed. Gary Genosko (Cambridge MA and Oxford: Blackwell, 1996), pp. 262–272, here p. 264.

infrastructuring. Her collective and ongoing mattering thus evolves not least as a figure of speech and "powerful thinking tool."[40]

Situated Aesthetics involve material-semiotic *poetics*—not in the sense of poetry, but of the Latin *poeisis*, creation or fabrication. Although Haraway's considerations on situating are originally formulated in the context of critical science studies and ethical epistemology, they imply an aesthetic theory, too. Not only do they rely on metaphors of the visual (like "gaze" or "perspective") to emphasize that knowledge and science are always materially embodied and located practices of sense-making; also Haraway, who herself as a writer practices situated poetics, shows throughout her work how all knowledge is composed of images, figurations, metaphors and narratives, which in turn have world-making effects—and clearly not in a radical-constructivist way, since all poetic sense-making is material-semiotic and entangled within more-than-human ecologies. "We shape our tools and our tools shape us. Diversity is essential to also create diversity of expression,"[41] was also a conclusion of the *Feminist Server Summit.* If the Feminist Server(s) are imaginary, they are so neither as phantasmas detached from the present reality nor in an uncritical manner. Sophie Toupin and Spideralex call for reimagining hacking as a "feminist techno-speculative storytelling, fiction and design." And just like Haraway they do so not to turn their backs on the material world, but quite the contrary—since speculative fabulation is a way

> to re-imagine technological and infrastructural entanglements that shape our world. It also serves to expose technologies and infrastructures that have furthered (neo)colonial processes such as the stealing and erasing of indigenous scientific knowledges and techniques, and the shattering of liberation struggles. By shedding light on these contradictions, doing *speculatively* also attempts to de-privilege and de-glorify science and technology. De-privileging the assemblage of humans and technology (non-human) echoes the act of making visible and valuing other types of assemblage with the non-human, such as with land, animals and plants.[42]

40 Snelting, "Forms of Ongoingness," transcript p. 6.
41 Constant, https://areyoubeingserved.constantvzw.org/Summit.xhtml
42 Sophie Toupin and Spideralex,"Radical Feminist Storytelling and Speculative Fiction: Creating new worlds by re-imagining hacking," *Ada: A Journal of Gender, New Media, and Technology* 13 (2018); https://adanewmedia.org/2018/05/issue13-toupin-spideralex/

The Feminist Server(s) practice(s) infrastructuring within the more-than-human ecologies of a commonly but unequally shared world. Situated Aesthetics of Feminist Server Art are thereby even more differentiating than the Relational Critique of the 1970s Maintenance Art: The Feminist Server's intertwining of critical analysis and relational transformation happens (firstly) in *collaborations,* which, according to Constant member Peter Westenberg, pivotally involve friction and potential conflict—fortunately, since: "Finding points of non-community […] and areas of dissent might open up routinious ways of working together and inspire doing togetherness differently."[43] Within conflicts and heterogeneities the Feminist Server processes new material-semiotic modes of thinking and doing infrastructures differently. Thereby her aesthetics (secondly) indicate how situating is not a mere matter of empiricist enumeration, but rather an active relating and speculative fabulation—because semiotic-material tools, which allow for less masterly infrastructuring, have partially yet to be fabricated. The Feminist Server is not least an aesthetic training ground for what is not present yet but could and should become. Also for this reason (thirdly) Constant does not publish "final cut" monological and overview representations of the Feminist Server(s), but only "evolving documentaries," i.e. open infrastructures for "complex stories that would develop over time, and which could best be told from a variety of points of view."[44]

43 Peter Westenberg, http://media.constantvzw.org/v/iterations_2017_2020/2_intro_itera-tions.html
44 Michael Murtaugh, "What's wrong with the YouTube documentary?," (2008), http://ac-tivearchives.org/wiki/What%27s_wrong_with_the_YouTube_documentary%3F

Sophie Toupin

The Commons, Sociotechnical Imaginaries and Resistance

Introduction

When Stefanie Wuschitz was working as a Digital Art Fellow at the University of Umea, Sweden, in 2008, she had an idea. Wuschitz wanted to set up a feminist hackspace[1] to generate a culture of fearless making and hacking for women and gender nonconforming people. A year later, Mz* Baltazar's Laboratory was born in Vienna. The feminist hackspace situated at the intersection of art and technology was to grow over the years through, among others, Wuschitz's Ph.D. dissertation on the subject. This feminist lab, which at the time was quite unique—feminist hackerspaces and makerspaces were to start emerging more widely around 2013–2014—was rooted in the philosophy of "open source," as it allowed furthering an open culture of sharing and collaboration. What animated the vision of Mz* Baltazar was an idea of science and technology grounded in feminist and commons perspectives. This type of practice, that aims at prefiguring a future at the intersection of the social and the technical as Mz* Baltazar's Laboratory did, was to be conceptualized in 2015 as *sociotechnical imaginary* by theorist Sheila Jasanoff in collaboration with Sang-Hyun Kim.[2] The concept referred to visions of science and technology that carried ideas about public purposes, collective futures, and the common good.

The practice and imaginary embraced by Mz* Baltazar's Laboratory are in striking contrast with mainstream tech culture. In fact, most technological interactions and encounters follow the sociotechnical imaginaries of Silicon Valley's tech companies. It is the Jeff Bezoses and Mark Zuckerbergs of this world who create and modulate many

---

1   I use the term hackspace when speaking about Mz* Baltazar's Laboratory because it is their preferred designation. Otherwise, I use hackerspaces.

2   Sheila Jasanoff and Sang-Hyun Kim, eds., *Dreamscapes of Modernity: Sociotechnical Imaginaries and the Fabrication of Power* (Chicago: University of Chicago Press, 2016).

aspects of our digital and non-digital realities: how we interact and participate online, what is done with the data we produce, what we are shown by the algorithms, the labor conditions and the impact on digital and non-digital workers. Far from embracing a collective future of genuine open culture oriented toward social justice, these technologies are based on an extractivist logic that is powered by our data, data sets and metadata that are gendered and raced. Nick Couldry and Ulises Ali Mejias discuss this new condition that is affecting us all and identify it as "colonization by data."[3] This new form of colonization, they suggest, is a key dimension of how capitalism has evolved by making our data and metadata the target of profitable extraction.

Until about the year 2000, when data extractivist logic had not yet fully permeated our digital lives, we lived in a world where there was a clearer opposition between the digital commons, developed as part of the non-market orientation, and what was then called e-commerce and the emerging knowledge economy. On the one hand there were free and open source software, copyleft, copyfarleft and Creative Commons licenses that enabled a practice grounded in open or *libre* culture, while on the other hand, there were proprietary software and digital copyrights that furthered a strictly commercial logic. As the border between the two aforementioned logics has become more porous, with tech companies using open source code for their consumer products, part of the struggle lies in the kind of sociotechnical imaginaries that power our technologies and sociotechnical practices.

In what follows, I focus on three main case studies of organizations, namely Mz* Baltazar's Laboratory, Tactical Tech and Nossas Cidades, that all place the digital and non-digital commons at the center of their practice and imaginaries. I use these case studies to discuss the type of practices associated with the commons that these organizations have developed, and which enable them to showcase their sociotechnical imaginary. I ask two interrelated questions: First, what are the types of infrastructure and/or methodologies these organizations build to further the digital and non-digital commons? Second, what are the sociotechnical imaginaries associated with them?

3   Nick Couldry and Ulises Ali Mejias, *The Costs of Connection: How Data Is Colonizing Human Life and Appropriating It for Capitalism.* Culture and Economic Life (Stanford: Stanford University Press, 2019).

I start from the general premise that resistance is a form of aesthetics, because it demands a creative process to think about the ways in which to resist. Free and open source software is such an example at the sociotechnical level, but it also goes beyond a form of resistance to proprietary software, as it can be considered a form of craft in and of itself. Gabriella Coleman points to free and open source communities as having an ethic and aesthetics of tinkering.[4] As we will see below, the examples under study all have an aesthetic of tinkering which materializes with the infrastructure, sociotechnical imaginaries and methodologies they build, update and maintain. In this sense, thinking and enacting alternative sociotechnical imaginaries that propose new ways of conceiving sociotechnical practice are a form of aesthetic.

Commons: Digital and Space-Based

I begin with a short history of what we call today the digital commons and how it is interrelated with a space-based commons practice. It sets the stage to show how the organizations under study have come up with methodologies and/or infrastructures that foreground open culture despite the blurring between open source software and capital. At least one of the stories of the digital commons and their relationship to space-based commons may be traced back to the free/libre and open source software (FLOSS) movement, which originated in the hacker culture of the early 1960s. I focus on this narrative, because it underlies the work of the three organizations under study.

At the Massachusetts Institute of Technology (MIT) Tech Model Railroad Club (TMRC), students tinkered collectively and in a common(s) space with model railroads, technical objects and mainframe computers. Many of these students were also members of the MIT Artificial Intelligence Laboratory where computer programming and AI were tinkered with, and where an aesthetic of tinkering emerged as part of the hacker culture.[5] The type of commons created through the

---

4   Gabriella Coleman, *Coding Freedom: The Ethics and Aesthetics of Hacking* (Princeton: Princeton University Press, 2013).
5   Ibid.

emergence of this computer practice involved both online and space-based activities. Open culture has been an essential part of the hacker practice where the ideal was to allow anyone to participate, share and collaborate. The open culture ideal is still visible today within hacker spaces, hacker conferences and hacker camps where hackers meet face to face to enjoy one another's comradeship, show each other's projects and collaborate in real life.[6]

It is however only in the 1980s that FLOSS crystallized around a number of projects, among which was Gnu is Not Unix (GNU). GNU was an alternative to Unix, insofar as it was freely available for everyone to modify, use, study, or redistribute. Then, after the creation of the Free Software Foundation in 1985, the organization published a General Public License (GPL) four years later and framed it as a legal hack. The GPL guaranteed four freedoms for users: the freedom to access the software code, the freedom to copy the software, the freedom to modify it, and the freedom to release modified versions under the same conditions. This license provided a legal framing for the creation and sharing of free software, but also created a sociotechnical practice and imaginary that subverted copyrights. In doing so, the community of commoners behind this movement challenged the assumptions and imaginary about software and competition, self-interest, and the maximization of private profit. Instead, it foregrounded a sociotechnical imaginary of sharing, a belief in productive freedom and a different understanding of what values are and how they circulate within communities.[7] While the ideas, philosophy and imaginary emanating from these projects were oriented towards social justice—Femke Snelting maintains that FLOSS principles are feminist at their core[8]—the community around FLOSS is

6 Gabriella Coleman, "The Hacker Conference: A Ritual Condensation and Celebration of a Lifeworld," *Anthropological Quarterly* 83, no. 1 (2010): pp. 47–72.
7 Benjamin J. Birkinbine, *Incorporating the Digital Commons: Corporate Involvement in Free and Open Source Software*. Critical, Digital and Social Media Studies (London: University of Westminster Press, 2020); Coleman, *Coding Freedom*.
8 Snelting states that the group she is part of—Constant, an artist-run organization in the fields of art, media and technology—understands that "our radical choice to work with free software [is a] conviction that the free software manifesto was a feminist manifesto. Because [...] it connects to feminist values" (transcript p. 3). It is in this way that Snelting affirms that collaboration, sharing and libre culture at the center of free software are also feminist values, and that feminists should embrace FLOSS. See Cornelia Sollfrank, "Forms of Ongoingness, Interview with Femke Snelting and spideralex," October 19, 2019, *Creating Commons*. http://creatingcommons.zhdk.ch/forms-of-ongoingness/ (all links in this text were last accessed October 22, 2020).

well known for being composed of white males,[9] with low participation of women and lack of diversity, and for reinforcing patriarchy in both digital and offline worlds.[10] The FLOSS imaginary is too often represented by Steven Levy's hacker ethics of an idealized meritocratic community, full of blind spots towards gender, class, race and politics and hence dominated by white men unaware of their privileges.[11]

In the early 2000s, ideas about the digital commons continued to flourish and caught the interest of scholars.[12] Researching FLOSS communities, Yochai Benkler understood this practice as a form of commons-based peer production.[13] He defined this form of production as "a new modality of organizing production: radically decentralized, collaborative, and non-proprietary; based on sharing resources and outputs among widely distributed, loosely connected individuals who cooperate with each other without relying on either market signals or managerial commands."[14] Benkler's theorization furthered Elinor Ostrom's understanding of the commons. In her pioneering work, Ostrom showed that self-organized forms of governance within groups or collectives represented an alternative to either the state or the

9   In 2001, Ghosh, Glott, Krieger and Robles found that only 1.1% of free/libre and open source software developers within the European Union were women. See A. Rishab Ghosh, Ruediger Glott, Bernhard Krieger and Gregorio Robles, *Free/libre and open source software: Survey and study* (2002) www.math.unipd.it/ ~ bellio/FLOSS%20Final%20 Report%20-%20Part%204%20-%20Survey%20of%20Developers.pdf (accessed July 25, 2020). More recently, Github made a study to understand the demographic that was using its platform and only 5% of respondents were women. See Github, *Open source survey* (2017). https://opensourcesurvey.org/2017/#about
10 Last year, Richard Stallman resigned from his position as president of the Free Software Foundation and from its board of directors. His resignation followed major criticisms regarding a misogynist message he sent to a mailing list concerning the Jeffrey Epstein sex trafficking affair. Apart from this particular example, Stallman was known for his sexist and misogynist behavior towards women over the years. See Geek Feminism Wiki, Richard Stallman, n.d. https://geekfeminism.wikia.org/wiki/Richard_Stallman
11 Steven Levy, *Hackers: Heroes of the Computer Revolution*, 25th anniversary edition (Sebastopol CA: O'Reilly Media, 2010).
12 Kleiner discusses how, before professionals such as lawyers and professors started the fight against copyright, artists had been at the forefront of the struggle. He also lays out an important criticism of creative commons. See Dmytri Kleiner, *The Telekommunist Manifesto* (Amsterdam: Network Notebooks 3, 2010). https://media.telekommunisten.net/manifesto.pdf
13 Yochai Benkler, *The Wealth of Networks: How Social Production Transforms Markets and Freedom* (New Haven NJ: Yale University Press, 2006).
14 Yochai Benkler, "Coase's Penguin, or, Linux and The nature of the firm," *The Yale Law Journal* 112, no. 3 (2002): pp. 369–446.

market.[15] Benkler thus applied the theory of the commons to FLOSS and what was later to be termed digital commons.

To experiment with the commons, to socialize and tinker with technologies, hackers, makers and geeks have created hackerspaces which are volunteer-run spaces. Hackerspaces have existed since the 1990s, but the more open variety began to mushroom after 2007.[16] These self-organized spaces constitute a commons which is space-based, and where members often produce digital commons, thereby bridging the digital and space-based commons. In these spaces, hackers, makers and geeks actualize their sociotechnical imaginary grounded in open culture. They create spaces they consider open and within those spaces work on all sorts of digital and/or non-digital commons projects.

In 2003, Lawrence Lessig, who had written an influential book[17] affirming that code is law, created the Creative Commons licenses, another influential legal hack to further an open culture (though not as free as in *libre* culture[18]). This consisted in a second phase of the history of the digital commons, as it went beyond hackers and computer programmers. Creative Commons created legal tools that enabled not only computer programmers but other creators (artists, academics, etc.), to choose the type of licenses under which they wanted to place their work. The goal of Creative Commons was to give creators the choice to grant users a different degree of freedom in the ways in which they could re-use or modify their work.[19]

These shifts corresponded to the "digital rights" movement that grew in the 2000s as an alternative to the expansion of a regime of intellectual property. While it represents an opposition to intellectual property often active in the advocacy and policy realms, it remains that this movement generally adopts a rights-based framework. One of the

15 Elinor Ostrom, *Governing the Commons: The Evolution of Institutions for Collective Action.* The Political Economy of Institutions and Decisions (Cambridge: Cambridge University Press, 1990).
16 Sophie Toupin, "Feminist hackerspaces: The synthesis of feminist and hacker cultures," *Journal of Peer Production* 10 (2014). http://peerproduction.net/editsuite/issues/issue-5-shared-machine-shops/peer-reviewed-articles/feminist-hackerspaces-the-synthesis-of-feminist-and-hacker-cultures/ (accessed July 1, 2020)
17 Lawrence Lessig, *Code and Other Laws of Cyberspace* (New York: Basic Books, 1999).
18 For a critique see Kleiner, *The Telekommunist Manifesto.*
19 As for the non-commercial and the non-derivative clauses of the Creative Commons and open source licenses, they were introduced at the request of artists, who wanted to retain the commercial incomes and creative control (no remixes).

organizations under study, Tactical Tech, grew out of this momentum in the early 2000s, while the Brazilian organization Nossas Cidades came out of a similar impetus about ten years later. Non-profit organizations that are part of the digital rights movement usually do not question the rights-based framework, which is rooted in a liberal imaginary of autonomous individuals that is part and parcel of capitalism.[20]

There is currently a major risk of the digital commons being privatized and enclosed. This is done on multiple fronts of which I state a handful. Digital commons advocates argue that the Internet should be seen as part of the common good, having been funded by public money and allowing for the circulation of content and artifacts.[21] However, since the turn toward the commercialization of the Internet in 1995, the appropriation of digital commons has expanded and has become a cause of great concern. Companies are enclosing the Internet into closed platforms (Netflix, Amazon Prime, Facebook, etc.) which are built on public infrastructures. Another reason for concern with the digital commons is that GAFAM (Google, Apple, Facebook, Amazon and Microsoft) are using the digital commons to further some of their services. As a case in point, Wikipedia and its content, which are under a Creative Commons license, are being used by Apple and Amazon to render Siri (Apple) and Alexa (Amazon), their virtual assistants (chat bots), more powerful. The Wikimedia foundation has asked GAFAM to give them more funding and as a result this situation is creating issues of dependency.[22] The new process of enclosure at play is that Wikipedia entries made by volunteers provide part of the intelligence and intelligible data for GAFAM chat bots, which are then sold to customers through smart speaker devices like Amazon Echo. GAFAM are leeching off intelligible data and datasets from the Internet that are considered as part of the digital commons for their profit and market dominance through new products. The digital commons are

---

20 For a critique of rights, a rights-based approach and its entanglement with capitalism, see Radha D'Souza, *What's Wrong with Rights? Social Movements, Law and Liberal Imaginations* (London: Pluto Press, 2018).

21 François Soulard, "The Internet as a Common Good: Framework and Perspectives for a Citizen Internet," *Wall Street International*, October 31, 2018. https://wsimag.com/science-and-technology/44147-the-internet-as-a-common-good

22 Rachel Withers, "Amazon Owes Wikipedia Big-Time," *Slate*, October 11, 2018. Retrieved from https://slate.com/technology/2018/10/amazon-echo-wikipedia-wikimedia-donation.html

also bought back by capital such as Github, a major platform to host and develop open source software projects, which Microsoft acquired in 2018.[23] GAFAM's interest in digital commons and the use of FLOSS is to reduce costs, go faster with the production of software and access pools of data and datasets to train their powered AI devices. What happens then is that the work—such as FLOSS, data and Wikipedia entries—produced as part of the digital commons is re-appropriated by companies which privatize it in the final product they sell to consumers. In these scenarios the digital commons are at great risk of being privatized and owned through the making of new products. The question arises: what needs to be done to deal with new types of enclosures that profit from the digital commons? Part of the work that needs to be done might be to create commons datasets that can only be used according to certain principles and modalities. Could the GPL be expanded to include data and datasets?

While the above picture of how digital commons have become re-appropriated by capital is a cause of concern, there are new methodologies for creating the commons that are emerging. In no way do the methodologies that I will present challenge the power of capital as briefly laid out above, but they are no less micro examples of resistance. Before I focus on a handful of these new practices, however, I will give an overview of what sociotechnical imaginaries are and mean, and where they come from.

Sociotechnical Imaginaries

Recently, activists have developed methodologies to create narratives to imagine alternatives to existing oppressive and dystopian models of technologies.[24] Spideralex, a sociologist, doctor in social economy and founder of the Catalan cyberfeminist collective Donestech, has developed exciting methodologies to collectively dream about desired futures and to unleash new sociotechnical imaginaries. She calls her

23 Gavin Mueller, "Microsoft and the Yeoman Coders," *The Jacobin Magazine*, June 13, 2018. https://jacobinmag.com/2018/06/github-microsoft-open-source-code-technology
24 Spideralex, "Futurotopias: Speculative fiction workshops on feminist technologies," Anarchaserver, May 29, 2019. https://zoiahorn.anarchaserver.org/specfic/2019/05/29/futurotopias-speculative-fiction-workshops-on-feminist-technologies/

methodology for crafting collectively new socio-technical imaginaries "futurotopia." The workshops she organizes aim at prefiguring desired futures; they take, though not explicitly, a Black feminist approach that recognizes the patriarchal, colonial, and imperial past that is shaping our present and future, including science and technology. These workshops have supported the feminist servers a number of feminist tech collectives run and maintain, in addition to reprogramming the minds of the participants on creating narratives of how to speak about and think about technology from feminist decolonial perspectives.

There is a long tradition of thinking about collective imaginaries as social practices. It has been studied in several disciplines including philosophy, sociology, Black feminism and more recently in science and technology studies (STS). As there are multiple histories of how to understand the emergence of sociotechnical imaginaries, I give below a few references for how the term has been built in scholarship. Benedict Anderson imagined communities coalesce around a number of defining values to assert the development of nations.[25] He comes to define a nation as "an imagined community–and imagined as both inherently limited and sovereign."[26] His main argument can be extended to other groups in the sense that communities emerge around shared ideas of collectivity. Adding an important layer to the conversation about social imaginaries, Arjun Appadurai showed that a plurality of imaginaries could coexist.[27] The existence of many imaginaries, as Appadurai asserts, has become an organized field of social practices, and a form of negotiation between sites of agency which define the fields of possibilities.

Drawing on Anderson, the philosopher Charles Taylor proposes the concept to explain how people imagine their collective social life.[28] His definition of the imaginary emphasizes its social and normative dimensions:

25 Benedict Anderson, *Imagined Communities: Reflections on the Origin and Spread of Nationalism* Revised ed. (London: Verso, 2006 [1983]).
26 Ibid., p. 1.
27 Arjun Appadurai, *Modernity at Large: Cultural Dimensions of Globalization* (Minneapolis: University of Minnesota Press, 1996).
28 Charles Taylor, *Modern Social Imaginaries*. Public Planet Books (Durham NC: Duke University Press, 2004).

By social imaginary, I mean something much broader and deeper than the intellectual schemes people may entertain when they think about reality in a disengaged mode. I am thinking, rather, of the ways people imagine their social existence, how they fit together with others, how things go on between them and their fellows, the expectations that are normally met, and the deeper normative notions and images that underlie these expectations.[29]

Black radical feminists are also important to the story of imaginaries, especially when it comes to thinking about liberation from multi-layered forms of oppression. In fact, their understanding of freedom has enlarged and deepened the Black radical imagination in producing a vision of liberation for all.[30] The emancipation of Black women is being understood as a commitment to liberating all people, and necessitating the reconstruction of social relations. In this vision of transforming society, reparation from slavery, colonialism, and other forms of oppression are at the core. Robin Kelley documents the history of radical intellectuals and artists from the African diaspora in the United States, and suggests that creating new knowledge and new dreams is an act of liberation in and of itself. In other words, he argues that the collective Black imagination constitutes an actual liberation movement. In this framework, imagination and politics are closely tied together. Understanding the Black imagination to be part of an act of liberation also opens new aesthetic forms of understanding politics.

Science and technology is often the forgotten dimension of the aforementioned approaches. It is the work of STS scholars that has emphasized the imaginary as a social practice and as a vision of a future (utopian and/or dystopian) mediated by technology. The work of Sheila Jasanoff with Sang-Hyun Kim is particularly interesting, since it focuses specifically on sociotechnical imaginaries. Jasanoff and Kim define sociotechnical imaginaries as "collectively held, institutionally stabilized, and publicly performed visions of desirable futures, animated by shared understandings of forms of social life and social order attainable

---

29 Ibid., p. 23.
30 bell hooks, *Feminism Is for Everybody: Passionate Politics* (Cambridge MA: South End Press, 2000); Robin D. G. Kelley, *Freedom Dreams: The Black Radical Imagination* (Boston MA: Beacon Press, 2002).

through, and supportive of, advances in science and technology."[31] According to their definition, science and technology are seen as a central component of the social imagination of modernity. By emphasizing the aspect of desired or desirable futures, Jasanoff and Kim link these ideas to a positive vision of social progress brought about by science and technology. Further, Jasanoff and Kim demonstrate that technological development, like science fiction, is in constant interaction with the social context that inspires and supports its production. Interesting for this chapter, Jasanoff and Kim point to how visions of scientific and technological progress carry with them implicit ideas about public purposes, collective futures, and the common good. They state that "through the imaginative work of varied social actors, science and technology becomes enmeshed in performing and producing diverse visions of the collective good, at expanding scales of governance from communities to nation-states to the planet."[32]

Intersectional Feminist Sociotechnical Imaginaries: Three Examples

The three case studies to follow, namely Nossas Cidades, Mz* Baltazar's Laboratory and Tactical Tech aim at better understanding the relationship between sociotechnical imaginaries, the commons, and infrastructures and/or methodologies. All share the belief that technologies play an important role in bringing about desired futures, and may be used toward progressive goals, as highlighted by Jasanoff and Kim. Further, all of the case studies selected are examples of how sociotechnical imaginaries are collectively held, institutionally stabilized, and publicly performed. The principles of open culture that are embraced by the organizations under study include, among others, open source software and Creative Commons licensing. In this sense, the organizations build on the sociotechnical imaginaries of the FLOSS community, but also go beyond it. They do so by focusing on the social actors engaged in the spaces created, the developers of the said technologies/spaces, the purposes for which the technologies are built

---

31 Jasanoff and Kim, *Dreamscapes of Modernity*, p. 4.
32 Ibid., p. 11.

and the pedagogical dimension necessary for sociotechnical imaginaries to collectively emerge.

Nossas Cidades

In 2017, a group of activists in Brazil designed a feminist open source chat bot called *Betânia* or *Beta* for short. *Beta* was a feminist text-based chat bot programmed to provide intersectional feminists, including Afro-Brazilian feminists and LGBTQI+ in Brazil, a tool for organizing around reproductive justice.[33] It was specifically designed to stop an anti-reproductive justice amendment to the Brazilian constitution that was proposed by a right-wing political MP and which would have criminalized abortion among other measures. *Beta* was initiated by the Brazilian non-profit laboratory for activism called Nossas Cidades (Our Cities) as a way to support and amplify street activism, and to continue pre-figuring the type of feminist future they want to live in. Despite the problematic politics of Facebook, Nossas Cidades built a bot that was compatible with Messenger—widely available and well-known[34]—to open new ways of engaging in the political process. What they realized from past online actions is that sending emails for mobilization purposes had little traction anymore, so they prototyped a new channel for political mobilization capable of generating more engagement with the tools used by feminist activists.[35] Once you downloaded the bot, *Beta* sent mass messages to its entire base inviting them to action. Nossas Cidades had identified the limitation of using Facebook to further their campaign, but decided to make a compromise to reach their short term goal. In this way they were able to meet feminists where they are and mobilize them in a time of crisis. *Beta* used to its advantage the new automated personalized advertisement feature

---

33 Sophie Toupin and Stephane Couture, "Feminist Chatbots as part of the feminist toolbox," *Feminist Media Studies* 20, no. 5 (2020): pp. 737–740. https://doi.org/10.1080/14680777.2020.1783802

34 Feminists in Brazil are widely using Facebook for their activism and Brazil is the country in the world with the fourth highest number of Facebook users. https://www.statista.com/statistics/268136/top-15-countries-based-on-number-of-facebook-users/

35 Caio Calado, "Beta Feminista —Uma Entrevista Com o Time Responsável Pela Criação Do Bot Feminista," *Medium*, February 25, 2018. https://medium.com/botsbrasil/beta-feminista-uma-entrevista-com-o-time-respons%C3%A1vel-pela-cria%C3%A7%C3%A3o-do-bot-feminista-bba17-6c3fa285e41

launched by Facebook a year earlier.[36] Anyone who downloaded the
bot on Messenger could converse with *Beta* about the importance of
feminist reproductive justice, but one of its main features was to automate the process of sending emails to Brazilian MPs regarding *Beta*
users' disagreement with the proposed bill. You only had to provide
your email address and *Beta* automated the process. Ultimately, the
huge street and online activism succeeded in defeating the bill.[37]

With *Beta* a group of activists managed to develop a successful
mobilization and pedagogical tool embodying a feminist sociotechnical imaginary, in effect overriding the dominant imaginary of the corporate platform. But what is a bot? A bot is a general term to describe
any software that automates tasks. Chat bots can automate text-based
or voice conversations on a number of platforms including Facebook
Messenger, Telegram and Twitter. Chat bots and other types of bots
are widely used by governments and companies to provide services to
customers and citizens. In these scenarios, chat bots are simply providing information to those using them, and as the aforementioned
example of Siri and Alexa show, these chat bots use content built as
part of the digital commons and re-appropriate it for new consumer
products. These bots are often thought of as replacing the labor of
people, articulating a dystopian view about automation and the loss
of jobs. Moreover, bots including chat bots have been widely used
for misinformation and disinformation campaigns, such as for climate
change denialism and for influencing elections in Brazil, India, the
United States and elsewhere.[38]

Beta's source code is free and open, and since the beginning of its
design phase has been available on Github, thus making it accessible
as a digital commons for all to replicate for other activists campaign-
ing. Those who worked on *Beta*, who are from all genders, furthered
the imaginary of the FLOSS community, but for and from an intersectional feminist perspective. The imaginary that sustains *Beta* is a

36 David Marcus, "Messenger Platform at F8," April 12, 2016. https://about.fb.com/news
    /2016/04/messenger-platform-at-f8/
37 Calado, "Beta Feminista."
38 Oliver Milman, "Revealed: quarter of all tweets about climate crisis produced by bots,"
    The Guardian, February 21, 2020. https://www.theguardian.com/technology/2020/
    feb/21/climate-tweets-twitter-bots-analysis; Luca Luceri, Ashok Deb, Silvia Giordano and
    Emilio Ferrara, "Evolution of Bot and Human Behavior During Elections," *First Mon-
    day* 24, no. 9 (2019), https://doi.org/10.5210/fm.v24i9.10213

technology that empowers feminists and their self-determination over reproduction through mobilization and pedagogy. Moreover, the virtual chat bot refers back to the body, not separating the virtual and the face-to-face, but making them intrinsically connected. *Beta* is an example of a technology that foregrounds a feminist sociotechnical imaginary that is about understanding bots as a new form of media that can be strategically used by feminist activists to amplify their actions. This new objective for using bots is not a way to replace activism by bots. Rather it is about how feminists can add a chat bot to their toolbox, to make their goal of living a feminist world closer to home.[39]

Mz* Baltazar's Laboratory

The lab is run by a collective that offers a hackspace for women, trans and non-binary people, in addition to a gallery space for feminist exhibitions.[40] Mz* Baltazar's Laboratory was one of the first feminist hackspaces working at the intersection of technology, art and feminism. To enlarge the notion of what a feminist hackspace is and does, Mz* Baltazar's Laboratory *is* involved in a process of creating a sociotechnical imaginary around it. In writing an auto-ethnography of their hackspace, Selena Savic and Stefanie Wuschitz suggest "speculating together about what a feminist hackspace could be like, is a way of world-making."[41] Referring to the concept of world-making echoes Donna Haraway's views about the importance of stories, and how we tell them.

It matters what ideas we use to think other ideas (with). It matters what matters we use to think other matters with; it matters what stories we tell to tell other stories with; it matters what knots knot knots, what thoughts think thoughts, what descriptions describe descriptions, what ties tie ties. It matters what stories make worlds, what worlds make stories.[42]

39   Toupin and Couture, "Feminist chatbots."
40   Shusha Niederberger, "Feminist Hackspace. Interview with Patricia Reis and Stephanie Wuschitz," *Creating Commons*, March 4, 2018. http://creatingcommons.zhdk.ch/wp-content/uploads/2019/05/feminist-hackspace_transscript.pdf
41   Selena Savic and Stefanie Wuschitz, "Feminist Hackerspace as a Place of Infrastructure Production," *Ada: A Journal of Gender, New Media and Technology* 13 (2018), https://adanewmedia.org/2018/05/issue13-savic-wuschitz/
42   Donna Haraway, *Staying with the Trouble: Making Kin in the Chthulucene* (Durham NC: Duke University Press, 2016), p. 29.

World-making through the provision of a space is demonstrated by the feminist intentionality behind Mz* Baltazar's Laboratory, which is supported by a code of conduct that applies at both the digital and physical level, where harassment and discrimination are not tolerated. In this way, the collective makes clear the type of intersectional feminist world they want to embrace and actualize. They extend these ideas to the wider world, dreaming of how to prefigure in their lives such principles. Elsewhere, I have documented the practices of feminist hackerspaces, noting their use of the notion of safe(r) spaces for learning and sharing, and their implementation of codes of conduct to embody the type of culture they want to see in their space.[43] Here, I move away from the term safe(r) space—though I recognize and acknowledge *Mz* Baltazar's* attachment to the term—and rather use the term *intentional space*. While both intentional and safe(r) space are associated with world-making, over the years I have come to understand that commoning practices or creating commons, digital or otherwise, are less about being/feeling safe or safer—though this might be one of the intended goals—but rather about being intentional. By using this concept, the possibility of opening up a feminist imaginary that affirms proudly one's belief and intention, is much stronger than the imaginary associated with protection.

In an interview with Creating Commons, two of Mz* Baltazar's Laboratory's founders/members said that they don't use the term "commons," though the term would apply to them, but instead they use the term "open source." This is made clear in Savic and Wuschitz's auto-ethnography, when they say that their space not only provides open source tools and equipment to all participants, but also encourages members to perform gender in a new, unexpected way, [to] break with technology related stereotypes and [to] unlearn trained feelings of deficiency.[44]

The originality of their understanding of open source as being more than open source technology, which they refer to as *cultural open source*, reaffirms a feminist and queer sociotechnical imaginary that

---

43 Sophie Toupin, "Feminist Hackerspaces as Safer Spaces?" *dpi: Feminist Journal of Art and Digital Culture* 27 (2013). http://dpi.studioxx.org/fr/feminist-hackerspaces-safer-spaces

44 Savic and Wuschitz, "Feminist Hackerspace as a Place of Infrastructure Production," para 19.

includes the openness of gender and allows for "reprogramming" feelings and affect. Just like Nossas Cidades they extend a concept that is usually applied to software or hardware to the body with the fluidity of gender. In terms of feelings, it is not only about an affective community being created like in other hackerspaces, but also about a shifting of affective dispositions, from that of an open culture and its digital commons to one that does all that plus foregrounding transformative social relations.[45] Moreover, the way Mz* Baltazar's Laboratory understands its space as a commons to imagine new social relations among humans and between human and non-humans is shared by a community, which aims at empowerment, solidary and trust. Wuschitz in an interview says: "I think the word commons actually applies 100% to us. (…) I think everyone can use our network, but no one really owns it."[46]

Tactical Tech

Tactical Tech describes itself as "an international non-governmental organization that explores and mitigates the impact of technology on society."[47] It started in 2003 and is currently based in Berlin. From their first project, *NGO in a Box*, which gave NGOs FLOSS software, to their more recent Glass Room project, Tactical Tech has furthered an idea of the commons within civil society. This is explicitly referred to on their website where they state that: "Our vision is a world where digital technologies can contribute to a more equitable, democratic and sustainable society."[48]

In an interview, Marek Tuszynski, one of the co-founders of Tactical Tech said: "a focus of Tactical Tech at the beginning was on free and open source software, because for us that was the political toolbox that enables the users, gives them agency and autonomy and the right to use this technology freely."[49] All of the software created by and How Tos available on the Tactical Tech website have been released as FLOSS software and under Creative Commons licensing. As we have

45 Niederberger, "Feminist Hackspace."
46 Ibid.
47 https://tacticaltech.org/#/about
48 Ibid.
49 Felix Stalder, "Working with the Paradoxes of Technology, Interview with Marek Tuszynski," *Creating Commons*, September 16, 2018. http://creatingcommons.zhdk.ch/working-with-the-paradoxes-of-technology/ (accessed June 11, 2020)

seen earlier, the ideas that buttress Tactical Tech came out of a digital rights movement in the 2000s, which is informed by a liberal imaginary with the individual at the center. In other words, the type of projects Tactical Tech is involved in provide a sociotechnical imaginary where human rights are the guiding principles.

More recently, Tactical Tech has used artistic projects and strategies to enlarge their methodological repertoire of what can be considered as part of the commons. With their project the Glass Room, which was started in 2016, Tactical Tech has put together an exhibition of art, design, and technology objects that allow visitors to explore their relationship to technology, data, privacy and surveillance. Grounded in human rights, the sociotechnical imaginary that supports this space of learning is one that makes visible the process of data collection, demonstrating to the visitors that all technologies are designed for a purpose. The imaginary is an educated public that understands the processes at play with the technologies they use, the methodology to attain this sociotechnical imaginary being a pedagogical endeavor. In this way the Glass Room reconfigures the public sphere—the realm of social life where public opinion takes shape—to address and reveal how surveillance and data colonialism function. People come together as a non-privatized public in the Glass Room to inform themselves about and debate matters of general interest and common concern. The hope is that it will lead to action.

The Glass Room project is conceived not only as a place of learning and pedagogy, but also as a concept that anyone can make their own. In this sense, the project's concept is free and open source, as anyone can print and reproduce Tactical Tech's exhibit. The Glass Room is being offered to communities as a commons that can be copied and modified to raise awareness about, debate and experiment with new sensibilities on how our technologies work and their impact on people's daily lives. The Glass Room is in opposition to typical art exhibitions, which are usually not open as a concept, but rather closed and non-replicable. The Glass Room is composed of a kit you can order and install. It reminds me of a maker kit that can be assembled and played with while learning about the technological process at play.

Conclusion

Sociotechnical imaginaries play an important role in developing alternatives to the current crisis. The three examples above show how sociotechnical imaginaries rooted in intersectional feminism and/or human rights promote a vision of technology that is grounded in the commons. This extends the FLOSS community's imaginary that aims at subverting copyrights and promoting a culture of sharing, but which for the most part does ignore gender, race, class and politics. Both Nossas Cidades and Mz* Baltazar's Laboratory build on the FLOSS digital commons imaginary, while at the same time coming up with an intersectional feminist imaginary, a situated practice and a place of learning. Further, both practice and imaginary refer back to the body: either through the fight over reproductive justice or the creation of a commons space reserved for an intentional community which freely experiments with the digital commons, gender and affect. The last case study's sociotechnical imaginary surrounds Tactical Tech and its vision of actualizing human rights when it comes to the relationship between technology and society. This is done through the creation of spaces aimed at educating the public through an intentional pedagogy, which functions as a public sphere to debate issues related to the digital sphere.

These examples have stressed the importance of transformative social relations, including at the level of gender and race in addition to the self-determination of people and individuals over their online and offline destinies. The takeaway of this article is that while the (digital and non-digital) commons as we know them are in danger of being enclosed by capital and its extractive logic, social actors are inventing new methodologies and/or infrastructures to expand commoning practices. While none of the examples studied will stop the encroaching upon the commons, the lesson is that such forms of politics nevertheless can create freedom(s).

Rahel Puffert

What is "In Common" Here?

Transformed Relationships Between Art and Education on the Path to (Digital) Commons

"People adapt to a possibility for change, and
by doing this, they change.
In this way, they are already in transition."
Frigga Haug

The following considerations are based on my preference for a type of art that is characterized by the fact that it does not delegate its mediation and distribution, but rather takes these processes into consideration, or even treats them as a theme or central object. Art of this sort, rooted in the precedents established by early twentieth-century Russian Constructivism, Productivism, and their wider context, carries with it that art may be instrumentalized politically, but does not conclude thereby that art should avoid any "social intention." On the contrary, and in contrast to the practitioners of bourgeois art theory and of *l'art pour l'art* (who are still active today), and their stipulations, I proceed from the ultimately trivial but by no means self-evident assumption that all art emerges from specific socio-political parameters, and art (and artists) necessarily functions accordingly.[1]

Art, Society, ...

My particular interest lies in artistic practices that consciously make the organization and formation of a social framework part of their

1   Rahel Puffert, *Die Kunst und ihre Folgen: Genealogien der Kunstvermittlung* (Bielefeld: transcript, 2013), pp. 9–11.

approach. Only in *this* sense do I call such artistic practices "social"—my use of this adjective has nothing to do with normative qualifications, such as "fair," "ethical," "sustainable," "socially engaged," etc.[2] Such practices show their awareness of art as a *fait social* (in Durkheim's formulation), both on the levels of their reception and of their production.

... Commons, and the Question of What "In Common" Means

In various statements on the topic, commons are usually thought to be positioned "beyond the market and the state."[3] If they once formed the point of departure for developing, to a greater extent, alternative or solidary forms of the (environmental) economy,[4] they have since come to be regarded more often as an innovative way out of today's crisis-ridden global social order.[5] More skeptical voices have therefore drawn attention to the fact that an uncritical conceptualization of the commons threatens to leave them vulnerable to the exploitative interests of capitalism. Instead one should approach the commons from the angle of reproductive labor and insist on its conditionality and inalienable substance. The term "commoning" is understood to denote self-sustaining, non-instrumental activities undertaken for and with one another. In the case of such activities, the traditional separation between immaterial (or emotional) labor and material labor no longer applies. Understood in this way, commoning is ultimately a matter of using non-technologizable forms of reproduction in the sense of collective *praxis*—at least according to *one* thesis.[6]

---

2   Ibid.
3   See the various formulations along these lines in the Wikipedia entry on commons.
4   Elinor Ostrom, *Governing the Commons: The Evolution of Institutions for Collective Action* (Cambridge: Cambridge University Press, 1990).
5   Silke Helfrich and David Bollier, *Frei, fair und lebendig: Die Macht der Commons* (Bielefeld: transcript, 2019).
6   Silvia Federici, "Women, Reproduction and the Construction of Commons," a lecture delivered on April 18, 2013, https://www.youtube.com/watch?v = zBBbVpbmRP0: "Unless we come together and reconstruct the social fabric of our towns, creating new solidarity bonds, we will not be able to wage the type of struggle that we need to regain control over our lives and reclaim the wealth that we have produced. We have to see the commons not only as an objective to be reached in the future, but as the base for our struggle." (All URLs in this text have been last accessed October 20, 2020).

In this contribution, I would like to address the question of whether and to what extent the discourse of the commons benefits from three artist-initiated projects. To be more precise, I intend to take a closer look at what the mediation of these projects contributes to the commons. The very title of this research project suggests that a good deal of preliminary work has already been done. The project name *Creating Commons* can be interpreted in three ways: first as a sort of prescribed definition or as a hypothetical umbrella term for the various (sub)projects associated with it; second as a description of the activity that takes place on the project's website (which includes all other contributions such as texts, interviews, images of workshops, references, surface design, etc., and acknowledges the work of the project's initiators and administrators); and third as a programmatic statement that distinguishes the project from the *Creative Commons*, for instance.[7] The latter project has created an Internet culture out of "freely licensed" operating forums (such as Wikipedia) that allow for relatively easy access (especially knowledge-related resources) or complete open access in the academic sphere. The problem is that techniques of control behind this project remain invisible and therefore resemble neoliberalism's techniques of domination.[8] The *praxis* of the *Creative Commons* thus represents a proto-concept of the commons, whereas *Creating Commons* is about producing what could be called commons in the sense of a collective, social process.

A pedagogical grasp of *Creating Commons* and its various meanings begs even further examination. All three levels of meaning contained in the project's title (an umbrella term, a description of activity, a programmatic statement) become even more complicated or are multiplied by the fact that all uses of the term "commons" are at first somewhat unclear or open-ended, regardless of whether it revolves around commonly shared goods, communality, communities, commonalities, or all commons in the plural. In any case, it revolves around something—or, as it were: it circulates.

---

7   See https://de.creativecommons.net/was-ist-cc/
8   For a more detailed discussion of this point, see Cornelia Sollfrank and Felix Stalder, "From Creative Commons to Creating Commons," *Blickpunkt: Zeitschrift der IG Bildende Kunst* 44 (2017): pp. 22–25.

In order to arrest the endless circulation of signification loops, interruptions are necessary.[9] Below, when I adopt a pedagogical perspective to engage with three production sites that are run by artists and make use of open-source technologies, my limited aim is simply to learn more about whether and to what extent these projects contribute to a narrower definition of what the word "common" means within the context of *Creating Commons*.

Art Mediation as an Institutional Critique

With this aim in mind, to what extent can a pedagogical perspective (of all things) be of any significance? A few remarks should be made about this before I proceed.

My orientation toward pedagogical and education-theoretical lines of inquiry derives from my theoretical work and *praxis* in the field of critical art mediation. Primarily employed in the German-speaking area, the concept of "art mediation" denotes a way of rethinking things that came to prominence a few years before the end of the last millennium, when it first began to cause a stir in museum outreach and education (as it was still called then) as well as in school-based or community-targeted art education. In tandem with the institutional-critical art of the 1990s, which, for the sake of establishing a self-imposed socio-political space, endeavored to "create its own public sphere," artists, teachers, and activists adopted a critical position against the aggressive exploitative logic of the art market, which was vehemently being implemented at the time and which attempted to reduce art and artistic labor to the function of (symbolic) capital investments. In addition, art mediators distanced themselves from a tradition of art education that—in defiance of all critical impulses from sociology, pedagogy, post-structural philosophy, cultural studies, and art itself—adhered to the representation of a traditional autonomous concept of art and perceived itself as being of service to this obsolete concept. The objection is that this approach too quickly resolves and "makes safe"

9   See http://creating-commons.zhdk.com

art's sometimes undefined and ambiguous status.[10] As a consequence, the aim of the field of art mediation, which has since become highly differentiated, has been to create situations that raise the question of whether a given event or perception has something to do with art, while also leaving this question as open and unresolved as possible. This, too, is precisely the institutional-critical gesture of art-mediating activity: instead of merely conveying institutionally established knowledge *about* art, it is intent on raising the socio-politically relevant question of who is allowed to participate in it. Thus, for example: What concept of art is mediated to whom, and under what conditions? And: To whom is this concept not being conveyed, and why not? Or: What means of address fail to engage entire segments of the public?

Aesthetics and Inequalities

Affective reactions such as familiarity, admiration, feelings of exclusion, fascination, repulsion, wanting to belong, or alienation: thanks to Pierre Bourdieu's concept of "habitus," such approaches to art could no longer only be understood as subjective reactions that can be derived directly from the relationship between a work of art and its viewers. This idea shook up the concept of "aesthetic experience," which had previously been above criticism in the discourse of art education. Now, diverse affects could be interpreted as being distinctively situated—that is, acquired via social interaction—and this situatedness allowed them to be practiced and actualized in social space.

In Bourdieu's sense, habitus can be described as a structure made up of one's background, gender, and social status, the interplay of which determines many of our lifestyle decisions. These structures, which can change over time and space, are based on taste-related schemata of classification that have been formed from the historical work of many generations.[11]

With his concept of habitus, Bourdieu subjected Kant's conception of aesthetic judgment to a fundamental critique, and was able to dem-

---

10 Pierangelo Maset, *Praxis Kunst Pädagogik: Ästhetische Operationen in der Kunstvermittlung* (Lüneburg: Edition Hyde, 2001), p. 16.
11 Pierre Bourdieu and Loïc Wacquant, *An Invitation to Reflexive Anthropology* (Chicago: The University of Chicago Press, 1992), p. 139.

onstrate on the basis of empirical studies that Kant's theory is classicist at heart and that it is best suited for "legitimating social differences." By means of Bourdieu's "social critique of the judgment of taste," the universalization of Kant's theory of art turns out to be a form of "symbolic violence," because it makes "pleasure without any interest" a condition of aesthetic judgment.[12] Thus, a certain way of perceiving art—one based on the privileges of a lifestyle unhampered by economic hardship—is taken to be a general and naturalized standard, though it is difficult or impossible for those with different social situations to adopt this aesthetic approach. This knowledge is not only discomforting or unsettling for teachers; it also calls into question the authority and role of anyone who claims, with the backing of institutional power, to want to mediate art to others.

If the discourse of art mediation arose from the periphery in order to perforate, expand, or frustrate the official and powerfully implemented definitions of what should be recognized as art,[13] it did so with the aim of achieving the self-empowering effects that can be gained from laying bare hidden codifications and rules or from changing the canon in general. This latter concern in particular has been supplemented by art mediators operating in museums and exhibitions, who have since shifted the canon to include feminist and queer art and media theory (for instance).[14] Embracing the perspective of postcolonial testimonies, moreover, art mediation has made use of migration-oriented teaching in order to draw attention to racism and cultural differences.[15]

Generally skeptical of institutional mechanisms of social exclusion and distinction, critical art mediators make it their task "to expose the violent relationships that are inherent to dominant narratives, promises, and manners of legitimation."[16] Because art mediators often work

12 Pierre Bourdieu, *Distinction: A Social Critique of the Judgement of Taste*, trans. Richard Nice (Cambridge MA: Harvard University Press, 1984), p. 7.

13 See Pierangelo Maset, *Ästhetische Bildung der Differenz: Kunst und Pädagogik im technischen Zeitalter* (Stuttgart: Radius, 1996), p. 167.

14 See Nanna Lüth, "Radical Drag! Varianten einer nicht-binären Kunstpädagogik," *Kritische Berichte: Zeitschrift für Kunst- und Kulturwissenschaften* 4 (2016): pp. 64–73.

15 See Nora Sternfeld, *Verlernen vermitteln* (Hamburg: Universitätsdruckerei, 2014); and Carmen Mörsch, *Die Bildung der Anderen mit Kunst: Ein Beitrag zu einer postkolonialen Geschichte der kulturellen Bildung* (Hamburg: Universitätsdruckerei, 2017).

16 Carmen Mörsch, "Sich selbst widersprechen. Kunstvermittlung als kritische Praxis innerhalb des educational turn in curating," in *Educational Turn: Handlungsräume der Kunst- und Kulturvermittlung, Ausstellungstheorie & Praxis*, vol. 5, ed. Nora Sternfeld and Beatrice Jaschke (Vienna: Turia + Kant, 2012), pp. 55–77, here p. 64.

for or are contracted by these institutions (museums, galleries, schools, universities, and so on), "their work is contradictory in nature."[17] For art mediators, however, working *toward* such contradiction is a programmatic aspect of their approach. In this regard, there are decisive differences in the roles and functions that individual art mediators attribute to art. For instance, the slogan "from the art itself,"[18] which was originally directed against certain pedagogical and didacticizing tendencies in the field, has since been refined, and now it is more often a question of "from which art" one really ought to proceed.[19]

In recent decades, a transformation has taken place in the relationship between institutional art mediation and art, and it is possible to regard this as a reciprocal shift. This shift has changed our concepts of community and has reformulated how the notion of "common meaning" should be understood. The transformation in question can be divided into the following three phases:

Phase One: Works of art become tests of communal connections. In Pierangelo Maset's words: "The education of the gaze that we cast on an object is a (pedagogical) act of social significance, an act that creates a connection between members of a community but can also abolish this connection. Works of art thus serve to verify such a connection, which has to be created and dissolved and whose *possibility* of dissolution is a constitutive component of democratic societies."[20]

Phase Two: Art makes mediation its material and object. A *sensus communis* is created in tandem with a long-term practical and theoretical development of notions of art:[21] "The material of art no longer consists of just things. It also consists of forms of knowledge, structures, processes, strategies, and perceptions that can also be situated outside of the system of art."[22] Art mediation thereby finds itself in a new position; it can now adopt artistic features itself, with the aim of

17 Ibid.
18 Eva Sturm, *Von Kunst aus: Kunstvermittlung mit Gilles Deleuze* (Vienna: Turia + Kant, 2011).
19 Puffert, *Die Kunst und ihre Folgen*, p. 257.
20 Maset, *Ästhetische Bildung der Differenz*, p. 99.
21 See Maset, *Praxis Kunst Pädagogik*, pp. 8–9: "The *sensus communis* is not something that can be conveyed in small educational steps; rather, it is the result of a long period of theoretical and practical work on concepts of art. It does not merge with the aesthetic experience of the subject but rather, in the best case, keeps the outside open to communal perception."
22 Ibid., p. 32.

"leading traditional art education away from 'art' and developing it into *art*-education (*KunstPädagogik*)."[23]

Phase Three: "Art" rhetorically appropriates the critical discourses, including their social concerns about mediation, so skillfully and practically that it can discard the option of community altogether. As before, a "*different*" sort of art then becomes essential to generating the elements and forms of an "improbable community."[24] "For education as well as for art," according to Maset, "it is fatal that the techniques of control are increasingly adopted by institutions and those who work for them. It is psycho-technicians who imbue attention and thought with their ever-adjustable matrix of control. [...] Increasingly, art is playing a highly problematic role. It is no longer just a medium of distinction; it has meanwhile also become a medium of repression."[25]

The Sites of Three Commons-Based Projects

In what follows, I will focus on three projects that are located in Vienna, Brussels, and London, that are not only online but also operate bricks-and-mortar locations. The projects in question are the Viennese hackspace Mz* Baltazar's Laboratory, which was founded in 2006 and is managed by Stephanie Wuschitz and Patricia Reis; the art school e.r.g. in Brussels, which has been directed by Laurence Rassel since 2016; and the artist-governed space Furtherfield in northern London, which was initiated in 1996 by Ruth Catlow and Marc Garrett. In addition to parts of the surrounding parkland (which is often put to use), the latter project consists primarily of two buildings or workspaces: a non-commercial gallery and a multi-functional work room in which workshops and other events regularly take place.

My discussion is supported predominantly by what was said and conveyed in the interviews produced within the research context of *Creating Commons*. Well aware that these interviews do not replace or reproduce the social happenings that are taking place on location at these projects, I regard them as performative conceptualizations

---

23 Ibid., pp. 32–33.
24 Pierangelo Maset, *Kunstvermittlung heute: Zwischen Anpassung und Widerstand,* ed. Andrea Sabisch et al. (Hamburg: REPRO Lüdcke, 2012), p. 19.
25 Ibid., p. 21.

of the sites themselves—as acts of mediation. The questions that I asked myself about these projects are the following: Which roles do the speakers adopt with respect to collective activity? How is this activity legitimated, and which references describe and circumscribe it? Which forms of inclusion and exclusion condition the social and thus also pedagogical events in each of these respective places? To what extent do these projects contribute to "social reorganization"?[26] My aim was thus to learn more about the notion of community that these projects wish to convey.

Established in the Name of Secession and Participation: Mz* Baltazar's Laboratory, Vienna

Mz* Baltazar's Laboratory is a feminist hacklab in Vienna that is located in an unassuming storefront and serves as a meeting place for members of the LGBTQ community. The story of its origin is as briefly told as it is conceptually significant: in the beginning, as Stephanie Wuschitz has reported, there was a feeling of dissatisfaction with a particular form of masculine techno-fetishism in traditional hacker labs, which hindered equal participation from those in different social and gender positions. This led to the secession and formation of a group of people who decided to establish a hacklab of their own with a clearly feminist agenda.[27] When explaining their project, Stephanie Wuschitz and Patricia Reis complement each other and share authority in defining the project. Sprinkled with the language of coding theory, their descriptions reveal that the orientation of the project lies at the intersection of "gender, technology, hacking, and art" (as Reis puts it). At least to those familiar with Virginia Woolf's essay, their mention of "a room of one's own" is a clear reference to the necessary condition of having material and discursive independence. Woolf had spoken out in favor of the right of women to own private property as a fundamental precondition for their individual artistic production.[28]

26 Sollfrank and Stalder, "From Creative Commons to Creating Commons."
27 See "Feminist Hackspace," an interview with Patricia Reis and Stephanie Wuschitz (March 1, 2018) available at http://creatingcommons.zhdk.ch/feminist-hackspace
28 Virginia Woolf, *A Room of One's Own and Three Guineas*, ed. Morag Shiach (Oxford: Oxford University Press, 2001), pp. 1–150. Originally published in 1929.

What she meant by this was simply a room, in a specific architectonic sense, in which the literary work of women could take place in an uninhibited way. Reis and Wuschitz have transplanted this artistic production from a private room into a semi-open store space, where it can be carried out independently or collectively. Not only for themselves have the operators of the project secured material independence by applying for government funding; they also share this independence with others. They have made an infrastructure available, but they reserve the right to regulate its accessibility and design the content of its agenda.

Unburdened Separation

The hetero-normative structures of the hacker scene have had the effect that a woman is not perceived as someone who is interested in hacking or in exploring new technologies, but rather as a woman who wants to be as masculine, so to speak, as "the other guys" engaged in this activity (in Wuschitz's words). Thus, the need arose to establish a space in which *different* self-perceptions and external perceptions were possible. By using the term "safer space," Wuschitz and Reis poignantly express their wish to create a space that may not be able to guarantee total safety, but is safe enough to enable the formation of a "*different* culture of technology."

By limiting access to "bias-people" (in Wuschitz's terms), Mz* Baltazar's Laboratory also revives the idea of androgyny—another of Woolf's necessary conditions for the artistic productivity of women— under a changed set of historical and political conditions. By claiming that androgyny is part of every person's consciousness, Woolf problematizes the idea of classifying people according to a single gender, and she goes beyond that by describing good literature as androgynous.[29] Although the more differentiated gender-specific categorization LGBTQ shields Woolf's concept of "androgyny" from the feminist charge that it is essentialist, this new and more finely differentiated term also has the effect that it has made it easier to determine who belongs and who does not. In any case, whoever wants to know how to become a feminist hacker in the sense supported by Mz* Baltazar's Laboratory must be aware that the development of a feminist technology culture here depends on people who perceive themselves as

---

29   Ibid., pp. 135–36.

non-binary, who have a self-determined relationship to themselves, and who are accustomed to contemplating and trying out technologies. As Wuschitz has mentioned elsewhere, this very separatism lies at the heart of the project.[30] This self-affirming and stabilizing framework for interaction is consciously based on a discriminating act: the decision to allow only women and trans-persons to participate has the advantage that it enables members to learn from one another without the burdens of gender normativity, thereby creating a space for them to deal with technologies freely and without anxiety: "Within the collective, the individual overcomes hesitations, self-censorship, and the limitations of gender-normed behavior."[31] The ambitions of the group include engaging with hardware, learning soldering and welding, and the first steps toward learning how to code. In doing so, the group also and inevitably deviates from established gender norms: "Disassembling an electronic device on purpose not only breaks the hardware, but also breaks with feminine gender scripts […], the norm on how to perform femininity (not be 'aggressive' and to not avidly 'destroy')."[32]

And Outside?
In addition to the curated exhibition and workshop program, which is offered free of charge by invited (and compensated) international artists, Wuschitz and Reis also stress the importance of on-site community work. If, for instance, someone wants to offer additional workshops on open-source programming languages or to use the space in another way, this is entirely possible so long as there are no scheduling conflicts. The project's offerings are directed toward anyone who is interested in interacting with international artists in Vienna. As Wuschitz admits, the latter are predominantly English-speaking "white middle-class academics." It is not easy, Reis adds, "to reach out to people who have a different background."

The approach to commons practiced here is based on a clearly established separation from the "outside," which in this case literally means whatever is happening beyond the confines of the lab. That

---

30 See Selena Savic and Stephanie Wuschitz, "Feminist Hackerspace as a Place of Infrastructure Production," *Ada: A Journal of Gender, New Media and Technology* 13 (2018), https://adanewmedia.org/2018/05/issue13-savic-wuschitz
31 Ibid.
32 Ibid.

said, Wuschitz and Reis nevertheless insist that the boundary between the inside of the former store and the "street" is always in flux. Paradoxically, however, what they say about this outside does not seem to allow for much permeability. The project's basis on its own feminist technology culture has had the unsurprising effect that, in our times of intensified geographical and body-related differences, conflicts and socio-political antagonism are seldom far away. They can be observed, as Reis has remarked, right outside of the project's open door in the form of "little troubles."

Care and Closure

The architectonic limitation of this inner space suits the hackers well; indeed, they have explained that the physical capacity of the location is, in cognitive and social respects, one of the conditions for the success of their commons. After a group grows beyond a certain size, it is not easy to maintain its heterogeneity. Wuschitz and Reis thus touch upon a mundane question that is nevertheless relevant for teachers: How large can a group become before its member lose awareness of their uniqueness and thus no longer feel as though "they are being seen"?

It is the hosts themselves who, through their commitment to the project, organize its on-site events, enact their "philosophy," and continuously cultivate a sense of "trust" and "love" (as Reis puts it). Only in such a way is it possible not only to establish a certain set of rules for dealing with the commons (here understood as common goods and services) but also, so as to avoid a rigid order, to revise or reject these rules in a permanent process of negotiation. This becomes difficult when it comes to sharing undesirable tasks such as tidying up, cleaning, or managing the project's finances. If the group's communication and interaction are to take place without any rules whatsoever, and if this lawlessness is glorified to some extent with an aura of solidarity, trust, and love, then the project predisposes itself to accusations of being naïvely romantic and aggressively (and excessively) unstructured.[33]

However, it is precisely these indeterminant immaterial qualities that reveal the fragility of the feminist hackspace and make it all the

---

[33] See, for instance, Isabel de Sena: Thick Webs & Continuous Relays: Feminist Epistemologies for the Digital Commons (October 11, 2019), available at http://creatingcommons. zhdk.ch/thick-webs-continuous-relays

more defensible as an experiment. Because the purpose of the project is to safeguard a certain way of dealing with technology and to foster a discrimination-critical awareness of difference, it also has a moral dimension. At stake is nothing less than testing out a necessarily unstable technology culture that relies neither on normative ideas of technology nor on the latter's typical expression of gender relations.

Instituting the Institution: e.r.g., Brussels

Whereas the feminist hackers in Vienna founded their artist-run space in a self-organized manner, Laurence Rassel, a long-time member of the collective Constant, recently (in 2016) became the director of an institution that has existed since 1972. When it was founded, the Brussels-based art school École de recherche graphique (*e.r.g*) was devoted to the experiment and idea of an exciting combination of transdisciplinarity and collective forms of work. Here, one works within the framework of workshops, gets by without any formal course structure, and engages with a variety of artistic methods and media, whereby particular importance is ascribed to practices that are traditionally described as "applied" (commercial graphics, illustration, photography, animation, etc.). Rassel joined this institution with the hope of reviving its experimental basic ideas. She wanted to loosen up the rigid culture that had gradually built up there over the course of various institutional processes, and replace it with a state of mutability and flux.

Deconstructing an Institution
By consistently calling into question the infrastructure of the school, Rassel made many of its elements available anew; at the same time, she explained that this process would gradually lead to the development of a flexible and self-governing institution for collective activity: "How can we build, construct an art school that is conscious about the conditions of production, conscious about gender, I mean the narrative needed [...]? It was really to imagine a space that exists and has its own rules, but how can we build something *together*?"[34]

---

34 "Experimenting with Institutional Formats, Interview with Laurence Rassel," http://creatingcommons.zhdk.ch/experimenting-with-institutional-formats/ (emphasis in original).

As the Director of an institution, Laurence Rassel speaks as someone who is aware of her function and her powerful role, and she uses the latter to initiate collective processes and thus to include potentially all participants in the responsibility for steering the institution itself. Rassel has therefore been following a risky pedagogical imperative that leads to open-endedness—to the "wild world of uncertainty in which pedagogical activity takes place," in the words of Paul Mecheril and Britta Hoffarth. These authors also stress that without uncertainty, openness, and inaccessibility, there would be no pedagogical activity at all.[35] Rassel demonstrates that the pedagogical connection is always one of mutual relatedness and, given existing hierarchical conditions, must encompass more than principles of instruction/implementation or decision-making/participation. By sharing and relinquishing the power of her office of Director, Rassel has declared the institution an open experiment—a process in which possibilities of collaboration are newly tested and the idea of exchanging and distributing opportunities is freshly explored.

Rassel makes it clear that she does not imagine a social system of pure equality, but she intentionally harnesses the freedom that comes with her function as a Director to promote and enable collective processes. In order to accomplish this, she relies on the toolkits of three discourses that coexist in what she refers to as a contaminated system: open source, feminism, and institutional therapy.

Three Discourses for Reviving an Institution
1. Open source: For Rassel, leading a public institution means making its principles and decision-making processes transparent and comprehensible, but it also means making its resources broadly accessible. On every possible (legal) level and in every committee, she thus works to achieve a high standard of collectivity. To this end, she has initiated working groups that aim to make institutional policies more fluid, open up channels of communication, and evaluate the current usefulness of traditional decision-making structures.

---

35 Paul Mecheril and Britta Hoffarth, "Ironie: Erkundung eines vergnüglichen Bildungsereignisses," in *Ironie in der Pädagogik: Theoretische und empirische Studien zur pädagogischen Bedeutsamkeit der Ironie*, ed. Alex Aßmann and Jens Oliver Krüger (Weinheim: Juventa, 2011), p. 29.

2. Feminism: These processes concern a wide range of structures that pertain to such things as access rules, waste disposal, hiring policies, pedagogical self-perceptions, the cafeteria, media concepts, and thus also to certain resources that often function on the inside of an institution without any general awareness of who really does what and why. Rassel gives special attention to processes of reproductive labor; she goes out of her way to ensure their visibility and she ascribes value to them that society often denies. For Rassel, her feminist approach also entails the acknowledgement of "situated knowledge" (in Donna Haraway's terms), which is tied to a critique of any universal claims to objectivity. She makes efforts to emphasize the partiality of different points of view and to consider the specificity of these perspectives, which can be shaped (for example) by social conditions or gender differences. Thus, she also accepts the limitations that come with any given viewpoint. By understanding herself as part of the world— and not as someone who exists outside of it—Rassel does not simply regard the institution under her charge as a spatial shell but rather as an influential structure that gives rise to subjectivities. With this understanding in mind, her aspiration is to create an institution that is self-aware.

3. Institutional therapy: Inspired by Marxist proponents of the (anti-) psychiatry movement such as François Tosquelles, Jean Oury, and Félix Guattari, Rassel is striving to create an institution that places the "ambience of communication" in the foreground. Instead of regarding such things as medical treatment, parenting, or education exclusively as the result of a dual relationship (between doctor/patient, mother/child, teacher/student), Rassel takes into account the institutional conditions, settings, and constellations that affect human relationships. Hierarchies, restrictions, bureaucratic hurdles, and the conditions caused by social differences are examined as potential sources of illness that need to be treated as though one is treating a patient.[36]

Accordingly, Rassel regards the institution as ailing or at least poisoned by neoliberal techniques of control and by the demands for efficiency, profitability, and arbitrary authority, which affect the bodies and relationships of those attempting to create culture. Because

---

[36] See Mauricio Novello and David Reggio, "The Hospital is Ill: Interview with Jean Oury," *Radical Philosophy* 143 (2007): pp. 32–45.

the institution had gradually been permeated by alienating structures a sort of soft infiltration has been needed to transform it back into a lively environment. This has required the development of collective structures, and this means more than simply working in groups. Rather, it calls for an awareness of the reciprocal process that combines singular activity with a network of heterogeneous social relations.

Unorthodox Intersections of Knowledge

When Rassel talks, she successfully combines areas of knowledge in an unorthodox way, while relating them to one another in such a way that their individual elements as well as their interrelations become palpable, though not completely encapsulated.

Rassel claims that it is necessary to get ahead of and capture rapidly developing lines of thought and also, at the same time, to lend structure to these intellectual developments by means of certain theoretical concepts. By means of a broadly metonymic narrative, she manages in a short time to span a broad framework of references and to pique the curiosity of her audience, and this is because she invokes familiar ideas, supplements them with something new, combines them in an unorthodox way, and discusses their practical applications. Rassel goes against the grain of traditional academic orders of knowledge. Her surprising combinations of disciplines such as Marxist-feminist film theory, open-source culture, institutional psychotherapy, cyber-feminism, museum *praxis*, science fiction, and decolonial theory give rise to new and slightly shifted perspectives, draw lines of connection between previously known and recently learned areas of knowledge, and also (in the best case) put formerly separate cultural scenes in contact with one another.

An Unheard-of but Appropriate Excessiveness

Aware of the neoliberal restructuring of the educational system and higher education, the culture of quantification established by the Bologna Process, the push toward more and more evaluations, and the successive research that has become available on the deadening methods of quality management, Rassel's approach is refreshingly (and unabashedly) offensive and exciting on account of its excessiveness. Instead of subscribing to the dystopian projections that have become common currency since Foucault, Rassel instead designs a decidedly utopian scenario—she uses metaphors such as "spaceship," "biotope," and "enclosed society" —her ideas have long seemed somewhat outrageous. At the same time, however, because they are concerned with very specific materializations, because their economic implications have been thought through, and because they are aimed at creating long-term change, Rassel's ideas should hardly be regarded as fanciful or scandalous. In light of the logic of European educational policy, her excessiveness is an all too appropriate response to the culture of quantification that afflicts so many of today's colleges and universities.[37]

"Creating a Canon of Your Own": Furtherfield, London

With a history stretching back more than twenty years, Furtherfield, which is located in Finsbury Park, London, is a mature structure that can almost be called an alternative institution. It was founded at a time when radical changes were taking place in the art world, changes which contributed (especially in Great Britain) to a market-oriented and individualistic understanding of art and increasingly pushed critical and experimental methods into the background. Today, Ruth Catlow and Marc Garrett are, as they put it, the last remaining active founders of the collective. In the 1990s, the idea to create a self-organized independent space and a network of heterogeneous activities was inspired by the newly discovered possibilities of the World Wide Web. Catlow has stressed how influential the Internet was on her artistic *praxis*. Internet-based communication enabled new audience relations "across difference and distance" as well as new temporal conditions (real time, feedback loops) and, it was hoped, the general opportunity "to shape the world together." Influenced by punk, pirate, and DIY culture, Furtherfield used the Internet to create "infrastructures of resistance." Catlow and Garrett thus emphasize the specific quality of an artistic space that brings together diverse audiences on different levels, and constantly changes its own form in conjunction with its ever-changing public.

37   See Sabine Hark and Johanna Hofbauer, eds. *Vermessene Räume, gespannte Beziehungen: Unternehmerische Universitäten und Geschlechterdynamiken* (Berlin: Suhrkamp, 2018).

Another Body Politic

The combination of a local meeting place in one of London's last public parks and web-based activities constitutes the specific quality of Furtherfield: here, the classical art exhibit in a gallery space is combined with the needs of an ongoing culture of homeless people, as well as feminist groups, refugees, artists in residence, collaborators, and families from the community, all of whom meet together in Furtherfield's common space. For Garrett and Catlow, the idea of the public space is also significant to the extent that both of them are guided by an interest in enlightenment. Motivated by the question of how technologies change our forms of communication and our relationships, the exhibits in Furtherfield's gallery often have highly abstract themes and serve to make the technology-conditioned changes of our everyday lives "feelable." An example of this is an exhibit put on by Liz Sterry in 2014. By means of a sort of forensic analysis, the artist (legally) tracked the YouTube videos and Internet searches of a young woman over three months, and in this way she was able to reconstruct the bedroom of the woman in question. Regarding the parents of young Internet users, for instance, her exhibit brought attention to the uncomfortable question of how much personal information remains available as saved online data. The fact is that social media are fed information every day without the awareness of their users, who thereby unwittingly invite an anonymous audience to participate in their private lives.

Catlow and Garrett practice a culture of openness and invite a highly diverse audience to participate in technology-critical discourses by engaging with art. In so doing, they consider the entire broad scope of social life. Catlow formulated their goal as follows: "Making things that are hidden and not talked about available to whoever comes through the door."

Organization

Just as diverse as the audience are the forms of collaboration that Furtherfield has developed over time. As directors, Ruth Catlow and Marc Garrett are the initiators, founders, and those who take care of the project's entire structure on site and online. In this regard, they are supported by a few employees and freelancers, among whom there is no separation between conceptual, bureaucratic, or mediating work. Each of the collaborators sometimes takes on the role of the participant and sometimes that of the initiator of one of many projects. The porous nature of Furtherfield has been one of its important concerns since the beginning: it has always experimented with curatorial ideas in order to provide opportunities for people to be involved in artistic events and activities. Because one of the core ideas of Furtherfield has been to create platforms for discussion, its organizational form is based on the greatest possible openness and on exchanging ideas, critique, and networks. It is thus no coincidence that Catlow and Garrett, when speaking about the project, do not treat its organizational structure as a small issue. They also make a point of mentioning that, for many years, they have needed to have jobs on the side and that the application procedures for EU funding have become so demanding that larger institutions now have entire accounting departments that work on nothing else. The fact that Catlow and Garrett have nevertheless succeeded in realizing diverse forms of work and participation has influenced their relationship with audiences; or—conversely—such achievements are perhaps a result of this very relationship. "Its purpose," according to Penny Travlou, "is to sustain the potential for a more open relationship between artists and audiences through experimentation with contemporary digital networks and social media," and she refers to Furtherfield's stated ambition to change the relationship between works of art and their audience.[38] The entire project is permeated by this basic idea, and this has consequences for the structure of collaboration as well.

Commons and the Role of Art

The two "parents" of Furtherfield expressly refer to the discourse of the commons and especially to its history in Great Britain. The enclosure of land parcels by the gentry in the middle of the seventeenth century can be regarded as the first incidence in which commonly used goods were arbitrarily expropriated. The efforts of the "True Levelers" and the "Diggers" to tear down the fences and win back this land raised awareness of the unjust appropriation of common property and can be seen as the beginning of today's commons movements, with their focus on technology, data, or laws. What Marx observed in nineteenth-

38 Penny Travlou, "Ethnographies of Co-Creation and Collaboration as Models of Creativity," in *Electronic Literature as a Model of Creativity and Innovation in Practice: A Report from the HERA Joint Research Project*, ed. Scott Rettberg and Sandy Baldwin (Morgantown: West Virginia University Press, 2014), pp. 245–304.

century England, which can be considered the beginning of capitalist accumulation, is now to a great extent standard practice in the global South or in Latin America. In today's era of neoliberalism, in which governments have reduced public resources and ceded responsibilities for them to the private sector (thereby turning them into commodities that citizens have to pay for), the aforementioned enclosures are no longer restricted to the appropriation of land or water sources, as has been the case in the global South and Latin America for some time. According to Catlow, social media have brought about the privatization of consciousness and social relationships. Data shared in interactions between individuals can now be possessed and exploited by others, and this affects every area of subjective expression. In light of the comprehensive neoliberal tendencies toward privatization, which, via data use, have penetrated into every crevice of human existence, Garrett argues that it is now of the utmost importance to redefine the commons. In this context, Catlow and Garrett define the role of art in two ways. First, the discourse concerning the commons demands that artists permanently question the value of art. When this is not a matter of satisfying market demands or assigning art an educational value, what specific value does art have for the individual and, in particular, for those within a community that is interested in knowing what it means to live a good and self-determined life? According to Catlow's observation, the role of art is to interrogate normative processes and to expand people's perspectives of experience, affect, and the creation of meaning. This also applies to the commons discourse itself, which tends to become utilitarian. In Catlow's opinion, artistic interventions enable people to recognize problems and keep the horizon of human experience as open as possible.

Who is the Commons?

The context-specific modes of operation practiced by the three artistic projects discussed above differ considerably with respect to the groups that they intend to address. Whereas Mz* Baltazar's Laboratory is committed to serving a part of society determined by identity politics—upon which it bases its own self-perception and situates itself in a position that is critical of discrimination—Furtherfield endeavors to affect public opinion by infiltrating it with alternative discourses. Both projects create contexts of their own (which are as independent as possible) in order to stabilize and empower critical discourses and promote de-canonization. Rassel's concept of a different sort of institution is also based on the question of what truly distinguishes the public character of an establishment such an art school.[39] For her vision of the art school e.r.g., Rassel employs the image of a machine or an open-source structure: students have potential access to this structure; they can copy elements of it, change them, and leave behind traces. The more it is worked on, the more sustainable the machine will be and the more likely it will lead to the production of timely and significant art.

In a quite literal sense, Mz* Baltazar's Laboratory functions as a laboratory that has created a social experimental arrangement—a form of being together—in order to cultivate and explore feminist ways of dealing with technologies and, under these conditions, to set novel learning processes in motion. Furtherfield's spirit seems to be more firmly based on raising awareness of a broader range of non-mainstream discourses. Here, participants strongly believe in the mutability of culture, which can be reoriented to suit the needs of a multifaceted community and which can aim to unify separate public spheres because their respective daily lives are pervaded by common technological conditions. Furtherfield's objective is to demystify and critically examine these conditions. Unlike the self-organized structures of Mz* Baltazar's Laboratory and Furtherfield, the art school e.r.g. is an established institution whose long-term goal is in fact to change the regulatory system of its existing institutional structure by gradually introducing different, critical, and above all collective standards of value. In general, working toward changing conceptions of value is a goal that all three projects share in common.

All three projects also operate with the conviction that it is necessary to understand knowledge as a resource that can be tapped into via collaborative work and can be used and actualized to shape the world. This conviction runs counter to the idea that knowledge

---

39   That all three projects are financed with public funding and thus, to this extent, do not operate "beyond the market and the state" changes nothing about their intentions to establish critical alternatives to the cultural, educational, and political status quo.

should be left to proven experts and that already existing knowledge should be apportioned according to exclusive rules. The role of artists has therefore shifted away from producing work and away from their temporary mediating role, toward the exemplary and long-term goal of testing out social configurations within which education can take place as an inter-subjective event. Artists have taken on co-responsibility for an understanding of education that regards the latter not as something individualistic, but rather as a process of aesthetic and social difference, especially because the latter is a precondition for artistic production.

Whereas e.r.g. and Furtherfield consciously build upon the aesthetic and communicative quality of their respective environments and thus treat the development of infrastructure itself as a component of their transformative agendas, Catlow and Garrett also draw attention to the convincing nature of artistic interventions when they succeed in raising and addressing problems that affect their audiences.

One of the obvious components of these projects is the acquisition and mediation of technological skills within the framework of workshops, but this aspect is not their main focal point. The ability to deal with digital technologies in an enlightened and uninhibited way is rather regarded as a cultural technique that should be treated on the same level as reading a book, planting a tree, or making a mathematical calculation. However, being aware of the omnipotence of digital technologies and their part in a logic of commercial interests also requires reciprocal forms of education to be put in place that do not ignore or leave to others important socio-economic questions and powerful differences but rather actively appropriate them and stimulate alternative practices. The task at hand, as it were, is to work toward a future digital culture that endeavors to redistribute cultural capital.

E.r.g. and Furtherfield in particular espouse a concept of art that is critical of the individualistic artistic subject. Rassel's concept of a "less toxic institution" can be understood as a reference to her goal of using the heft of institutional structures to raise awareness of (self-)perception instead of reducing the critique of power and domination to personal problems between people (which has today become a side-effect of approaches based on identity politics). Rassel has since become painfully aware, however, that affects are also *produced* and implemented by the very machine aesthetics, which, today, are difficult to construe as anything more than an "objective counterpart."

Regarding all three approaches, it can be said that they neither evoke the idea of an imagined community nor offer collective forms of work as a solution. What harmonizes the three approaches is their shared pursuit of a more abstract form of communality in which attempts are made to compensate for the lack or decline of community without lamenting the situation at hand or contributing to further fragmentation. Paul Mecheril has referred to this sort of community spirit as post-communitarian "solidarity among strangers," and he has described this type of relationship as one that exists "beyond any feeling of close togetherness."[40] This type of relationship is characterized by the fact it is empirically definable, it possesses a high degree of integrative potential, and it is also desirable under the conditions of increasingly diverse ways of life: "Solidarity is characterized by a sort of engagement that is based on changing—or, better yet, preventing—the conditions in which my familiar and unfamiliar collaborative partners cannot develop themselves." [41]

Translation by Valentine Pakis

---

40 Paul Mecheril, "Postkommunitäre Solidarität als Motiv kritischer (Migrations-)Forschung," in *Solidarität in der Migrationsgesellschaft: Befragung einer normativen Grundlage*, ed. Anne Broden and Paul Mecheril (Bielefeld: transcript, 2014), p. 82.
41 Ibid., p. 86.

Christoph Brunner

Concatenated Commons and Operational Aesthetics

This chapter deals with the specific potentials of what I call an *operational aesthetics* as part and parcel of alternative online video platforms. These platforms, I will argue, engage in operative logics of programming and interface design as well as a merger of data and metadata with the aim to resist capitalist modes of value extraction tied to the digital image. I will particularly look at the platforms 0xDB and pad.ma as projects dedicated to collaborative practices of collecting, sharing and remodeling vast databases of moving images in relation to cinema *(0xDB)* and to activist film making and discourse around digital film archives (pad.ma).[1] Key to both platforms is the operative logic of timelines that allow engagement with the object in an asynchronous, texturally annotated and heavily flow-based appearance. To give a concrete example of such flows and lines from 0xDB: I choose Makoto Shinkai's animated short movie *She and her Cat* [Kanojo to kanojo no neko] (1999)—a cat narrating her relationship to a single woman in urban Japan while moving across the four seasons of a year full of experiences and encounters.[2] I check the film information from one of the drop-down menus, afterwards I watch the movie once in its entirety in low resolution of 96p, then I switch to timeline view and the entire movie appears as a stream of different monochrome variations, reminding me of some of Ryoji Ikeda's audio-visual performances and installations. The full timeline view's color-variation flows open up a very different engagement with the way I am used to perceiving movies while watching them. In another encounter on pad.ma, I skim through the contributions of the seminar *Fwd:Re Archive*, held by the artist collective CAMP in 2018 at the Goethe Institute in Mumbai to mark the 10th anniversary of the platform.[3] I find

---

1   See oxdb.org and pad.ma.org (All URLs in this text have been last accessed October 20, 2020)
2   https://0xdb.org/0373960/info
3   https://pad.ma/grid/title/fwd&project = = Fwd:_Re:_Archive

information, people, contexts, lines of relations and friendships, but also a community of humans gathered around digital platforms and moving images that have become digital objects imbued with activating potential for new forms of sociality. A sensation arises of shared life-lines and practices combined with the timelines available through the platform itself. It is through the relaying of different operational aesthetics as they move and amplify through digital platforms that a different perceptual account of the present comes to the fore. It is a present that is under negotiation and open for different ways of gathering through sensation, or rather, through the varying temporal encounters these platforms create. They "accrete durations" and concatenate the present into an asynchronous yet common relational field that I term concatenated commons.[4]

The main difference between pad.ma and 0xDB resides in their content, the latter being mostly cinema and different kinds of professionally-produced series, whereas the former contains more amateur footage and material gathered around specific events. Much of the material on pad.ma takes on documentary forms, often interviewing people and collecting testimonials on particular circumstances. These scenes are often annotated and sometimes geo-located in the different menus of the graphic user interface. The range of material is broad, from intense workshop-like discussions such as *Fwd:Re Archive* footage to shopping mall surveillance cameras as part of the project *CCTV Social*.[5] Both platforms turn the logic of the production, circulation and meaning of structures of moving images towards themselves in a (post-)digital era of excessive visual cultures. The proliferation of 'the poor image' provides the material and visual ground for cultural practices based on a "relational aesthetics" beyond the realm of institutionalized art. While both platforms engage with cinema and art in different ways, their main focus resides in fostering encounters through practices of engagement and experimentation. The notion of concatenated commons asks how platforms like pad.ma and 0xDB are able to engage digital objects that open up processes of relating in and through experience.

---

4   Amit Rai, "Here We Accrete Durations: Toward a Practice of Intervals in the Perceptual Mode of Power," in *Beyond Biopolitics: Essays on the Governance of Life and Death*, ed. Patricia Ticineto Clough and Craig Willse (Durham NC: Duke University Press, 2011), pp. 307–331.

5   https://pad.ma/grid/date/cctv_social&project = =CCTV_Social

Platforms are the zones for relaying temporalities, affects, and operations through which modes of sensing and sense-making arise. pad.
ma's and 0xDB's engagement with an operational aesthetics takes
account of the infrastructural affordances which condition processes
of sense(-making) and at the same time emphasize these media materialities as processes rather than products. Such media are concatenated
in the sense that they generate relations between different processes,
that is, between durations that differ in kind while sharing the potential of shaping experience. The question of concatenated commons
challenges not only where to situate perception beyond the human
scope but also pertains to the operational underpinnings which move
through technical ensembles. As practiced, commons are temporalizing activations rather than groups, or places. I will attempt to formulate a temporal conception of commons as an affective and aesthetic
politics of sense/making. The movement or direction of such sense
courses through the sensible and inserts into processes of sense making, while itself activating potentialities: opening up modes of becoming through the actual process of experience.

Time, Affect, and Commons

The process of concatenation is crucial for William James' concept
of experience as the "stuff of which everything is composed." [6] Such
a conception of experience liberates its operation from being tied to
an embodied subject of perception. Concatenation is the term James
deploys to hint at experience's pluralist ontology. In his book *Essays
in Radical Empiricism* he states:

The world it [Radical Empiricism] represents as a collection, some parts
of which are conjunctively and others disjunctively related. Two parts,
themselves disjoined, may nevertheless hang together by intermediaries
with which they are severally connected, and the whole world eventu-
ally may hang together similarly, inasmuch as some path of conjunctive
transition by which to pass from one of its parts to another may always

6   William James, *Essays in Radical Empiricism* (Lincoln: University of Nebraska Press,
    1996), p. 4.

be discernible. Such determinately various hanging-together may be called *concatenated* union, to distinguish it from the "through-and through" type of union, "each in all and all in each" (union of total conflux, as one might call it), which monistic systems hold to obtain when things are taken in their absolute reality. In a concatenated world a partial conflux often is experienced.[7]

In emphasizing the "partial conflux," James provides a take on reality which can never be totalizing while being part of larger relational movements. His remarks lead me to outline three different aspects of relation that pose the concept as different from mere connections.

Primarily, as James states, "the relations that connect experience must themselves be experienced relation, and any kind of relation experienced must be accounted as 'real' as anything else in the system."[8] This means that the composition of experience is by nature relational and what is experienced as an embodied sensation is the experience of relations relating, rather than the recognition of form or *Gestalt*. Relations are ontologically prior to the formation of subjects and objects, substances and forms and thus exceed a connectivist logic.

The relational foundation of experience brings with it the second aspect, that of movement. Rather than considering relation as static or fixed, it should be conceived as a trajectory or tendency. Shifting from entity to tendency means to also underline movement as the defining feature of relations. Unbound, movement is absolute: "Motion originally simply *is*; only later is it confined to this thing or that."[9] The general fact of movement also means that whatever becomes partially perceived in an embodied experience emanates from a "bare activity" which permeates the entirety of experience.[10] The question, I want to pose with James, concerns the specificity of relation as a movement. This means, what distinguishes one relation from another is defined by *how* relations share a time of co-emergence while expressing their singular movement (or tendency).

Concatenation means this very process of resonances of relations as movements, while differentiations occur in their unique mode of mov-

---

7   Ibid., pp. 107–108 (emphasis in the original).
8   Ibid., p. 42 (emphasis in the original).
9   Ibid., p. 145.
10 Ibid., p. 161 (emphasis in the original).

ing. In that sense, what comes to shape an embodied experience from the base-layer ground of activity through the differential relations can be addressed as tendencies, rather than substances. "The experiences of tendency are sufficient to act upon."[11] With this statement, James emphasizes that the partiality of the concatenated union which makes up the present of experience is sufficient to act upon, or as he states elsewhere: "To continue thinking unchallenged is, ninety-nine times out of a hundred, our practical substitute for knowing in the complete sense."[12]

A conception of a world in flux, and of concatenated union as what composes the present, requires a third aspect, that of rhythm. It is Deleuze's work on Spinoza and his casting of the concepts of bodies and affect which provide a fruitful liaison with the relational foundation of experience. Here, a body is not a substance or a subject but a mode. "A mode is *a complex relation of speed and slowness*, in the body but also in thought, and it is a capacity for affecting or being affected, pertaining to the body or to thought."[13] Defining things, humans or animals not by their form, organs (parts), or functions, but by "the affect of which [they are] capable" turns them into relational composites that actively contribute to the fabric of experience by means of their capacity.[14] Existence or the fabrication of the real, for Deleuze, is a polyrhythmic relaying of affects which shapes experience as a *concatenated commons*—meaning it relates "bodies" along their temporal differences without subsuming their differences under a unifying present. A commons, as I propose the term here, is a potential of relating, of resonating across different durations, a power to concatenate that can take many forms but does not predetermine the form it takes.

With the term concatenated union and the affective outline of relations and movement, I am suggesting an emphasis on *the fabrication of the real as temporal processing*. Commons as primarily polyrhythmic and temporal compositions conceive neither of a community, nor of a site or land as commons or common good, as sufficient for a conception of an aesthetics of the commons in relation to online and digital media

---

11   Ibid., p. 69.
12   Ibid (emphasis in the original).
13   Gilles Deleuze, *Spinoza, Practical Philosophy* (San Francisco: City Lights Books, 1988), p. 124 (my emphasis).
14   Ibid.

practices and their platforms. The partial logic of experience and the relational fabrication of a present both hint at a commons as the relational co-emergence of affective capacities that become felt in experience as tendencies. Concatenation defines the relational making of a present that exceeds the momentary while pointing at the contemporaneous. It draws on relations as the very building blocks of experience, and on experience as the active movement enabling the formation of embodied sensation, memory and communication across different matters, thoughts, and activities. In James' radical empiricism, the relational outline of experience of the world is always on the limit of its actual appearance, and the present, as "specious present," defines that margin of concrete enough formation in its potential becoming.[15]

Platforms beyond Infrastructures

The project 0xDB was first initiated by Jan Gerber and Sebastian Luetgert in 2007. An adaptation of the platform was conceived as base for the project pad.ma in collaboration with Sanjay Bhangar from the artist collective CAMP in Bombay. In the aftermath of these first two initiatives, the media archive framework Pan.do/ra was developed and led to a reimplementation of both 0xDB and pad.ma based on Pan.do/ra in 2011. Gerber and Luetgert also form the group *0x2620*—Collaborative Archiving and Networked Distribution. Overall, the primary impetus of both initiatives, 0xDB and pad.ma, resides in enabling specific encounters with (formerly private) collections. Their ethos aligns not only with open source and *libre* ideas of sharing and distribution but relates more crucially to a strong emphasis on programming and software development as an activist practice. In a statement for the tenth anniversary of 0xDB Gerber and Luetgert write: "a functioning piece of software can function as an argument: one that is impossible to make if you can only refer to an idea, or a plan, or a theory."[16] And they further underline the entanglements between aesthetic desire and the control thereof through capitalist censorship:

---

15 William James, *The Principles of Psychology* (New York: H. Holt and Company, 1893), p. 609.
16 Pirate Cinema Berlin, "10 Years of 0xDB,' https://pad.ma/documents/AJY/100

Just like there are protest songs, there is protest software. 0xDB is such a case: an act of protest against the grotesque piles of junk that are the online film archives of almost all official institutions, against the obscene amounts of public funding that are being spent on digital graveyards, and against the perverse fantasy at the core of cinema—which has many names: censorship, commodity, copyright—that it has to be hard, if not impossible, to watch a film. If you think that you've heard this one before, then you know that we're coming to the chorus now: The history of cinema is the story of the wealth of technological possibilities and the poverty of their use.[17]

This statement foregrounds the relation between the archive and power, viewed through the prism of film and cinema, as being highly restricted commercial spheres whose aesthetic operational powers are captured by commercial interest. Lawrence Liang points at a similar issue when he writes about national film archives which, instead of making material available to the public, often function as gatekeepers, where the "mythic value of films arise from their non-availability."[18] The imperial undertones of the archive—sharing its etymological root with the *archaeon* (the official house of the magistrate)—emphasize the archive's heavy baggage as a place of power, control and the governance of knowledge. For these reasons, I want to follow the critique of capitalist modes of control and value production but detach them from a notion of the archive, even though its meaning and possible critiques are manifold. In the case of 0xDB and pad.ma, I consider the term platform as more adequate, in relation to both the late liberal modes of digital operationality of value generation and extraction, and in terms of their specific temporalizing potentialities.

Both 0xDB and pad.ma are open source platforms, databases and repositories with a primary focus on time-based audio-visual material, mainly film and filmed footage. As part of their infrastructures, they also allow for the inclusion of documents, still images and annotations. Their software basis is the open source platform for media archives called Pan.do/ra, which "allows you to manage large, decen-

17 Pirate Cinema Berlin, "10 Years of 0xDB."
18 Lawrence Liang, "The Dominant, the Residual and the Emergent in Archival Imagination," in *Autonomous Archiving*, ed. Artikişler Collective (Barcelona: dpr-barcelona, 2016), p. 106.

tralized collections of video, to collaboratively create metadata and time-based annotations, and to serve your archive as a desktop-class web application."[19] The base-structure of Pan.do/ra is the combination of a Python backend and a JavaScript front end relayed by a JSON API (Application Programming Interface). It serves as a server and as a client, allowing the database infrastructure to be used for one's own collections and plugging this structure into highly customized front ends. The operational capacities of the API are relevant here. Adrian Mackenzie describes the API as "a gateway for centralization and decentralization" which operates between the database with its contents and the front end in the case of 0xDB and pad.ma.[20] The API is a relaying device which enables relations between data and their sentient capacities as part of a GUI (graphic user interface). The API is a "central element of programmability," as Mackenzie writes, where programmability "supports the social and economic entanglements" of commercial platforms like Facebook.[21] The social and economic entanglements Mackenzie is pointing at refer to the decentralized logic of API programming, which nonetheless contributes to the building of a platform, such as Facebook, where universal equivalents—user data—take over. This aspect is relevant due to its operational connotations, and I will further develop the concept of operation and operative logic in the last part of this chapter.

In the commercial sector, platforms "enact their programmability to decentralize data production and recentralize data collection."[22] The way Anne Helmond describes commercial platforms stands in stark contrast to Pan.do/ra's emphasis on decentralization of data collections and the open handle that defines the API coming with it. Obviously, data collection as a practice of social media platforms, and the data collections made available through 0xDB and pad.ma, relate to highly different contexts while sharing the activity of collecting. The same accounts for the question of decentralization, which, in the case

19 Pirate Cinema Berlin, "10 Years of 0xDB."
20 Adrian Mackenzie, "From API to AI: Platforms and Their Opacities," *Information, Communication & Society* 22, no. 13 (November 10, 2019): pp. 1-18, https://doi.org/10.1080/1369118X.2018.1476569
21 Ibid., p. 1.
22 Anne Helmond, "The Platformization of the Web: Making Web Data Platform Ready," *Social Media + Society* 1, no. 2 (September 22, 2015): 205630511560308, https://doi.org/10.1177/2056305115603080

of commercial platforms, provides the distribution of programming activity and the inclusion of its results into a universalizing operation, and in the case of 0xDB and pad.ma engages in a decentralized sharing of content and collaborative/collective engagements with data. Put differently, data production in relation to commercial platforms refers to the open-ended logic of API programming, where "platforms engage the flexibility and mutability of programming and programmability to modulate interfaces, devices, protocols, and increasingly, infrastructures in the interests of connectivity."[23] The empowering logic behind Pan.do/ra, on the other hand, points into a very different direction: Here we find decentralized infrastructures built on an ethos of co-production and co-emergence which defines the platform, rather than the universalizing tendencies weaving through heterogeneous elements of API programming.

Collecting and connecting, as the paradigms of APIs and platforms, bifurcate in the way that open source projects such as pad.ma and 0xDB and commercial social media platforms deploy their capacity for engaging relations. In either case, the role of data is crucial. For 0xDB and pad.ma, audio-visual data becomes an active digital object in its own right and thus is available for use and encounter as much as being generative of new relations through meta-data. The merger of data and meta-data cannot be underestimated here. It makes both simultaneously available for the processing of information and engagement with digital objects, amplifying different temporal layers in the process of information sharing and the collecting of data. For instance, in pad.ma and 0xDB each frame can receive its own URL, which becomes linkable for annotations and cross-referencing, mostly containing information such as subtitles, but also providing further aesthetic detail, such as sense of color and tone of each frame as part of a visual timeline of the entire video at hand. In the language of James, each of these hyperlinks becomes a derivative tendency which opens up new movements while referring to the rhythm of its former context. What is being shared and collaboratively worked at are not mere encoded information packages, as a more classic conception of language as code and data as information would suggest. It is rather the open-ended processual nature of the data and meta-data

---

23 Mackenzie, "API to AI," pp. 3–4.

in their interplay which distinguishes platforms such as 0xDB and pad.ma from commercial platforms like YouTube.

Contrary to this logic of shared amplification of data, commercial social media platforms turn data into an obscured resource for value extraction which equals data with information value, rendering its curation into an extractive activity.[24] Alternative platforms such as pad.ma and 0xDB neither understand collections as finite nor do they strive for capture or control as key operations of commercial platforms. Their collections result from highly individual compulsion and the potential of the Internet to distribute audio-visual material in a manner that invites reworking, commentary and cross-referencing. Connecting then is nothing goal-oriented, as would be the case in interlinking APIs to the building of a platform or algorithmic extraction from big data repositories. On the contrary, it means to engage a field of potential relations and *to formulate operational activations* for the different expressive qualities of the material (data) to be engaged. Commercial platforms are open-ended yet enclosed systems which cater to both a potential mode of identification and thus voluntary contribution of one's data for the sake of participating, and the need to adapt and capture new elements which contribute to a platform's attractiveness. The way to generate engagement in platforms such as 0xDB and pad.ma follows a very different route, while deploying similar advantages of an open system that is crucial to platforms. An example could be the quest for openness and adaptability in Pan.do/ra's API logic: It fosters insertion and adaptation of specific pieces of software and their functions across different realms, such as a user interface and a database. By inserting different elements of Pan.do/ra's coded (API) as well as physical (server space) into one's own projects, or contributing one's own films for further use to the platform, radically alters the logic of commercial platform operations. In these platforms, the distributive model aims at a final insertion and enclosure of programmed elements, contributing to the "whole" of a platform. pad.ma and 0xDB, on the other hand, remain open while

24 Nick Couldry and Ulises Ali Mejias, *The Costs of Connection: How Data Is Colonizing Human Life and Appropriating It for Capitalism*, Culture and Economic Life (Stanford: Stanford University Press, 2019), pp. 88–108.

providing tools for adaptation and the proliferation of different activations.

The key difference I want to stress between commercial platforms and alternative ones is the open circulation, the embracing of the indeterminacy of sharing code, in order to generate modes of value that exceed the capitalist surplus at the root of data extractivism. Beyond circulation, these alternative platforms allow for the transformation of digital objects into processes of relating. Such a shift happens through an active embracing of the relational nature at the heart of digital platforms. The audio-visual material enables a thinking of potential platform-based activations. Since we deal with sensuous material in the first place, these activations move through multiple processes of staging encounters with the material, both perceptually and semantically. The different functions of annotating or video-editing and watching through different temporal and visual representations, creates an immediate linkage between code as idea, its computational processing and the activation of bodies and thought, all of which concatenate in experience. Rather than creating identification-value, as commercial platforms do, alternative platforms create time-values of co-creative engagement as concatenated commons.

It is therefore crucial to distinguish platforms from infrastructures: A platform, as outlined above, comprises aspects pertaining to infrastructuralization and platformization. Infrastructuralization is "the process of rendering certain technical operations widely and immediately available."[25] Platformization, on the other hand, describes "the process of constructing a somewhat lifted-out or well-bounded domain as a relational intersection for different groups."[26] In relation to pad.ma and 0xDB the concept of platform provides a useful approach, since it underlines the collaborative, modular and temporalizing aspects of both its mostly video content and its possibilities of engaging with the material working with and through the interface. While Mackenzie and others, such as Plantin et al., focus on modes of late liberal value extraction on commercial social media platforms, projects such as pad.ma and 0xDB comprise a different notion of value that is attached to

---

25 Mackenzie, "API to AI," p. 6.
26 Ibid.

the operational aesthetics of video-based material activating a sense of temporal concatenations.[27]

The availability that Mackenzie attributes to infrastructures requires some clarification. I would productively challenge and extend the way Laurent Berlant describes infrastructures, as "defined by the movement or patterning of social form" which she distinguishes from structure.[28] Berlant writes:

> I am redefining "structure" here as that which organizes transformation and "infrastructure" as that which binds us to the world in movement and keeps the world practically bound to itself; and I am proposing that one task for makers of critical social form is to offer not just judgment about positions and practices in the world, but terms of transition that alter the harder and softer, tighter and looser infrastructures of sociality itself.[29]

What are these infrastructures of sociality? Following a Jamesian take on experience as explored above, infrastructures need to be considered as infrastructures of existence rather than infrastructures of sociality. Or, one would have to "reassemble the social" as Bruno Latour has done, turning the social into a more-than-human and collective process.[30] A third tuning of the social would then require a movement character at the base of what might come to take shape as human sociality. If infrastructures are infrastructures of the social, then it would be a society of forces and relations as the connective tissue of experience, and human sociality a sub-form of such operations. It is for these reasons that I want to address infrastructures at a more material and operational level while accounting for their inclusion of an extended understanding of the social. Ned Rossiter writes "if infrastructure makes worlds, then software coordinates it," and he further

---

27 Jean-Christophe Plantin et al., "Infrastructure Studies Meet Platform Studies in the Age of Google and Facebook," *New Media & Society* 20, no. 1 (January 2018): pp. 293–310, https://doi.org/10.1177/1461444816661553. It is worth mentioning the filmmaker Harun Farocki and his conception of the "operational image," which shares some of the techno-social aspects of an operational aesthetics.

28 Lauren Berlant, "The commons: Infrastructures for troubling times," *Environment and Planning D: Society and Space* 34, no. 3 (June 2016): pp. 393–419, https://doi.org/10.1177/0263775816645989, here p. 393.

29 Ibid., p. 394.

30 Bruno Latour, *Reassembling the Social: An Introduction to Actor-Network-Theory*, Clarendon Lectures in Management Studies (Oxford: Oxford University Press, 2007).

suggests that logistics infrastructures "enable the movement of labor, commodities, and data across global supply chains."[31] These operational logics move between physically bound enablement and proprietary powers while acknowledging their movement character, which becomes apparent in the entanglements with the algorithmic outline of contemporary software.[32] In resonance with 0xDB's aim to render video a digital object, I want to emphasize this material yet certainly more-than-human sociality immanent to the fabrication of the platform and its contents. The flux of the moving image moves through the materiality and the constraints of hardwired infrastructures, while its operational capacities as a being encountered on the platform shape possible activations of sense.

Infrastructures, taken as the more material enablement of social relational practices, allow me to foreground the platform-logic as an interstice of the material and the social, or, more precisely, as their operational common ground. Following Anja Kanngieser, Brett Neilson and Ned Rossiter, I want to conceive of platforms "as social and technical apparatuses through which to experiment with institutional forms in both on- and offline worlds."[33] The authors stress the deployment of the term—way before its commercial adaptation in the heyday of Web 2.0 infinite connectivity talk—in Communist organizational structures of the 1920s as well as its wide adaptation in activist and artistic projects.[34] It is the latter with which I want to associate 0xDB and pad.ma. While software might underpin the operationalization of a material infrastructure, it is the platform which renders them into a co-emergent processing. This inter-relation between the material and the operational feeds forward into specific modes of social co-production and experimentation. The open API allows for using the code to

---

31 Ned Rossiter, *Software, Infrastructure, Labor: A Media Theory of Logistical Nightmares* (New York: Routledge, 2016).

32 On operations, see Sandro Mezzadra and Brett Neilson, *The Politics of Operations: Excavating Contemporary Capitalism* (Durham NC: Duke University Press, 2019). On the materiality of infrastructures, see Nicole Starosielski, *The Undersea Network*, Sign, Storage, Transmission (Durham NC: Duke University Press, 2015). On proprietary powers and infrastructures, see several contributions in Lisa Parks and Nicole Starosielski, eds., *Signal Traffic: Critical Studies of Media Infrastructures*, The Geopolitics of Information (Urbana: University of Illinois Press, 2015).

33 Anja Kanngieser, Brett Neilson, and Ned Rossiter, "What is a Research Platform? Mapping Methods, Mobilities and Subjectivities," *Media, Culture & Society* 36, no. 3 (April 2014): pp. 302–318, here p. 305, https://doi.org/10.1177/0163443714521089

34 Ibid.

generate multiple relays between the database, its content and the different websites for potential cross-pollination. I would consider this platformatized process as a kind of process of sense/making, where the material, processual, programmable and the sensuous converge. Infrastructures need to be made available, as Mackenzie states, in terms of the server-structure and the database, as well as the source code and its open building blocks. Sense emerges in the practice and process of working with and through the materials. While this seems like a romantic "human-centered" mode of interaction with an archive or repository, I want to stress that both the infrastructural affordances and the platforms built around the digital objects on either 0xDB and pad.ma can only make sense if the processing of "stuff," or "experience" in the Jamesian sense, are considered alongside their mutually emergent and activating capacities.

Platforms, as Kanngieser et al. underline, are different from infrastructures because they are defined and nurtured by user interactivity and participation, creating "an environment of reciprocity, knowledge sharing and relationality."[35] This notion of platforms includes the social dimensions of co-producing and sharing while at the same time accounting for the infrastructural affordances and their potential constraints. Following the work of Olga Goriunova, the authors emphasize the affective dimensions of platforms: "The platform offers an ecology that makes possible the invention of cultural aesthetic phenomena by opening spaces in which creative praxis and co-conceptualisations can be stimulated and supported."[36] However, the differences and commonalities of commercial and alternative platforms not only revolve around open source code, decentralization, and an adaptable API-logic but also emphasize the different modes of labor immanent to the making, maintaining and use of platforms. While the making of platforms implies resources and the power of definition by the initiators, the maintenance of a platform results from active use and participation. This operational logic of engagement and participation shapes a platform's temporal and procedural nature, while taking account of the material infrastructural affordances and capacities. Finally, the aes-

---

35 Ibid., p. 306.
36 Ibid.; Olga Goriunova, *Art Platforms and Cultural Production on the Internet* (New York and London: Routledge, 2012). See also this volume.

thetic configurations of the interface, which can be modified to a certain extent in the case of 0xDB and pad.ma, condition but also enable the fabrication of sense as being activated through engagements with the platform. The encounter with material on these platforms differs vastly, whether I switch into "player" or "timeline" view, or if I look at the timeline depicted as key-frames or as waveform. In the case of my first example *She and her Cat*, the former leads to seeing the animated film become a manga produced by key frames and the latter moves into a more sonic representation in the waveform, similar to *Soundcloud* timelines.

I want to stress that such engagements are not a mere coming together of a set of materials and the perceiving user/subject, but rather result from the experiential ground which is commonly, yet differentially, shared between humans and more-than-human actors as concatenated. Particularly in the case of pad.ma, the embodied dimensions of content and perceptual experience of a user are moored in the thoroughgoing relaying between on- and offline spaces and practices. While the platform facilitates a processual encounter based on infrastructural capacities, the temporal activations abound across processes of sense-making. The time-sensitive aspects of pad.ma and 0xDB foreground the aesthetic political relevance immanent to the infrastructures and interfaces co-composing a platformed experience. In that sense, I want to understand both pad.ma and 0xDB as artistic and activist platforms rather than archives. As Kanngieser et al. write:

In art and activist realms platforms have been a key tool in opening up global networks of communication and organisation. Platforms provide a means to share knowledge, skills and research, to connect to possible collaborators and to propel a sense of immediate solidarity and commons over geographical space and time. Similarly, they provide a model for social networking and self-valorisation, which feeds into an accumulation of cultural capital both within global and local, online and offline worlds.[37]

---

37   Kanngieser et al., "What is a Research Platform?," p. 312.

In relation to pad.ma in particular, I would also want to stress the aesthetic dimension of this artistic and activist take on platforms.[38] The image-worlds of pad.ma are augmented by documents, transcripts, additional information; rendering the platform into a workstation for collaborative practice. Instead of being a mere repository, the platforms at stake generate an aesthetic experimental zone, with an emphasis that "vision is better from below" as Donna Haraway states in her work on situated knowledges.[39] In this subjugated and "submerged" perspective the operational power of the platforms presides over a stable account of content or finite truth.[40] In relation to the situatedness that Haraway emphasizes in its partial and tendential character, as I have outlined through James, the genealogical surges from the depths of temporal contortions across the different modalities of pad.ma and 0xDB.[41] As platforms they enable a commoning of sensuous encounters along the time-based capacities of the data and the way these data generate relations across fields of experience, on- and offline, between machines or technical ensembles and the sensuous making of the perceptual subject. Thus, the platform provides what Brian Massumi terms an "'activation contour:' a variation in intensity of feeling over time."[42] In that sense, platforms compose a contemporaneity of collective becoming while at the same time containing traces and layers of digital objects that carry an intensity of feeling across genealogical lines. From such a time-sensitive point of view, alternative activist and artistic experiments with platforms exceed the potential of making available and making present dear to the archival desires of many art projects. For what they do is to open up the temporal orders of the material, the processual and the social, making their intensities felt over time.

38 Hito Steyerl, "In Defense of the Poor Image," *e-flux* 10 (November 2009), https://www.e-flux.com/journal/10/61362/in-defense-of-the-poor-image/
39 Donna Haraway, "Situated Knowledges: The Science Question in Feminism and the Privilege of Partial Perspective," *Feminist Studies* 14, no. 3 (1988): pp. 575–599, here p. 583, https://doi.org/10.2307/3178066
40 Macarena Gómez-Barris, *The Extractive Zone: Social Ecologies and Decolonial Perspectives*, Dissident Acts (Durham NC and London: Duke University Press, 2017).
41 On partiality, see Marilyn Strathern, *Partial Connections*, updated edition, ASAO Special Publications 3 (Walnut Creek, Lanham, New York, Toronto and Oxford: AltaMira Press, 2004).
42 Rai, "Here We Accrete Durations," p. 309.

Beyond the Archive

While the archive maintains an important role in critical reflections on power relations in statist and institutional contexts, it usually under-cuts the question of the temporal dynamics immanent to the materials that populate the archive in digital contexts.[43] It is not just the content, its ordering, classification and re-emergence through the act of making a "lost" item relevant again, but the temporalizing forces which co-compose a present beyond perceptual encounter. A platform as pro-cess of platformization relates different processes and allows them to seek a certain degree of temporal autonomy. In the "10 Theses on the Archive" the group of authors deeply involved in pad.ma propose to disentangle the notion of the archive from institutional power imagi-naries and their undoing. They propose to conceive of the archive as "a possibility of creating alliances" between humans and more-than-humans, "between time and the untimely";[44] casting this altered archive into something that will "remain radically incomplete" rather than "representational."[45] Finally, and most crucially for a platform-thinking of moving images and the political work around such mate-rial, an archival impulse would allow them "to create ad-hoc networks with mobile cores and dense peripheries, to trade our master copies for a myriad of offsite backups, and to practically abandon the technically obsolete dichotomy of providers and consumers."[46] The platform-logic of a well-bounded yet distributed mode of relating takes its very pro-cessual nature as defining core: it is the movement that brings infra-structures to specific modes of encounter and expression, which make the platform a potentially more engaged mode of thinking the archive as political procedure.

I see much potential in the temporal openings of the processual and operational of the platform-specific interlacing of temporalities. It links with radical political practices while also including some of

43 On digital memory and temporality, see Wolfgang Ernst and Jussi Parikka, *Digital Mem-ory and the Archive*, Electronic Mediations, vol. 39 (Minneapolis: University of Minnesota Press, 2013), pp. 95–101.
44 Lawrence Liang, Sebastian Luetgert and Ashok Sukumaran, "10 Theses on the Archive," (text co-authored during the 'Don't wait for the Archive – I' workshop, Homeworks, Bei-rut, April 2010), https://pad.ma/documents/OH
45 Ibid.
46 Ibid.

the more contemporary digital divergencies, which otherwise easily tip over into neoliberal logics of throughput. In an interview Luetgert and Gerber speak more about repositories and collections rather than archives.[47] At the same time they explain the shift in funding structures for initiatives such as 0xDB and pad.ma. At the beginning the projects received European funding, which helped to build digital infrastructures and institutions. In more recent years funding for the projects has exclusively shifted towards the art world. This shift in funding also highlights one of the problems of late liberal inclusions into speculative markets, such as the art market. The archive, despite all its militant potentialities, was one of the art theoretical buzzwords of the 2000s and 2010s. A rather broad and deliberate deployment of the term archive is itself a hint at specific power relations and the economies of the global art market, much as the term platform might be. From this point of view, I will consider the notion of archive in the context of pad.ma and 0xDB as an umbrella term allowing communication across different fields, disciplines and practices in art, academia and activism.[48]

The "10 Theses" address the archive in its sensuous and affective registers. In the Theses the authors write: "To dwell in the affective potential of the archive is to think of how archives can animate intensities."[49] Animating or rather activating intensities is the relational processing of a concatenated commons, where modes of expression contract from the temporal continuum of experience. In that sense, the on- and offline potentials of platforms are extended towards the timely and untimely movements traversing servers, cables, glances, and sensuous shocks. The motion and rest immanent to the circulation of intensity make an affective relaying of archival matter a question of processing without beginning and end. This does not mean that we have to celebrate the instant or the momentarily. Rather, as Gilles Deleuze and Félix Guattari suggest, it is a question of inhabiting the

---

47 See http://creatingcommons.zhdk.ch/expanding-cinema/ and https://pad.ma/documents/OH

48 On the archive in relation to artistic research practices, see Christoph Brunner and Michael Hiltbrunner, "Anarchive künstlerischer Forschung. Vom Umgang mit Archiven experimenteller und forschender Kunst," *Archivalische Zeitschrift* 95, no. 1 (May 2017): pp.175–190, https://doi.org/10.7788/az-2017-950110

49 Liang et al., "10 Theses on the Archive."

contemporary as a "resistance to the present."⁵⁰ Affect is not the here
and now and intensity does not mark a peak of feeling. Similarly, the
time-sensitive and genealogical aspects of 0xDB and pad.ma contain
a concatenated sense of future-past that moves across the present but
is never "of" the present as a reducible instant. The contemporary
always is a concatenated commons of pushing and pulling intensities
of material's temporal capacities to activate and being activated, to
affect and being affected.

How does a platform become such a practical "device" to resist the
present? Deleuze and Guattari refute a present that divides, orders and
subjugates, a stratified present of a capitalist logic. The authors of the
Theses suggest that the archive is an "apparatus which engages our
experience and perception of time."⁵¹ Rather than making perception
and experience "our," I suggest to dislodge them from the human,
putting them in a submerged state of the concatenated union that is
the partiality of experience marking a present through the feeling of
tendencies. This differential and partial expression of a time of the
present allows for the constitution and emergence of a platform and
its political powers. The platform as "a scene of intervention" binds
temporalities of the "contingent, ephemeral, and the unintended" that
are "the challenge of the moving image as archive [and] recovery of
lost time."⁵² However, the experiences and perceptions which course
through a human embodied relay are imbued with an affective sociality beyond the human. Such experiences are socio-technical in the
literal sense, a fusion of operations of sense/making that the relational
processing of a platform enables and shapes. Platforms such as pad.
ma and 0xDB allow for collective experimentations with temporalities, which contribute to and shape a concatenated commons across
different matters and operations. To engage in the *how* of commoning means to relate with the tendencies' movement potential as processes of amplifying resonances. In that sense, the repository or collection requires tending and care, wants to be maintained and engaged,
needs to be made accessible and given elbow-room for its structures
to evolve. A platform is like a cephalopod, on the move, following

50 Gilles Deleuze and Félix Guattari, *What Is Philosophy?* (New York: Columbia University Press, 2014), p. 108.
51 Liang et al., "10 Theses on the Archive."
52 Ibid.

flows on its hunt, changing color, shape-shifting textures while being held through an entire ecology of caring and supporting material and moving relations.

Resisting the present with and through platforms such as pad.ma or 0xDB happens through the unruly operational value of the "poor image" providing this sphere with its vital powers.[53] The 10 Theses, also Ravi Sundaram and Hito Steyerl attest to the proliferation of poor images and that "these mundane images attain value, not in and of themselves, but as part of a database and as information."[54] pad.ma contains manifold series of engagements with CCTV footage and draws them into small research projects, not only of interviews in control rooms but also in sticking to the redundant and residual image worlds of surveillance cameras operating in empty shops. What comes to the fore in these images is less an acknowledgment of infinite image dumps occurring across the Internet and its kinds of storage devices, but more a conception of these images as a "vast swathe of residual time."[55] The dimension of time and temporality in archives often refers to militant practices as "making present" some knowledge or historical fact that was left irrelevant by the elective engagements and setups of archives. Eric Kluitenberg opposes this linear treatment of temporality, building on the tension between Tactical Media and the "archive":

Tactical Media, activist practices and gatherings find their vitality in moments of crisis, through the participation of the body of the protestor in them, and the affective resonance patterns they generate. The "archive" (as a system of rules governing the appearance of definite and clear statements), in its function of capturing living moments and turning them into historical events, constitutes the very opposite of this dynamic.[56]

The author further underlines that the former treatment of media in activist contexts pertains to a logic of the present as instantaneous and immediate, while the latter creates a temporality that is actually atemporal. Both, he argues, require a readjustment to what I would call a

53 Steyerl, "In Defense of the Poor Image."
54 Liang, "The Dominant, the Residual and the Emergent in Archival Imagination," p. 103.
55 Ibid.
56 Eric Kluitenberg, "Commons and Digging Tunnels," in *Autonomous Archiving*, ed. Artiki ler Collective (Barcelona: dpr-barcelona, 2016), pp. 153–154

concatenated commons of the poor image in the case of pad.ma and
0xDB. The platforms' image resolution never exceeds 480p, both as an
infrastructural affordance (slow Internet connections) but also an aesthetics that aligns with the digital affordances of mobile media images
and their circulation. In a similar vein, Ravi Sundaram points out that
such a doubling of circulation and infrastructures is part and parcel of
an increasingly saturated mobile media landscape of the late-colonial
(he uses the term postcolonial) global South (another auxiliary term).[57]
Neither residual as lost time nor hyper-present, the poor image is not
a remnant but appears as "liberated from the vaults of cinemas and
archives and thrust into digital uncertainty, at the expense of its own
substance."[58] In that sense, these poor and wretched images resist a
presentist order of time, an order of the unified present while carrying
manifold engagements with subjugated knowledges that come to the
fore on experimental platforms such as pad.ma.

The poor image tends towards abstraction: it is a visual idea in its
very becoming. Steyerl's reflections on the digital conditions of the
wretched image are important for a differential temporality at stake
in 0xDB and pad.ma. She points out that the poor image becomes a
moveable time-capsule that can be individually stored, edited, and
circulated. As digital objects, these images and files are imbued with
activation potential beyond the classic archival orders and their atemporal logic. The poor image transports a former conception of "originality" into a "transience of the copy," which also means a transformation of single coherent time into a multiplication of temporalities.
Finally, Steyerl suggests that "the networks in which poor images
circulate thus constitute both a *platform* for a fragile new common
interest and a battleground for commercial and national agendas."[59] It
becomes clear that the poor image takes on a potentiality which lies
in its abstraction as visual idea in its very becoming. It is a speculative
device exceeding not only orders of time and place as finite but also
challenging commercial refinements of processes of platformization.
The poor images constitute a mode of temporal multiplicity whose circulation and openness engage a commons of potentialities rather than

---

57 Ravi Sundaram, "Post-Postcolonial Sensory Infrastructure," *e-flux* 64 (April 2015), https://
www.e-flux.com/journal/64/60858/post-postcolonial-sensory-infrastructure/
58 Ibid.
59 Steyerl, "In Defense of the Poor Image" (my emphasis).

imagined futures. Such a differential temporality is contemporaneous, but its contemporaneity is a fragmented, heterogenous, and heterochronic assembling of sense and sensation for which platforms such as pad.ma function as activating infrastructure.

The poor image cannot be detached from its geo-political contexts and the availability of online infrastructures in less urbanized areas of the world. Sundaram draws on the artist collective CAMP's film *From Gulf, to Gulf, to Gulf*, which is available on *Indiancine.ma* (a sister platform of pad.ma). The film consists of mobile phone footage of sailors travelling on cargo ships in the Indian Ocean between Somalia, Aden, Sharjah, Iran, Pakistan, and Western India. The images shift between material processes, from the building of the ships and their loading and unloading in different ports, to vernacular practices aboard such as playing games or cooking, and they frequently depict other boats caught on fire and sinking. The images are nothing specific on their own but create a consistency in the way they are assembled and brought into resonance. The circulation of the poor image becomes also a critique, as Sundaram points out, of dominant forms of logistical value extraction of the high-end and high-speed logics of contemporary media. This brings us back to the activist roots of platform logics as means of organizing along the operational capacities of technological and social potentials in becoming together. Sundaram writes:

These expanding media infrastructures have formed a dynamic loop between fragile postcolonial sovereignties and informal economies of circulation. Indifferent to property regimes that come with upscale technological culture, subaltern populations mobilize low-cost and mobile technologies to create horizontal networks that bypass state and corporate power. Simultaneously, we witness the expansion of informal networks of commodification and spatial transformation. This loop shapes much of contemporary media circulation, where medial objects move in and out of infrastructures and attach themselves *to new platforms of political-aesthetic action*, while also being drawn to or departing from the spectacular time of media events.[60]

---

60 Sundaram, "Post-Postcolonial Sensory Infrastructure" (my emphasis).

Against the spectacular time of media events, the poor images as shared, relayed, annotated, or reused through 0xDB and pad.ma foreground the temporal creating of concatenated commons in and through the differential rhythms which resist immediate value extraction and capture in late liberal economies colonizing the senses. The timeline logic at the heart of pad.ma and 0xDB functions as the key operation for different rhythms of sensing and making to intersect. As outlined throughout, the poor image is actually bearing potential because of its agility and fractured nature. It affords habits of cinematic perception trained by high quality experience to contend with low-resolution worlds of color patches, fuzzy light influxes and out of focus elements populating the screen. As a temporal lure, the poor image not only accelerates because its processing cost is low, but also creates new ways of valorizing the image as tied to a time beyond spectacle or the celebration of the vernacular, which receives much appraisal both in ethnographic and documentary film as well as voyeuristic reality TV shows. The poor image is the conductor of a commoning process where the concatenations of experience meld into temporalities underneath the capitalist structuring of time, which populate both spheres: the visible and sensible distribution through media platforms and the algorithmic foreclosure of sorting date leading to predetermined effects.

Premises of Lost Time—
Rhythms of an Operational Aesthetics

In an interview as part of the research project *Creating Commons*, Luetgert and Gerber describe the engagement with the platform 0xDB as creating a certain rhythm that differs decisively from the mode of consuming a movie. The timeline logic of the platform foregrounds what I call an operational aesthetics. Such an aesthetics takes account of the open API structure of Pan.do/ra as much as it includes the different ways of "perceiving" a film as digital object. Such digital objects, the way I have developed through the analysis of pad.ma and 0xDB, not only interlaces data and metadata but also opens up the audio-visual continuity of the film towards a multiplication of temporalities that occur when frames receive a unique URL and can be cross-linked or

cut together with different materials, or when commentary on pad.ma
provides vital information about the actual situation of a violent scene
of protest. The forensic character of such tools foregrounds the procedural nature of a polyphonous truth that bears continuously shifting
engagements with the real. This operationality moves through experience; it co-composes experience with the material, spatio-temporal
and potential realms of a concatenated commons. In pad.ma and 0xDB
timelines allow for both specific modes of representation, visualization
and expression while at the same time taking account of the operational nature of the poor images these platforms harbor. These timelines are the operational core of 0xDB and pad.ma: contracting and
concatenating temporalities in the actual experience of working with
the platform, they define the operation logic of the platforms.

Operations and operational logic are rather counterintuitive terms
when it comes to media practices of resistance or "protest software."
Brian Massumi defines an operative logic tied to a politics of perception as "forces for change."[61] These forces are not merely present or
confined actants—they belong less to a logic of agency, susceptible
to subsumption under the extractive rhythms of late liberalism. The
operative logic has transtemporal capacities of modulating a specific
engagement of forces over time. Massumi's writings primarily analyze military strategies of the twenty-first century and how they bank
on the active modulation of the entanglements of "time, perception,
action, and decision."[62] In the context of alternative video platforms, I
want to shift the term operations towards a temporal practice of commoning.

An operative logic hints at the envelopment of abstract relations into
the actual fabrication of the real as concatenated in the present—as
experience. This complex contraction, as I have argued throughout,
refers to temporal layers and relations intersecting beyond any pre-
given stasis or essence. In other word, it concerns the relational aesthetic process of feeling tendencies along their composition of experience. The real, or what comes to materialize in perception, is never
only what is felt in the here and now. It includes many dimensions

61 Brian Massumi, *Ontopower: War, Powers, and the State of Perception* (Durham NC: Duke
University Press, 2015), p. ix.
62 Ibid., p. vii.

of prior and future experience which are not merely ordered into discrete elements or moments, but which co-compose a present as concatenated. Foregrounding the concatenation of the present through perception can become one of the key potentials of alternative media platforms such as pad.ma and 0xDB. The operational aesthetic that is both—part of the programmed and coded structure, as much as the confluence of material, embodied, perceptual and conceptual infrastructures of sense/making—bear the power of resisting late liberal modes of extracting from experience and its assumed data.

The operative logic of platforms is their very capacity of contracting specific data and their different informational layers as relays of activation of sense. The platform nature is operational since it combines a specific logic of relating openly, in the case of 0xDB and pad. ma, through the temporal reconfiguration of data. In their different take on the space and time of cinema these platforms "lay down rhythms" as Deleuze writes: "One never commences; one never has a tabula rasa; one slips in, enters in the middle; one takes up or lays down rhythms."[63] This is a pragmatic and operational understanding beyond the infrastructural giveness of matter and its constraints, or the user adapting to these constraints or bending them. In their openness the analyzed platforms offer a temporal account of operative logics which interlace the fabrication of the present through a platformative operational logic. Such an operation is not merely emancipatory, but also part and parcel of the temporalizing politics of commercial social media and their algorithmic hunger for surplus extraction. For a creative engagement with an operational aesthetics, one has to take account of the temporal power of platformization that banks on the open structure of the poor image capable of fostering new perceptual encounters. These encounters are concatenated temporalities that can be felt collectively through the rhythms they produce.

The operational aesthetic power of the poor image and its capacity for accreting temporalities resides in seeding rhythms capable of suspending capitalist refrains. These rhythms are operative in the way that they allow for abstraction to actually inhabit the making of the real, inserting a modulation of sense, while actually not having to concretize in a finite object—a "visual idea" in Steyerl's words. The

---

63   Deleuze, *Spinoza*, p. 123.

operative logic of the poor image is informative of a "becoming of continuity," as a felt potentiality.[64] Such a felt potentiality becomes affectively contagious; it moves between database, the digital object, metadata, timelines and the perceiving body/mind engaging with the video platform. The formation of a continuity through becoming is the processing of heterogeneous elements into a conjunction which makes the present a potential common ground in experience.

pad.ma and 0xDB not only provide the potential of people collaborating through the possible features and functions, but they engage operative logics as relational aesthetic activations, capable of creating time relays of a commons. It is here, where the concept of protest software becomes a relational operation, that reconfigures the means of engagement with aesthetic material, such as film and video. These shifts occur through concrete operational elements of software and the fabrication of a space, the web-interface, which allows the composition of new concatenations of the present. Concatenated commons interlace the operational capacities of a platform with the sensuous dimension of an affective engagement with the digital objects made available through the database. The archive as platform is not only dynamic or open, but it comprises operational values and potential rhythms as integral to its vault.

In a short text Stefano Harney refers to Frantz Fanon's final passage of *The Wretched of the Earth*, where Fanon raises the question of rhythm in relation to colonization and capitalism. Developing a conception of the assembly line, "a line cut loose," that exceeds the boundaries of the factory, Harney argues for an operational understanding of modes of subjectivation in late liberal capitalism.[65] In this operational account the main target is not the human subject anymore but rather logistical processes. The principle Harney draws on refers to "operations management" as the key conduit of a logistical mode of value generated by movement and "throughput" rather than finite products. Following a *kaizen*-principle, processes take precedence over products and human embodiments are mobilized to "channel

64 Alfred North Whitehead, *Process and Reality: An Essay in Cosmology: Gifford Lectures Delivered in the University of Edinburgh during the Session 1927–28* (New York: Free Press, 1987), p. 35.
65 Stefano Harney, "Hapticality in the Undercommons," in *The Routledge Companion to Art and Politics*, ed. Randy Martin (London and New York: Routledge, 2015), p. 173.

affect towards new connections" where the worker "operates like a synapse, sparking new lines of assembly in life."[66] I want to emphasize how an operative logic can take different forms, similar to the way Steyerl and Sundaram depict the poor image. The question for a politics for concatenated commons has to activate modes of encounter with the operational aesthetics as potentials for sensing and feeling transindividually. The rhythm that "breaks" and "kills" can be transformed into very different rhythmic assemblages, opening up both ways of engaging with potential and concrete modes of expressing it.[67]

Sundaram depicts such an operational aesthetic shift when he writes that in digital platforms such as pad.ma the signal has replaced "the abstract labor/money, dis-embedding the 'mass' in the process of circulation." This signaletic shift links to "media that has become the infrastructural condition of *living*" in "affect-driven post-colonial media modernity," creating "new forms of unauthorized publicity."[68] Sundaram explicitly emphasizes the different platformization processes which revolve around the circulation, but also storage and archiving of poor images imbued with minor gestures, vernacular practices and different modes of political struggle. pad.ma and the example of *From Gulf to Gulf to Gulf* are both infrastructures of sense-making and commoning. Such commoning depends on the temporal activations immanent to the poor image. As Steyerl writes, "the circulation of poor images feeds into both capitalist *media assembly lines* and alternative audiovisual economies. In addition to a lot of confusion and stupefication, it also possibly creates disruptive movements of thought and affect."[69]

The assembly line reverberates throughout the logistical and operational logic of late liberal capitalism. However, the assembly line is but one model of a timeline; it preempts continuity rather than embracing the becoming of continuity. The deep engagement with polyrhythmic timelines at the heart of pad.ma and 0xDB actually exposes the temporal poverty of capitalist temporality while offering veritable alternative proliferations of time-sensitive commoning. For Harney, the assembly line is detached from the factory, cut loose, to implement a

---

66   Ibid., p. 176.
67   Frantz Fanon, *The Wretched of the Earth* (New York: Grove Press, 2004), p. 238.
68   Sundaram, "Post-Postcolonial Sensory Infrastructure."
69   Steyerl, "In Defense of the Poor Image" (my emphasis).

temporal order of its own, beyond the confinements of specific spaces of production and reproduction. In other words, the assembly line has become fully operational. The social factory becomes a processual operation through and through, in which material infrastructures, bodies and series of interrelated acts are temporarily patched together, always adaptable to more throughput and operation value. These operations are the operations that the dark side of capitalist platformization banks on—as an extensive line that mobilizes activity. In that sense, experience, the actual emergent quality enabling modes of existence to compound and constitute embodied expressions, is the territory on which the new modes of operationalized platform-logics dream their appropriative nightmares. Harney points out that from the plantation to late liberal capitalism, the line of improvements of processes has been extended to and implemented in all domains of organic and inorganic life. With this polyphonic yet universalizing rhythm, however, other rhythms and lines co-evolve. These are the lines of "arrhythmia"; of a different operationality beyond the capitalist platforms of throughput and improvement and their capture of the sensuous and sense-making.

An affective account of experience as pre-personal, relational, and building on tendencies, allows the sphere where an affective politics is most needed to be addressed. Resisting the operational managerial lust for surplus, and its subjugating and oppressive modes of appropriating life way beyond the human scope, means to engage at the level of relational formation of expression. It is here where I conceive of the arrhythmic potential of the poor image and of platforms such as 0xDB and pad.ma as potential platforms of critique. The critique that these platforms expose acts on the synaptic and sensuous, affective but also infrastructural and operational level. The general operationality which platform logics express is here turned into a counterpower along the relational aesthetic capacities of the poor image: "The poor image is no longer about the real thing—the originary original. Instead, it is about its own real conditions of existence: about swarm circulation, digital dispersion, fractured and flexible temporalities. It is about defiance and appropriation just as it is about conformism and exploitation. In short: it is about reality."[70]

70 Steyerl, "In Defense of the Poor Image."

How is such a reality of the poor image in an "affect-driven post-colonial media modernity" capable of seeding arrhythmia as a counterpower to capitalist capture of late liberal platformization? The aesthetic question is less how to bring something into a specific form, but rather pertains to an aesthetics of operational rhythmicality resonating across relations and their varying tendencies. Such an operational aesthetics concerns the manner of concatenating that shapes the fabrication of a commons in reality. Operational aesthetics engage bodily capacities of sensing, but extend these capacities into an ecological situatedness that is material, processual and transtemporal. pad.ma's platformatized staging of *From Gulf to Gulf to Gulf* not only allows the user to engage with an image world produced on the move, but moves the way perception is usually conceived. It creates a different optics that exceeds the realm of the visible, through a layering of data sets and their proliferation from geolocation, to commentary, to cross-referencing specific frames. The images themselves present a sense of contemporary forms of logistics and circulation of goods which actually intersects with the circulation and distribution of images, minor gestures of feeling, globalized processes of labor, and how they might resist the infinite capture of throughput while nurturing other becomings of continuity. Alternative platforms as open structures for sense/making engage the temporal fabric of the present as a polyrhythmic relaying of affects. Experimenting with these times-sensitive operations through the counterpowers of the poor image might lead to further amplificatory resonances of situated practices of resistance and struggle, a veritable "creating commons" through the concatenations of an operational aesthetics.

Authors and Editors

Christoph Brunner is Assistant Professor for Cultural Theory at the Institute for Philosophy and Art Studies, Leuphana University of Lüneburg. There, he directs the ArchipelagoLab for Transversal Practices, where students and researchers experiment with different formats and forms of collaboration between art, theory and activism. The Lab hosts artists in residence, conducts the Activist Sense Workshop and Lecture Series, hosts self-organized student reading groups, screenings and performances. Christoph's research revolves around the intersections between media, affect, and aesthetic politics. He focuses on contemporary social movements and their use of aesthetic techniques and strategies. The question of translocal modes of networking and organization, the use of embodied and affective forms of knowledge, and relational conceptions of subjectivity define guiding lines of this research.

Daphne Dragona is a curator and writer based in Berlin. Through her work, she engages with artistic practices and methodologies that challenge contemporary forms of power. Among her topics of interest have been: the controversies of connectivity, the promises of the commons, the challenges of artistic subversion, the instrumentalization of play, the problematics of care and empathy, and most recently the potential of kin-making technologies in the time of climate crisis. Her exhibitions have been hosted at Onassis Stegi, Laboral, Aksioma, EMST (National Museum of Contemporary Art, Athens), Alta Technologia Andina, and Le Lieu Unique. Dragona was the conference curator of transmediale from 2015 until 2019. Her articles have been published in various books, journals, magazines, and exhibition catalogs by the likes of Springer, Sternberg Press, and Leonardo Electronic Almanac. She holds a Ph.D. from the Faculty of Communication & Media Studies of the University of Athens.

Jeremy Gilbert is Professor of Cultural and Political Theory at the University of East London, where he has been based for many years. He has been involved with both mainstream party politics and extra-parliamentary activism throughout his adult life, having been an active participant in the social forum movement of the early 2000s, a member of the founding national committee of Momentum (the controversial organization established to sup-

AUTHORS AND EDITORS

port Corbyn's leadership of Labour), and being a current elected member of the management committee of Compass, a pluralist left-wing think tank and lobby group. His most recent publications include the translation of Maurizio Lazzarato's *Experimental Politics* and the book *Common Ground: Democracy and Collectivity in an Age of Individualism* (Pluto, 2014) and *Twenty-First-Century Socialism* (Polity, 2020).

Olga Goriunova is a cultural theorist working with technological cultures, media philosophy and aesthetics. Her research is interdisciplinary and draws upon theories of computing, art, philosophy, literature and film. Her main interests lie in the processes of subjectivation in relation to technology and aesthetics, but also in thinking beyond the human, in terms of posthuman ecologies. She is a founding co-editor of open access peer-reviewed journal *Computational Culture, a Journal of Software Studies*. Among her books are: *Art Platforms and Cultural Production on the Internet* (Routledge, 2012) and *Bleak Joys: Aesthetics of Ecology and Impossibility* (University of Minnesota Press, 2019). She edited *Readme. Software Arts and Cultures* (Aarhus University Press, 2004) and *Fun and Software: Exploring Pleasure, Pain and Paradox in Computing* (Bloomsbury, 2014).

Gary Hall is a critical theorist and media philosopher working in the areas of digital culture, politics and technology. He is Professor of Media in the Faculty of Arts and Humanities at Coventry University, UK, where he directs the Centre for Postdigital Cultures. He is the author of a number of books, including *Pirate Philosophy* (MIT Press, 2016) and *The Uberfication of the University* (University of Minnesota Press, 2016). His latest monograph, *A Stubborn Fury: How Writing Works in Elitist Britain*, is due to appear in Joanna Zylinska's new series: Media : Art : Write : Now for Open Humanities Press. He blogs at: www.garyhall.info

Ines Kleesattel is an art theorist and philosopher, teaching and researching at Zurich University of the Arts. Her research interests are political aesthetics, critical theories, situated knowledges in artistic research, aesthetics of post-colonial translocality, and the poetics of theory. Among the books she (co)authored are: *Politische Kunst-Kritik. Zwischen Rancière und Adorno* (Turia + Kant, 2016), *The Future is Unwritten. Position und Politik kunstkritischer Praxis* (Diaphanes, 2018); *Polyphone Ästhetik. Eine kritische Situierung* (transversal texts, 2019).

Shusha Niederberger is an artist and educator who has been active in the field of media art, autonomous technological practice, and education since 2000. Since 2014, she is directing the art education department of HeK (House of electronic arts Basel), devising new strategies for technological practice as a cultural/aesthetic practice. She has conceived new institutional formats of critical technological practice (*Critical Make Festival*, Basel 2015), and explored the gendered aspects of technology in publications, workshops, performative lectures, talks, and a festival she co-curated (*Electronnes*, Zürich 2017). She is a lecturer for contemporary net cultures at F + F Schule für Kunst und Gestaltung Zürich, and currently is research associate at the University of the Arts in Zürich for the project *Creating Commons*.

Rahel Puffert is a cultural theorist and Professor for Art and Education at the Hochschule der Künste, Braunschweig, Germany. She taught art and its mediation at Carl von Ossietzky Universität, Oldenburg, between 2012 and 2019 and is co-founder and artistic director of Werkhaus Münzviertel since 2013. The focus of her research is the educative and social function of art, and art in public space, for example in schools. Rahel worked in art mediation for Städtische Galerie Nordhorn and Kunstverein Springhornhof Neuenkirchen and as advisor for "ÜberLebenskunst. Schule," Bundeskulturstiftung/Freie Universität Berlin; she collaborated with the projects "target: autonopop," the archive for art and social movements and FRONTBILDUNG and was editor and founding member of the Internet platform THE THING, Hamburg. She works, publishes and researches on the diverse transitions between artistic, educative and (cultural-)political practices.

Judith Siegmund is Professor of Contemporary Aesthetics at the State University of Music and Performing Arts, Stuttgart. There she is, together with others, creating the "Campus Gegenwart." She comes from the fields of philosophy and the visual arts and was Assistant Professor for Theory of Design/Aesthetic Theory and Gender Theory at the Berlin University of the Arts from 2011 to 2018, where she instigated the research project "Autonomy and Functionalization." Among her books are *Die Evidenz der Kunst* (2007), *Zweck und Zweckfreiheit. Zum Funktionswandel der Künste im 21. Jahrhundert* (2019). She is co-editor of the series *Ästhetiken X.O—Zeitgenössische Konturen ästhetischen Denkens*.

Cornelia Sollfrank (Ph.D.) is an artist, researcher and educator living in Berlin. Recurring subjects in her artistic and academic work within and about digital cultures are artistic infrastructures, forms of (political) self-organization, authorship and intellectual property, techno-feminist practice and theory. She was co-founder of the collectives women-and-technology, –Innen, Old Boys Network and #purplenoise, and currently is research associate at the University of the Arts in Zürich for the project *Creating Commons*. Her recent book *The Beautiful Warriors: Technofeminist Praxis in the 21st Century* was published in October 2019 with minor compositions/Autonomedia, New York. More information at: artwarez.org

Felix Stalder is a Professor for Digital Culture in the Department Fine Arts, Zurich University of the Arts and Principal Investigator for the *Creating Commons* research project. His work focuses on the intersections of cultural, political and technological dynamics, in particular on commons, control society, copyright and transformation of subjectivity. He not only works as an academic, but also as a cultural producer, being a moderator of the mailing list < *nettime* > and a member of the *World Information Institute* as well as the *Technopolitics Working Group* (both in Vienna). Among his recent publications are *Digital Solidarity* (PML & Mute, 2014) and *The Digital Condition* (Polity Press, 2018). felix.openflows.com

Sophie Toupin is a Ph.D. candidate in the Department of Art History and Communication Studies at McGill University in Montreal, Québec, Canada. Her current research examines the relationship between communication technologies and revolutionary movements in the context of liberation struggles. She was awarded a Fonds de recherche du Québec – Société et culture (FRQSC) postdoctoral fellowship (2020–2022) at the University of Amsterdam to explore the linkages between feminism, data and infrastructure. She is one of the three co-editors for the upcoming book *The Handbook of Peer Production* (Wiley, 2021). Some of her publications can be found at: mcgill.academia.edu/SophieToupin

Magdalena Tyżlik-Carver is Assistant Professor in the Department of Digital Design and Information Studies at the School of Communication and Culture at Aarhus University, Denmark. She is also an independent curator and recent curated exhibitions and events include *ScreenShots: Desire and Automated Image* (2019), *Movement Code Notation* (2018), *Corrupting Data* (2017), *Ghost Factory: performative exhibition with humans and machines* (2015), *Common Practice* (2010, 2013). She is co-editor (with Helen Pritchard and Eric Snodgrass) of *Executing Practices* (Open Humanities Press, 2018) a collection of essays by artists, programmers, and theorists engaging in critical intervention into the broad concept of execution in software. She is a member of Critical Software Thing group and a member of the editorial board for the Data Browser series. She is also Associate Researcher with Centre for the Study of the Networked Image at London South Bank University.